Table of Contents

Introduction

Congratulations on your decision to join the field of nursing - few other professions are so rewarding! By purchasing this book, you've already made the first step towards succeeding in your career; and the second step is to do well on the TEAS exam, which will require you to demonstrate knowledge and competence of those subjects taught at the high school level.

This book will help refresh you on all of those subjects, as well as provide you with some inside-information on how to do well on this test. Even if it's been years since you've graduated high school, studied, or taken a test – don't worry, you'll be ready!

About the Test
The TEAS exam is three-and-a-half hours long, and is divided into the following sections:

Mathematics	
30 Questions: Numbers and operations, Measurement, Data Interpretation, Algebraic Expressions	51-Minute Time Limit.
English and Language Arts	
30 Questions: Grammar and Word meaning, Spelling and Punctuation, Structure	34-Minute Time Limit.
Reading	
42 Questions: Paragraph and passage comprehension, Informational Source Comprehension	58-Minute Time Limit.
Science	
48 Questions: Human Body Science, Life Science, Earth and Physical Science, and Scientific Reasoning	66-Minute Time Limit

There is a total of 170 questions on the TEAS exam, however 20 of them are unscored and used only for pre-test or "trial" questions for the test makers to gather information. That means you have 150 questions that are scored.

Scoring
You cannot "pass" or "fail" the TEAS exam. Your score is simply indicative of your current level of comprehension. However, each school has their own entrance requirements – some are higher than others. Be sure to check the requirements of the institutions you want to attend.

How This Book Works
The subsequent chapters in this book are divided into a review of those topics covered on the exam. This is not intended to "teach" or "re-teach" you these concepts – there is no way to cram all of that material into one book! Instead, we are going to help you recall all of the information that you've already learned. Even more importantly, we'll show you how to apply that knowledge.

Each chapter includes an extensive review, with practice drills at the end to test your knowledge. With time, practice, and determination, you'll be well-prepared for test day.

Chapter 1: Mathematics

This chapter will cover the many subjects included in the math section of the TEAS: basic algebra, geometry, and applied math.

The Most Common Mistakes

People make mistakes all the time – but during a test, those mistakes can make the difference between an excellent score, or one which falls below the requirements. Watch out for these common mistakes that people make on the TEAS:

- Answering with the wrong sign (positive / negative).
- Mixing up the Order of Operations.
- Misplacing a decimal.
- Not reading the question thoroughly (and therefore providing an answer that was not asked for.)
- Circling the wrong letter, or filling in wrong circle choice.

If you're thinking, "Those ideas are just common sense" – exactly! Most of the mistakes made on the TEAS are simple mistakes. Regardless, they still result in a wrong answer and the loss of a potential point.

Strategies for the Mathematics Section

1. **Go Back to the Basics**: First and foremost, practice your basic skills: sign changes, order of operations, simplifying fractions, and equation manipulation. These are the skills used most on the TEAS, though they are applied in different contexts. Remember that when it comes right down to it, all math problems rely on the four basic skills of addition, subtraction, multiplication, and division. All that changes is the order in which they are used to solve a problem.

2. **Don't Rely on Mental Math**: Using mental math is great for eliminating answer choices, but ALWAYS WRITE IT DOWN! This cannot be stressed enough. Use whatever paper is provided; by writing and/or drawing out the problem, you are more likely to catch any mistakes. The act of writing things down forces you to organize your calculations, leading to an improvement in your TEAS score.

3. **The Three-Times Rule**:
   - **Step One – Read the question**: Write out the given information.
   - **Step Two – Read the question**: Set up your equation(s) and solve.
   - **Step Three – Read the question:** Make sure that your answer makes sense (is the amount too large or small; is the answer in the correct unit of measure, etc.).

4. **Make an Educated Guess**: Eliminate those answer choices which you are relatively sure are incorrect, and then guess from the remaining choices. Educated guessing is critical to increasing your score.

Positive & Negative Number Rules

Adding, multiplying, and dividing positive and negative numbers has predictable results. Knowing these can help determine if your answer is correct.

(+) + (-) = Solution has the sign of the larger number.

(-) + (-) = Negative number.

(-) * (-) = Positive number.

(-) * (+) = Negative number.

(-) / (-) = Positive number.

(-) / (+) = Negative number.

Examples:

Find the product of -10 and 47.

(-) * (+) = (-)

-10 * 47 = **-470**

What is the sum of -65 and -32?

(-) + (-) = (-)

-65 + -32 = **-97**

Is the product of -7 and 4 less than -7, between -7 and 4, or greater than 4?

(-) * (+) = (-)

-7 * 4 = -28, which is **less than -7**

What is the value of -16 divided by 2.5?

(-) / (+) = (-)

-16 / 2.5 = -6.4

Order of Operations

PEMDAS – **P**arentheses/**E**xponents/**M**ultiply/**D**ivide/**A**dd/**S**ubtract

This describes the order that math steps are done within a problem.

Perform the operations within parentheses first, and then any exponents. After those steps, perform all multiplication and division. (These are done from left to right, as they appear in the problem).

Finally, do all required addition and subtraction, also from left to right as they appear in the problem.

Examples:

1. Solve $(-(2)^2 - (4 + 7))$

    First, complete operations within parentheses:

    $(-(2)^2 - (11))$

    Second, calculate the value of exponential numbers:

    $(-(4) - (11))$

    Finally, do addition and subtraction:

    $(-(4) - (11)) =$ **-15**

2. Solve $(5)^2 \div 5 + 4 * 2$

    First, calculate the value of exponential numbers:

    $(25) \div 5 + 4 * 2$

    Second, calculate division and multiplication from left to right:

    $5 + 8$

    Finally, do addition and subtraction:

    $5 + 8 =$ **13**

3. Solve the expression $15 * (4 + 8) - 3^3$

    First, complete operations within parentheses:

        $15 * (12) - 3^3$

    Second, calculate the value of exponential numbers:

        $15 * (12) - 27$

    Third, calculate division and multiplication from left to right:

        $180 - 27$

    Finally, do addition and subtraction from left to right:

        $180 - 27 = \mathbf{153}$

4. Solve the expression $(\frac{5}{2} * 4) + 23 - 4^2$

    First, complete operations within parentheses:

        $(10) + 23 - 4^2$

    Second, calculate the value of exponential numbers:

        $(10) + 23 - 16$

    Finally, do addition and subtraction from left to right:

        $(10) + 23 - 16$

        $33 - 16 = \mathbf{17}$

Greatest Common Factor (GCF)

The greatest common factor (GCF) of a group of numbers is the largest number that can evenly divide all of the numbers in the group. To find the GCF of a set, find all of the factors of each number in the set. A factor is a whole number that can be multiplied by another whole number to result in the original number. For example, the number 10 has four factors: 1, 2, 5, and 10. These are all of the whole numbers that can be multiplied by another whole number to equal the number 10.

When listing the factors of a number, remember to include 1 and the number itself.

The largest number that is a factor for each number in the set is the GCF.

Examples:

Find the GCF of 24 and 18.

Factors of 24: 1, 2, 3, 4, 6, 8, 12, 24

Factors of 18: 1, 2, 3, 6, 9, 18

The greatest common factor is **6**.

Find the GCF of 121 and 44.

Since these numbers are larger, it's easiest to start with the smaller number when listing factors.

Factors of 44: 1, 2, 4, 11, 22, 44

Now, it's not necessary to list all of the factors of 121. Instead, we can eliminate those factors of 44 which do not divide evenly into 121:

121 is not evenly divisible by 2, 4, 22, or 44 because it is an odd number. This leaves only 1 and 11 as common factors, so **11** is the GCF.

Greatest common factor problems can also appear as word problems. For example:

First aid kits are being assembled at a summer camp. A complete first aid kit requires bandages, sutures, and sterilizing swabs, and each of the kits must be identical to other kits. If the camp's total supplies include 52 bandages, 13 sutures, and 39 sterilizing swabs, how many complete first aid kits can be assembled without having any leftover materials?

This problem is asking for the greatest common factor of 52, 13, and 39. The first step is to find all of the factors of the smallest number, 13:

Factors of 13: 1, 13
13 is a prime number, meaning that its only factors are 1 and itself. Next, we check to see if 13 is also a factor of 39 and 52:

$13 * 2 = 26$
$13 * 3 = 39$
$13 * 4 = 52$

We can see that 39 and 52 are both multiples of 13. This means that **13 first aid kits** can be made without having any leftover materials.

Elena is making sundaes for her friends. She has 20 scoops of chocolate ice cream and 16 scoops of strawberry. If she wants to make identical sundaes and use all of her ice cream, how many sundaes can she make?

Arranging things into identical groups with no leftovers is always a tip that the problem calls for finding the greatest common factor. To find the GCF of 16 and 20, the first step is to factor both numbers:

Factors of 16: 1, 2, 4, 8, 16

Factors of 20: 1, 2, 4, 5, 10, 20

From these lists, we see that **4** is the GCF. Elena can make four sundaes, each with five scoops of chocolate ice cream and four scoops of strawberry. Any other combination would result in leftover ice cream or sundaes that are not identical.

Probabilities

A probability is found by dividing the number of desired outcomes by the number of total possible outcomes. Just as with percentages, a probability is the ratio of a part to a whole.

$$Probability = \frac{desired\ outcomes}{total\ possible\ outcomes}$$

Examples:

What is the probability of picking a blue marble if 3 of the 15 marbles are blue?

$$Probability = \frac{desired\ outcomes}{total\ possible\ outcomes}$$

In this problem, the desired outcome is choosing a blue marble, and the total possible outcomes are the total possible 15 marbles. Therefore the equation reads:

$$Probability = \frac{3}{15}$$

The probability is **1 in 5** that a blue marble is picked.

The probability that a ball selected from a bag of balls will be red is 0.6. If there are 75 balls in the bag, how many of them are red?

$$Probability = \frac{desired\ outcomes}{total\ possible\ outcomes}$$

In this problem, the desired outcome is choosing a red ball and the total possible outcomes are represented by the 75 total balls, so the equation should be written as:

$$0.6 = \frac{red\ balls}{75}$$

red balls = 0.6 * 75 = **45**

A theater has 230 seats. 75 seats are in the orchestra area, 100 seats are in the mezzanine, and 55 seats are in the balcony. If a ticket is selected at random, what is the probability that it will be for either a mezzanine or balcony seat?

In this problem, the desired outcome is a seat in either the mezzanine or balcony area and the total possible outcomes are represented by the 230 total seats, so the equation should be written as:

$$\text{Probability} = \frac{100 + 55}{230}$$

Probability = 0.67

The probability of selecting a student whose name begins with the letter S from a school attendance log is 7%. There are 42 students enrolled at the school whose names begin with S. How many total students attend the school?

In this problem, we are given a probability (7/100, or 0.07) and the number of desired outcomes (42). So the equation is set up as:

$$0.07 = \frac{42}{total\ possible\ outcomes}$$

Total possible outcomes = 42 / 0.07
Total possible outcomes = 600

Fractions

Adding and subtracting fractions requires a common denominator. The denominator is the number on the bottom of the fraction. The first step when adding or subtracting a set of fractions is the convert all of the fractions into numbers with common denominators. Once the denominators are the same, the numerators can be added or subtracted.

Find a common denominator for:

$$\frac{2}{3} - \frac{1}{5}$$

To find the common denominator, you can multiply each fraction by the number 1. With fractions, any number over itself is equivalent to 1. $\frac{5}{5}, \frac{12}{12},$ and $\frac{0.4}{0.4}$ are all equivalent to 1. By using these types of multipliers, you can change the denominators of fractions to be the same number for each fraction in the addition or subtraction problem. Just remember to also multiply the numerator. For example:

$$\frac{2}{3} - \frac{1}{5} = \frac{2}{3}\left(\frac{5}{5}\right) - \frac{1}{5}\left(\frac{3}{3}\right) = \frac{10}{15} - \frac{3}{15} = \frac{7}{15}.$$

To add mixed fractions, you can first add the whole numbers, and then the fractions.

$$2\frac{1}{4} + 1\frac{3}{4} = 3\frac{4}{4} = 4.$$

To subtract mixed fractions, convert to single fractions by multiplying the whole number by the denominator and adding the numerator. Then work as above.

$$2\frac{1}{4} - 1\frac{3}{4} = \frac{9}{4} - \frac{7}{4} = \frac{2}{4} = \frac{1}{2}.$$

To multiply fractions, convert any mixed fractions into single fractions and multiply the numerators together and the denominators together. Reduce to lowest terms if needed.

$$2\frac{1}{4} * 1\frac{3}{4} = \frac{9}{4} * \frac{7}{4} = \frac{63}{16} = 3\frac{15}{16}.$$

To divide fractions, first convert any mixed fractions into single fractions. Then invert the second fraction so that the denominator and numerator are switched. Last, multiply the fractions. Inverting a fraction changes multiplication to division.

$$2\frac{1}{4} \div 1\frac{3}{4} = \frac{9}{4} \div \frac{7}{4} = \frac{9}{4} * \frac{4}{7} = \frac{36}{28} = 1\frac{8}{28} = 1\frac{2}{7}.$$

Practice questions:

- $5\frac{2}{3} - 2\frac{1}{3} = ?$

  This is a mixed-fraction subtraction problem, so the first step is to subtract the whole numbers:

  $$5 - 2 = 3$$

  Then, subtract the fractions. They already have a common denominator, 3:

  $$\frac{2}{3} - \frac{1}{3} = \frac{1}{3}$$

  So the answer is $3\frac{1}{3}$.

- What is the product of $\frac{1}{12}$ and $\frac{6}{8}$?

  This is a fraction multiplication problem, so simply multiply the numerators together and the denominators together and then reduce:

  $$\frac{1}{12} * \frac{6}{8} = \frac{6}{96} = \frac{1}{16}$$

  Sometimes it's easier to reduce fractions before multiplying if you can:

  $$\frac{1}{12} * \frac{6}{8} = \frac{1}{12} * \frac{3}{4} = \frac{3}{48} = \frac{1}{16}$$

- Find $\frac{7}{8} \div \frac{1}{4}$.

  For a fraction division problem, invert the second fraction and then multiply and reduce:

  $$\frac{7}{8} \div \frac{1}{4} = \frac{7}{8} * \frac{4}{1} = \frac{28}{8} = \frac{7}{2}$$

- Find $2\frac{1}{3} - \frac{3}{2}$.

  This is a fraction subtraction problem with a mixed fraction, so the first step is to convert the mixed fraction to a normal fraction:

  $$2\frac{1}{3} = \frac{2*3}{3} + \frac{1}{3} = \frac{7}{3}$$

  Next, multiply each fraction by a factor of 1 to get a common denominator. How do you know which factor of 1 to use? Look at the other fraction and use the number found in that denominator:

  $$\frac{7}{3} * \frac{2}{2} = \frac{14}{6}$$

  $$\frac{3}{2} * \frac{3}{3} = \frac{9}{6}$$

  Now, subtract the fractions by subtracting the numerators:

  $$\frac{14}{6} - \frac{9}{6} = \frac{5}{6}$$

- Find the sum of $\frac{9}{16}, \frac{1}{2}$, and $\frac{7}{4}$.

  For this fraction addition problem, we need to find a common denominator. Notice that 2 and 4 are both factors of 16, so 16 can be the common denominator:

  $$\frac{1}{2} * \frac{8}{8} = \frac{8}{16}$$

  $$\frac{7}{4} * \frac{4}{4} = \frac{28}{16}$$

  $$\frac{9}{16} + \frac{8}{16} + \frac{28}{16} = \frac{45}{16}$$

- A recipe calls for $1/4$ of a cup of sugar. If 8 and a half batches of the recipe are needed, how many cups of sugar will be used?

  This is a fraction multiplication problem: $\frac{1}{4} * 8\frac{1}{2}$.

  First, we need to convert the mixed fraction into a full fraction:

  $$8\frac{1}{2} = \frac{8 * 2}{2} + \frac{1}{2} = \frac{17}{2}$$

  Now, multiply the fractions across the numerators and denominators, and then reduce:

  $$\frac{17}{2} * \frac{1}{4} = \frac{17}{8} \text{ cups of sugar.}$$

- Find the value of $\frac{2}{5} \div 1\frac{1}{5}$

  This is a fraction division problem, so the first step is to convert the mixed fraction to a full fraction:
  $$1\frac{1}{5} = \frac{5 * 1}{5} + \frac{1}{5} = \frac{6}{5}$$

  Now, divide the fractions. Remember to invert the second fraction, and then multiply normally:

  $$\frac{2}{5} * \frac{5}{6} = \frac{10}{30} = \frac{1}{3}$$

- Sabrina has $\frac{2}{3}$ of a can of red paint. Her friend Amos has $\frac{1}{6}$ of a can. How much red paint do they have combined?

  To add fractions, make sure that they have a common denominator. Since 3 is a factor of 6, 6 can be the common denominator:

  $$\frac{2}{3} * \frac{2}{2} = \frac{4}{6}$$

  Now, add the numerators:

  $$\frac{4}{6} + \frac{1}{6} = \frac{5}{6} \text{ of a can of red paint}$$

Absolute Value

The absolute value of a number is its distance from zero, not its value.

So in $|x| = a$, "x" can equal "$-a$" as well as "a."

Likewise, $|\,3\,| = 3$, and $|-3\,| = 3$.

Equations with absolute values will have two answers. Solve each absolute value possibility separately by rewriting the problem as two problems, one with the positive value of the number in the absolute value sign, and one with the negative value. All solutions can be checked by plugging them into the original equation.

Examples:

Solve for x: $|2x - 3| = x + 1$

Equation 1:

$2x - 3 = -(x + 1)$.

$2x - 3 = -x - 1$.
$3x = 2$.
$x = 2/3$.

Equation 2:

$2x - 3 = x + 1$.

$x = 4$.

x = 2/3 or 4

Solve for y: $2 * |y + 4| = 10$

Equation 1:

$2 * -(y + 4) = 10$

$-y - 4 = 5$
$-y = 9$
$y = -9$

Equation 2:

$2 * (y + 4) = 10$

$y + 4 = 5$
$y = 1$

$y = -9$ or 1

If the absolute value of x is equal to $4x + 3$, what is the value of x?

The first step is to rewrite this problem algebraically:
$|x| = 4x + 3$

Next, write the two equations and solve:

Equation 1: $-x = 4x + 3$

$-5x = 3$
$x = -3/5$

Equation 2: $x = 4x + 3$

$-3x = 3$
$x = -3/3$, or $x = -1$

$x = -1$ or $-3/5$

Mean, Median, Mode

Mean is a math term for "average." Total all terms and divide by the number of terms.

Find the mean of 24, 27, and 18.

$24 + 27 + 18 = 69 \div 3 = $ **23**.

Median is the middle number of a given set, found after the numbers have all been put in numerical order. In the case of a set of even numbers, the middle two numbers are averaged.

What is the median of 24, 27, and 18?

18, **24**, 27.

What is the median of 24, 27, 18, and 19?

18, 19, 24, 27 ($19 + 24 = 43$. $43/2 = $ **21.5**).

Mode is the number which occurs most frequently within a given set. If two different numbers both appear with the highest frequency, they are both the mode.

What is the mode of 2, 5, 4, 4, 3, 2, 8, 9, 2, 7, 2, and 2?

The mode would be **2** because it appears the most within the set.

Examples:

What is the mean of 15, 26, 26, 28, and 32?

$$(15 + 26 + 26 + 28 + 32) / 5 = 25.4$$

The mean of three numbers is 45. If two of the numbers are 38 and 43, what is the third number?

$$(38 + 43 + X) / 3 = 45$$

$$38 + 43 + X = 135$$

$$X = 54$$

What is the median of 0.5, 0.3, 1.5, -0.75, and 1?

$$-0.75, 0.3, \mathbf{0.5}, 1, 1.5$$

What is the median of 15, 18, 21, and 18?

15, **18, 18**, 21

$(18 + 18) / 2 = 18$

Find the mode of the set: 6, 22, 160, 21, 37, 22, 70, 76

The mode is 22, because it is the only number that appears more than once.

Find the mode of the set: 33, 58, 53, 31, 58, 42, 58, 33, 47, 51

33, 58, 53, 31, 58, 42, 58, **33**, 47, 51
33, **58**, 53, 31, **58**, 42, **58**, 33, 47, 51

58 appears more than any other number, so it is the mode.

Percent, Part, & Whole

$$Percent = \frac{Part}{Whole}$$

A percent is the ratio of the part to the whole. Questions may give the part and the whole and ask for the percent, or give the percent and the whole and ask for the   part, or give the part and the percent and ask for the value of the whole. The equation above can be rearranged to solve for any of these:

Percent = Part / Whole

Part = Whole * Percent

Whole = Part / Percent

Percents should always be expressed as a decimal number when solving. For example, if a problem uses the number 30%, change that number to 0.3 when solving. The percent sign (%) indicates that the decimal has been multiplied by 100, so divide the % by 100.

The word "of" usually indicates what the whole is in a problem. Remember that the part is smaller than the whole when the percent .

Examples:

Jim spent 30% of his paycheck at the fair. He spent $15 for a hat, $30 for a shirt, and $20 playing games. How much was his check? (Round to nearest dollar.)

Whole = Part / Percent

Whole = (15 + 30+ 20) / .30 = **$217.00**

45 is 15% of what number?

Whole = Part / Percent

Whole = 45 / 0.15

Whole = **300**

Greta and Max sell cable subscriptions. In a given month, Greta sells 45 subscriptions and Max sells 51. If 240 total subscriptions were sold in that month, what percent were not sold by Greta or Max?

Percent = Part / Whole

Percent = (51 + 45) / 240

Percent = 0.4, or 40%

This tells us that Greta and Max sold 40% of the subscriptions, so **60%** were sold by other employees.

What percent of 65 is 39?

Percent = Part / Whole

Percent = 39 / 65

Percent = 0.6, or 60%

Grant needs to score 75% on an exam. If the exam has 45 questions, at least how many does he need to answer correctly?

Part = Whole * Percent

Part = 45 * 0.75

Part = 33.75, so he needs to answer at least 34 questions correctly.

Emma scored 16% of her team's goals during a soccer season. If the team totaled 25 goals, how many did Emma score?

Part = Whole * Percent

Part = 25 * 0.16

Part = 4 goals

Percent Change

Percent Change = Amount of Change / Original Amount * 100.

Percent Increase = (New Amount – Original Amount) / Original Amount * 100.

Percent Decrease = (Original Amount – New Amount) / Original Amount * 100.

Amount Increase (or **Decrease**) = Original Price * Percent Markup (or Markdown).

Original Price = New Price / (Whole - Percent Markdown [or Markup]).

> **Example:** A car that was originally priced at $8300 has been reduced to $6995. What percent has it been reduced?
>
> (8300 – 6995) / 8300 * 100 = **15.72%**.

Ratios

A ratio tells how many of one thing exists in proportion to another thing. Unlike fractions, ratios do not give the amount of a part relative to a whole. To work with ratios, you can find the equivalent fraction. Do this by adding together the parts of the ratio to find the size of the whole.

Examples:

There are 90 voters in a room, and they are either Democrat or Republican. The ratio of Democrats to Republicans is 5:4. How many Republicans are there?

> We know that there are 5 Democrats for every 4 Republicans in the room; that is what the ratio 5:4 means. To convert the ratio to fractions, add the parts together to find the whole:
>
> 5 + 4 = 9
>
> Fraction of Democrats: $\frac{5}{9}$
>
> Fraction of Republicans: $\frac{4}{9}$
>
> If 4/9ths of the 90 voters are Republicans, then:
>
> $\frac{4}{9} * 90 = $ **40 voters** are Republicans.

The ratio of students to teachers in a school is 15:1. If there are 38 teachers, how many students attend the school?

To solve this ratio problem, we do **not** need to find the whole number of people in the school, since we are solving for one part of the population (students) given the size of the other population (teachers). We know that:

For every 1 teacher, there are 15 students.

Therefore for 38 teachers, there are 38 * 15 students.

38 * 15 = **570 students** in the school.

A variety pack of cereal bars contains peanut butter flavor and chocolate flavor in a ratio of 3:2. If there are 20 bars total, how many of them are peanut butter flavored?

Convert the ratio to fractions:

3 + 2 = 5

Fraction of peanut butter flavor: $\frac{3}{5}$

If there are 20 bars total, then $\frac{3}{5} * 20 = $ **12 bars** are peanut butter flavored.

Proportions

There are two types of proportionality:

Direct Proportions: Two quantities that are directly proportional will increase or decrease in tandem. They change in the same direction.

Inverse Proportions: Two quantities which are inversely proportional will change in opposite directions. As one increases, the other will decrease.

To solve **direct** proportions, set up a fraction equation. For example:

A train traveling 120 miles takes 3 hours to get to its destination. How long will it take for the train to travel 180 miles?

$$\frac{120\ miles}{3\ hours} = \frac{180\ miles}{x\ hours}$$

It is important to set up the equation so that types of quantities are in the same position in the fraction. For example, above, miles are in the numerator and hours are in the denominator. Now, solve for the missing quantity through cross-multiplication:

(120 miles)*(x hours) = (3 hours) * (180 miles)

$$x\ hours = \frac{(3\ hours)*(180\ miles)}{120\ miles}$$

$x =$ **4.5 hours**

One acre of wheat requires 500 gallons of water. How many acres can be watered with 2600 gallons?

This is a direct proportion – an increase in wheat requires an increase in gallons of water. Therefore it can be solved using a fraction equation:

$$\frac{1\ acre}{500\ gallons} = \frac{x\ acres}{2600\ gallons}$$

$$x\ ac\square es = \frac{(1\ acre)*(2600\ gallons)}{500\ gallons}$$

$$x = \frac{26}{5}\ acres,\ \text{or } \textbf{5.2 acres}$$

Check the answer – is it more or less acres than the initial value? It should be more, since there was an increase in the amount of water.

The price of a product is inversely proportional to how many are produced. If 100 products are made, they each cost $5. If 200 are made, they each cost $2.50. How much will each product cost if 400 are produced?

> *Inversely proportional* means that as one quantity increases, the other decreases. To solve an inversely proportional problem, figure out how much one quantity goes down as the other rises.
>
> In this example, when the number of products doubles, the price divides by 2. Therefore when quantity goes from 200 to 400, the price should go from $2.50 to $2.50/2 = **$1.25**.

Jason has realized that when more people are using his school's wifi connection, the internet speed is reduced. When there are 20 users, the speed is 3 megabits per second. When there are 60 users, the speed drops to 2 megabits per second. If the speed is inversely proportional to the number of users, what speed should Jason expect when 80 users are logged in?

> To solve, first examine the rates at which the two quantities change:
>
> When the number of users tripled from 20 to 60, the speed was reduced by 1/3rd. So if the number of users in increased by a factor of 4, how much will speed be reduced by? Solve using a fractional equation:
>
> $$\frac{3}{1/3} = \frac{4}{x}$$
>
> $$x = \frac{4}{3} * \frac{1}{3} = \frac{4}{9}$$
>
> When the amount of users is multiplied by 4, the speed should reduce by 4/9. Therefore, the new speed will be:
>
> $3 - (4/9)*3 = $ **1.67 megabits per second.**

Literal Equations

Equations with more than one variable. Solve in terms of one variable first.

Example: Solve for y: $4x + 3y = 3x + 2y$.

1. Combine like terms: $3y - 2y = 4x - 2x$.

2. Solve for y. $y = -x$.

Algebraic Equations

When simplifying or solving algebraic equations, you need to be able to utilize all math properties: exponents, roots, negatives, order of operations, etc.

1. Addition and subtraction: Only like terms can be added or subtracted. A like term is one with the same variable or combination of variables. Constants are numbers without variables attached, and those can be grouped together as well.

Examples:

Rewrite the expression $5xy + 7y + 2yz + 11xy - 5yz$

Group together xy terms, y terms, and yz terms:

$16xy + 7y - 3yz$

Find the value of x: $5x + 4y - 16 = 4x + y + 4$

Group together like terms:

$x + 3y = 20$

Then, isolate x:

$x = 20 - 3y$

2. Multiplication: First, multiply the coefficients. Then multiply the variables:

Example: Monomial * Monomial. (Remember: a variable with no exponent has an implied exponent of 1.)
- $(3x^4y^2z)(2y^4z^5) = 6x^4y^6z^6$.

Example: Monomial * Polynomial.
- $(2y^2)(y^3 + 2xy^2z + 4z) = 2y^5 + 4xy^4z + 8y^2z$

Example: Binomial * Binomial.
- $(5x + 2)(3x + 3)$. Remember: FOIL (First, Outer, Inner, Last).

   First: $5x * 3x = 15x^2$.

   Outer: $5x * 3 = 15x$.

   Inner: $2 * 3x = 6x$.

   Last: $2 * 3 = 6$.

   Combine like terms: $15x^2 + 21x + 6$.

Example: Binomial * Polynomial.
- $(x + 3)(2x^2 - 5x - 2)$.

   First Term: $x(2x^2 - 5x - 2) = 2x^3 - 5x^2 - 2x$.

   Second term: $3(2x^2 - 5x - 2) = 6x^2 - 15x - 6$.

   Added Together: $2x^3 + x^2 - 17x - 6$.

Inequalities

Inequality signs are the following:

> Greater than symbol, indicating that the expression left of the symbol is larger than the expression on the right

< Less than symbol, indicating that the expression left of the symbol is smaller than the expression on the right

≥ Greater than or equal to symbol, indicating that the expression left of the symbol is larger than or equal to the expression on the right

≤ Less than or equal to symbol, indicating that the expression left of the symbol is less than or equal to the expression on the right

Inequalities are solved like linear and algebraic equations, except the symbol must be reversed when dividing or multiplying both sides of the equation by a negative number.

Examples:

$-7x + 2 < 6 - 5x$. Solve for x.

Step 1 – Combine like terms: $-2x < 4$.

Step 2 – Solve for x. (Reverse the sign, because both sides of the equation are divided by -2): $x > -2$.

Solving compound inequalities will give a solution set rather than one answer.

Examples:

$-4 \leq 2x - 2 \leq 6$. Solve for x.

Step 1 – Add 2 to each term to isolate x: $-2 \leq 2x \leq 8$.

Step 2 – Divide by 2: **$-1 \leq x \leq 4$**. It is not necessary to reverse the sign, since we are not dividing or multiplying by a negative number.

Solution set is **[-1, 4]**.

Graphs and Charts

These questions require that you interpret information from graphs and charts. These questions are typically straightforward as long as you pay careful attention to detail. There are several different graph and chart types that may appear.

Bar Graphs

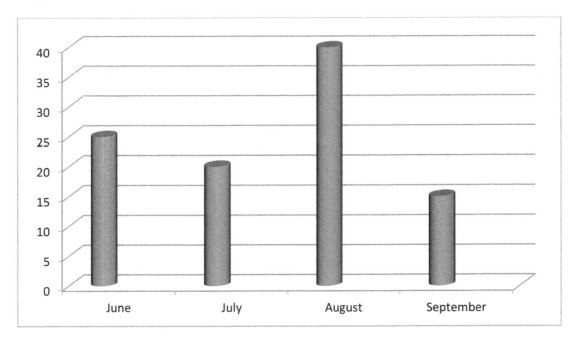

Using the above chart of ice cream sales per month, how many more sales are made in July than September?

As you can see, sales in July are 20 and September sales are 15. The correct answer is therefore **5**. If you see any answer choices which are grossly incorrect – such as -10 or 20 – immediately count them out. Don't over-think graphical questions.

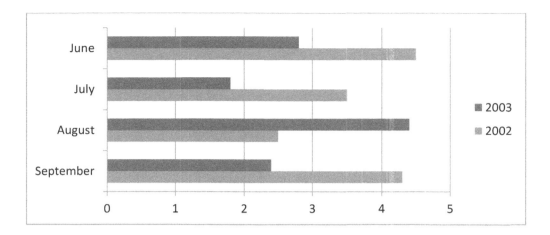

The chart above shows rainfall in inches per month. Which month shown had the least amount of rainfall?

> This bar chart presents four different months: June – September of 2002 and June – September of 2003. The month with the least amount of rainfall will be the one with the shortest bar. That month is **July 2003**.

Pie Charts

Pie charts present parts of a whole. Pie charts are sometimes used with percentages. Examples of pie chart questions are given below.

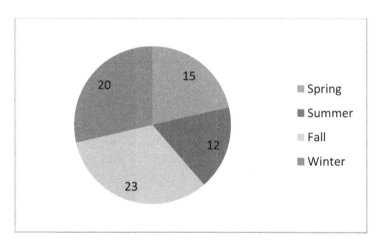

The pie chart above shows the distribution of birthdays in a class of students. How many students have birthdays in the spring or summer?
>   Spring birthdays – 15
>   Summer birthdays – 12
>   Total spring and summer birthdays: **27**

What fraction of birthdays occurs in the winter?

$$\frac{winter\ birthday}{total\ birthdays} = \frac{20}{20+15+23+12} = \frac{20}{70} = \frac{2}{7}$$

36

Line Graphs

Line graphs show trends over time. Examples are given below.

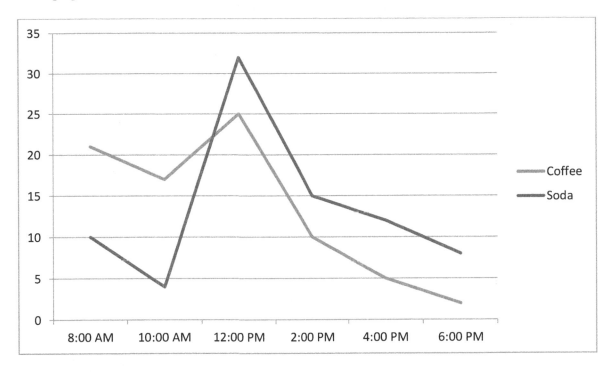

The line graph above shows beverage sales at an airport snack shop at different times through the day.

Which beverage sold more at 4:00 pm?

At 4:00, approximately 12 sodas and 5 coffees were sold, so more **soda** was sold.

At what time of day were the most beverages sold?

This question is asking for the time of day with the most sales of coffee and soda combined. It is not necessary to add up sales at each time of day to find the answer. Just from looking at the graph, you can see that sales for both beverages were highest at noon, so the answer must be **12:00 pm.**

Histograms

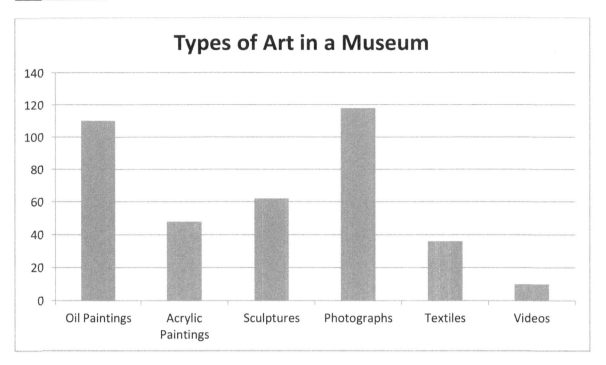

A histogram shows a distribution of types within a whole in bar chart form. The histogram above shows the distribution of types of art within a museum. Below are two example histogram questions:

Which type of art is the second most common type found in this museum?

The second most common would be the second tallest bar, which corresponds to **oil paintings.**

Approximately what fraction of the art pieces in this museum are sculptures?

To find the fraction, we need the part over the whole. Since the question specifies *approximate*, we can estimate the amount of each type:

$$\frac{sculptures}{total\ art\ pieces} = \frac{60}{110+50+60+120+40+10} = \frac{60}{390} = \frac{6}{39} = \frac{2}{13}$$

Roman Numbers

The Roman number system uses the following identities:

Roman Numeral	Value
I	1
V	5
X	10
L	50
C	100
D	500
M	1000

These 7 numerals are combined to form numbers through addition. Numerals are always arranged from greatest to least in value. For example, the number 157 would be written as:

$100 + 50 + 5 + 1 + 1$

CLVII

That is the standard way to write 157, even though Roman numerals could be combined in different ways to add up to that number. In standard Roman notation, the largest possible numerals have to be used to write a number. Here's another example: the number 3,621:

$1000 + 1000 + 1000 + 500 + 100 + 10 + 10 + 1$

MMMDCXXI

To avoid having to add four of the same numeral in a row, subtraction is used. If a numeral with a smaller value is placed *before* a numeral with a larger value, the smaller number is subtracted from the bigger number. For example:

$IX = 10 - 1 = 9$

Since I has a value of 1 and it is placed *before* X, which has a value of 10, the number is found by subtracting 1 from 10. Here are a few Roman numeral example problems:

Express the number 538 in Roman Numerals.

$538 = 500 + 30 + 8$

$538 = 500 + 10 + 10 + 10 + 5 + 1 + 1 + 1$

$538 = DXXXIII$

What number is expressed by the Roman Numeral CDVII?

$C = 100, D = 500, V = 5, I = 1, I = 1$

Since C is *before* D, 100 is subtracted from 500

$500 - 100 + 5 + 1 + 1 = 407$

Decimals

When adding and subtracting decimals, line up the numbers so that the decimals are aligned. You want to subtract the 1s place from the 1s place, the $1/10^{th}$ place from the $1/10^{th}$ place, etc. Addition follows the same rules. For example:

Find the sum of 17.07 and 2.52.

$$
\begin{array}{r}
17.07 \\
+ \quad 2.52 \\
= \quad \textbf{19.59}
\end{array}
$$

Jeannette has 7.4 gallons of gas in her tank. After driving, she has 6.8 gallons. How many gallons of gas did she use?

$$
\begin{array}{r}
7.4 \\
- \quad 6.8 \\
= \quad \textbf{0.6 gallons}
\end{array}
$$

When multiplying and dividing decimals, multiply or divide the numbers normally. Then determine the placement of the decimal point in the result by counting the number of digits after the decimal in each of the numbers you multiplied together. For example:

What is the product of 0.25 and 1.4?

25 * 14 = 350

There are 2 digits after the decimal in 0.25 and one digit after the decimal in 1.4. Therefore the product should have 3 digits after the decimal: **0.350** is the correct answer.

Determining the placement of the decimal point after division is simpler. Remember that with division, you can multiply the divisor and the dividend by any number as long as you multiply them by the same number, since those will cancel out. Change the divisor (the number you are dividing *by*) by moving the decimal point until it is a whole number. Then move the decimal point for the dividend (the number you are dividing) the same number of spaces in the same direction. After that, you can easily divide the new numbers normally to get the correct answer. For example:

Find 0.8 ÷ 0.2.

Change 0.2 to 2. The decimal moves on space to the right to accomplish this.

Next, move the decimal one space to the right on the dividend. 0.8 becomes 8.

Now, divide 8 by 2. 8/2 = **4**, which is the correct answer.

Find the quotient when 40 is divided by 0.25.

First, change the divisor to a whole number. 0.25 becomes 25.

41

Next, change the dividend to match the divisor. We moved the decimal two spaces to the right, so 40 becomes 4000.

4000/25 = **160**, which is correct.

Converting percentages, fractions, and decimals

This can be intimidating to some people since we are all used to simply punching in numbers into a calculator. Some are easy just because it's common knowledge for most folks that ½ equals 0.5 and ¼ equals 0.25 and so on. They know 65% is the same as 0.65 and 0.01 equals 1%. But how do you express a number like 3/16 in decimal form? What percent is that? That number probably doesn't just pop into your head for some people, but they might be able to figure it out. Others might be totally lost.

The easiest way to solve this problem is to set up a simple equation. Let's use the example 3/16.

3/16 is basically the same as saying 3 divided by 16, so let's set up that equation just like that:

$$16 \overline{)\ 3.0}$$

How many times 16 go into 3? Zero times obviously, which is why we add the decimal. Imagine the decimal isn't there, and think of it as the lowest number possible that is still bigger than 16, which is 30. So, how many times does 16 go into 30? Just 1 time, so the next step:

$$16 \overline{)\begin{array}{l} 1 \\ 3.0 \\ 14.0 \end{array}}$$

Now, of course we have a remainder we have to take care of in the next step. The remainder is 14, and since 14 is smaller than 16, we need to add a decimal and think of it as 140. So, how many times does 16 go into 140? The answer is 8 times. 8 times 16 equals 128, so 140-128 means we have another remainder of 12 this time.

$$16 \overline{)\begin{array}{l} 18 \\ 3.0 \\ 14.0 \\ \hline 12 \end{array}}$$

Once again, think of the 12 as 120 since 16 is bigger than 12. How many times does 16 go into 120? The answer is 7 with a remainder of 8.

$$
\begin{array}{r}
187 \\
16\overline{)\,3.0} \\
14.0 \\
\overline{12} \\
8.0
\end{array}
$$

The final step is we know that 16 can go into 80 exactly five times, so the final number = 5.

$$
\begin{array}{r}
1875 \\
16\overline{)\,3.0} \\
14.0 \\
\overline{12} \\
8.0
\end{array}
$$

The decimal will go in front of our answer, so we now know that 3/16 = 0.1875. On the real test, you'll get a mix of hard and easy ones. One of the best ways to prepare is to simply memorize as many fractions and their decimal equivalents as you can. If you already know that 5/8 is 0.625, you don't have to spend any time on that question working it out.

Another helpful trick is to approximate. Using 5/8 as an example again, we know that 4/8 is half or 0.50 so any answer choice less than 0.5 can be eliminated. We know 6/8 is the same as ¾ or 0.75, so anything above .75 can be eliminated as well. This can many times show you the right answer without having to work it out all the way. Also, you may not need to work the problem all the way out like we did in the example to .1875 since sometimes you'll see no other answer choice even starts with the 0.18xx.

A final helpful trick is if the denominator is easily divisible by 100, you can quickly find the answer. For example, 9/20. We know 20 goes into 100 five times, so 9x5=45. Move the decimal and you have the answer of 0.45! It obviously doesn't work that easily if the denominator is 13 or 17 or another number that is not easily divisible by 100, but this method is very useful to keep in mind.

Decimals into Fraction

Many people find converting decimals into fractions easier. We have this review section after "fractions into decimals" because it is best to get the hard stuff out of the way first.

First, we need to review a basic important aspect of decimals, which are the units following the decimal. Look at this example:

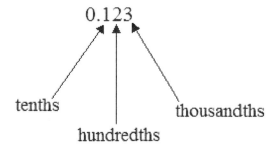

Here we see a zero with a decimal and three numbers after it. The first one is the "tenths" place, then the "hundredths", and the third one is the "thousandths". This is important to remember for solving decimal to fraction problems.

Let's work through an example: Convert 0.45 into a fraction.

Step 1: we see that this decimal number only goes to the "hundredths" place. This step almost seems to easy, but we simply start with:

$$\frac{45}{100}$$

Step 2: The next step is to simply reduce the fraction down to the lowest common denominator. For example, we know both 45 and 100 are divisible by 5, so start there. 45 divided by 5 is 9. 100 divided by 5 is 20. Therefore, we are left with:

$$\frac{9}{20}$$

And that's it! The answer is 9/20. In some cases, you might need to reduce a little further in case you accidentally did not start with the lowest common denominator. Now all that is left is to practice and you'll have the hang of it in no time. A great way to practice is to simply make your own questions since these are so straightforward unlike word problems. You can easily check yourself with an online conversion calculator if you aren't sure, and you will be a pro in no time.

Units of Measurement

You are expected to memorize some units of measurement. These are all given below:

United States Customary System	
Length	
1 foot	12 inches
1 yard	3 feet
Weight	
1 pound	16 ounces
1 ton	2000 pounds
Capacity	
1 pint	2 cups
1 quart	2 pints
1 quart	4 cups
1 gallon	4 quarts
1 gallon	8 pints
1 gallon	16 cups

Units of Time	
1 minute	60 seconds
1 hour	60 minutes
1 day	24 hours
1 week	7 days
1 year	365 days
1 year	52 weeks
1 year	12 months

Metric System	
Length	
1 kilometer	1000 meters
1 meter	100 centimeters
1 meter	1000 millimeters
1 centimeter	10 millimeters
Weight	
1 kilogram	1000 grams
1 gram	1000 milligrams
Capacity	
1 liter	1000 milliliters
1 millimeter	1 cubic centimeter

The metric system uses a standard set of prefixes that can apply to length, weight, and capacity. The most common ones are:

kilo – 1000

centi – 100

milli – 1/1000

When doing unit conversion problems, find the conversion factor. Then apply that factor to the given measurement to find the new measurement. Examples are shown below.

Practice problems:

A fence measures 15 feet long. How many yards long is the fence?

1 yard = 3 feet

15 / 3 = **5 yards**

A pitcher can hold 24 cups. How many gallons can it hold?

1 gallon = 16 cups

24 / 16 = **1.5 gallons**

A spool of wire holds 144 inches of wire. If Mario has three spools, how many feet of wire does he have?
12 inches = 1 foot

144 / 12 = 12 feet

12 feet * 3 spools = **36 feet of wire**

A ball rolling across a table travels 6 inches per second. How many feet will it travel in one minute?

This problem can be worked in two steps: finding how many inches in one minute, and then converting that to feet. It can also be worked the opposite way, by finding how many feet it travels in one second and then converting that to feet traveled per minute. The first method is shown below.

1 minute = 60 seconds

6 inches/second * 60 seconds = 360 inches

1 foot = 12 inches

360 inches/12 inches = **30 feet**

How many millimeters are in 0.5 meters?

1 meter = 1000 millimeters

0.5 meters = **500 millimeters**

A lead ball weighs 38 grams. How many kilograms does it weigh?

1 kilogram = 1000 grams

38 grams / 1000 grams = **0.038 kilograms**

How many cubic centimeters are in 10 liters?

1 liter = 1000 cubic centimeters

10 liters = 1000 * 10 cubic centimeters

10 liters = **10,000 cubic centimeters**

Jennifer's pencil was initially 10 centimeters long. After she sharpened it, it was 9.6 centimeters long. How many millimeters did she lose from her pencil by sharpening it?

1 centimeter = 10 millimeters

10 cm – 9.6 cm = 0.4 cm lost

0.4 centimeters = 10 * .4 millimeters = **4 millimeters** were lost

Comparison of rational numbers

Number comparison problems present numbers in different formats and ask which is larger or smaller, or whether the numbers are equivalent. The important step in solving these problems is to convert the numbers to the same format so that it is easier to see how they compare. If numbers are given in the same format, or after they have been converted, see which number is smaller or if the numbers are equal. Remember that for negative numbers, higher numbers are smaller.

Examples:

Is $4\frac{3}{4}$ greater than, equal to, or less than $\frac{18}{4}$?

These numbers are in different formats – one is a mixed fraction and the other is just a fraction. The first step is to convert the mixed fraction to a fraction:

$$4\frac{3}{4} = 4 * \frac{4}{4} + \frac{3}{4} = \frac{19}{4}$$

Once the mixed number is converted, it is easier to see that $\frac{19}{4}$ is **greater than** $\frac{18}{4}$.

Which of the following numbers has the greatest value: 104.56, 104.5, or 104.6?

These numbers are all already in the same format, so the decimal values just need to be compared. Remember that 0s can be added after the decimal without changing the value, so the three numbers can be rewritten as:

104.56

104.50

104.60

From this list, it is clearer to see that **104.60** is the greatest because .60 is larger than .50 and .56.

Is 65% greater than, less than, or equal to $\frac{13}{20}$?

The first step is to convert the numbers into the same format. 65% is the same as $\frac{65}{100}$. Next, the fractions need to be converted to have the same denominator. It is difficult to compare fractions with different denominators. Using a factor of $\frac{5}{5}$ on the second fraction will give common denominators:

$\frac{13}{20} * \frac{5}{5} = \frac{65}{100}$. Now, is easy to see that the numbers are equivalent.

Solving Word Problems

The most important step in solving any word problem is to read the entire problem before beginning to solve. You shouldn't skip over words or assume you know what the question is from the first sentence. The following are the general steps used to solve word problems:

General Steps for Word Problem Solving:

Step 1: Read the entire problem and determine what the problem is asking for.
Step 2: List all of the given data.
Step 3: Sketch diagrams with the given data.
Step 4: Determine formula(s) needed.
Step 5: Set up equation(s).
Step 6: Solve.
Step 7: Check your answer. Make sure that your answer makes sense. (Is the amount too large or small; are the answers in the correct unit of measure; etc.)

Note: Not all steps are needed for every problem.

One of the most commonly-made mistakes in mathematics applies especially for word problems is not reading the question all the way or providing an answer to a question that wasn't asked. Even if an answer you calculated is a given answer choice, that doesn't make it the correct answer. Remember that not all of the information given in a problem is needed to solve it.

> For example:

> Kathy had $12.45, John had $10.30, and Liz had $6.90. How much money did the girls have combined?

> The amount John has is not needed to solve the problem, since the problem is only asking for the combined amounts of Kathy and Liz.

Mistakes most commonly occur when answers for only a part of the problem are given as answer choices. It's very easy to get caught up in thinking, "That's the number I have here! It looks right, so I'll go with that." Trust yourself, and always check your answers. The best way to prepare for the arithmetic section is to practice! At first, don't concern yourself with how long it takes to solve problems; focus on understanding how to solve them, and then time yourself.

This section will go over some of the most common types of word problems found on the Arithmetic Reasoning Section, but keep in mind that any math concept can be turned into a word problem.

Key Words

Word problems generally contain key words that can help you determine what math processes may be required in order to solve them. Here are some commonly-used key words:

- **Addition:** Added, combined, increased by, in all, total, perimeter, sum, and more than.
- **Subtraction:** How much more, less than, fewer than, exceeds, difference, and decreased.
- **Multiplication:** Of, times, area, and product.
- **Division:** Distribute, share, average, per, out of, percent, and quotient.
- **Equals:** Is, was, are, amounts to, and were.

BASIC WORD PROBLEMS

A word problem in algebra is the equivalent of a story problem in math, only word problems are solved by separating information from the problems into two equal groups (one for each side of an equation). Examine this problem:

> Sara has 15 apples and 12 oranges. How many pieces of fruit does she have?

We know that the sum of 15 and 12 is equal to the total amount of fruit. An unknown number or value is represented by a letter. The total number of pieces of fruit is unknown, so we will represent that amount with x. When the value that a particular variable will represent is determined, it is defined by writing a statement like this:

> Let x = Total Amount of Fruit.

Once again, the sum of 15 apples and 12 oranges is equal to the total amount of fruit. This can be used to translate the problem into an equation:

> $15 + 12 = x$
> $x = 27$
> Sara has 27 pieces of fruit.

Of course, you could probably have solved this problem more quickly without having set up an algebraic equation. But knowing how to use an equation for this kind of problem builds your awareness of which concepts are useful; some of them are even critical to solving much harder problems.

Examples:

1. A salesman bought a case of 48 backpacks for $576. He sold 17 of them for $18 at the swap meet, and the rest were sold to a department store for $25 each. What was the salesman's profit?

> Calculate the total of the 17 backpacks, which you know the cost to be $18:
> 17 * $18 = $306.
>
> Calculate how many backpacks were sold at $25: 48 − 17 = 31.
>
> Calculate the total amount of profit for the backpacks sold at $25: 31 * $25 = $775.

51

Add the two dollar amounts for backpacks sold: $306 + $775 = $1081.

Subtract the salesman's initial cost: $1081 - $576 = $505.

The answer to the question asked about his profit is: $505.

2. Thirty students in Mr. Joyce's room are working on projects over the duration of two days. The first day, he gave them 3/5 of an hour to work. On the second day, he gave them half as much time as the first day. How much time did the students have altogether?

1st day = 3/5 of an hour.
2nd day = 1/2 (3/5) = 3/10 of an hour.
Total = 3/5 + 3/10 = 6/10 + 3/10 = 9/10 of an hour.

An hour has 60 minutes, so set up a ratio:

$9/10 = x/60$.
$x = 54$.
So the students had 54 minutes altogether to work on the projects.

Another way to do this problem is to calculate first the amount of time allotted on the first day: 3/5 * 60 minutes = 36 minutes.

Then take half of that to get the time allotted on the second day:
36 minutes * 1/2 = 18 minutes.

Add the two together for your total time! 36 + 18 = 54.

PERCENTAGE WORD PROBLEMS

Basic Equations:

Percent Change: Amount of Change ÷ Original Amount * 100

Percent Increase: (New Amount – Original Amount) ÷ Original Amount * 100

Percent Decrease: (Original Amount – New Amount) ÷ Original Amount * 100

Amount Increase (Or Amount Decrease): Original Price * Percent Markup
                                        (Or, for Amount Decrease, Markdown)

Original Price: New Price ÷ (Whole - Percent Markdown)

Original Price: New Price ÷ (Whole + Percent Markup)

Many percentage problems consist of markup and markdown. For these, you calculate how much the quantity changed, and then you calculate the percent change relative to the original value.

Examples:

1. A computer software retailer used a markup rate of 40%. Find the selling price of a computer game that cost the retailer $25.

    The markup is 40% of the $25 cost, so the equation to find markup is: $(0.40) * (25) = 10$.

    The selling price is the cost plus markup: $25 + 10 = 35$. The item sold for $35.

2. A golf shop pays its wholesaler $40 for a certain club, and then sells it to a golfer for $75. What is the markup rate?

    First calculate the markup: $75 – 40 = 35$.

    Then find the markup rate: $35 is (some percent) of $40, or: $35 = (x) * (40)$.

    ...so the markup over the original price is: $35 ÷ 40 = x$. $x = 0.875$.

    Since the problem asks for a percentage, you need to remember to convert the decimal value.

    The markup rate is 87.5%.

3. A shoe store uses a 40% markup on cost. Find the cost of a pair of shoes that sells for $63.

    This problem is somewhat backwards. You are given the selling price, which is "cost + markup", and the markup rate. You are not given the actual cost or markup.

    Let x be the cost. The markup, being 40% of the cost, is $0.40x$. The selling price of $63 is the sum of the cost and markup, so:

$63 = x + 0.40x.$

$63 = 1x + 0.40x.$

$63 = 1.40x.$

$63 \div 1.40 = x.$

$x = 45.$ The shoes cost the store $45.

4. An item originally priced at $55 is marked 25% off. What is the sale price?

    First, find the markdown. The markdown is 25% of the original price of $55, so: $x = (0.25) *$ (55). $x = 13.75.$

    By subtracting this markdown from the original price, you can find the sale price: $55 - 13.75 = 41.25.$ The sale price is $41.25.

5. An item that regularly sells for $425 is marked down to $318.75. What is the discount rate?

    First, find the amount of the markdown: $425 - 318.75 = 106.25.$ Then calculate "the markdown of the original price", or the markdown rate: $106.25 is (some percent) of $425, so:

    $106.25 = (x) * (425).$

    ...and the markdown over the original price is: $x - 106.25 \div 425.$ $x = 0.25.$

    Since the "x" stands for a percentage, remember to convert this decimal to percentage form. The markdown rate is 25%.

6. A bike is marked down 15%; the sale price is $127.46. What was the original price?

    This problem is backwards. You are given the sale price ($127.46) and the markdown rate (15%), but neither the markdown amount nor the original price.

    Let "x" stand for the original price. Then the markdown, being 15% of this price, will be $0.15x$. The sale price is the original price, minus the markdown, so: $x - 0.15x = 127.46.$

    $1x - 0.15x = 127.46.$

    $0.85x = 127.46.$
    $x = 127.46 \div 0.85.$

    $x = 149.95.$ The original price was $149.95.

    Note: In this last problem, we ended up – in the third line of calculations – with an equation that said "eighty-five percent of the original price is $127.46". You can save yourself some time if you think of discounts in this way: if the price is 15% off, then you're only actually paying 85%. Similarly, if the price is 25% off, then you're paying 75%, etc.

Note: While the values below do not refer to money, the procedures used to solve these problems are otherwise identical to the markup - markdown examples.

7. Growing up, you lived in a tiny country village. When you left for college, the population was 840. You recently heard that the population has grown by 5%. What is the present population?

    First, find the actual amount of the increase. Since the increase is five percent of the original population, then the increase is: (0.05) * (840) = 42.

    The new population is the old population plus the increase, or: 840 + 42 = 882.

    The population is now 882.

8. You put in an 18 X 51 foot garden along the whole back end of your backyard. It has reduced the backyard lawn area by 24%. What is the area of the remaining lawn area?

    The area of the garden is: (18) * (51) = 918. This represents 24% of the total yard area, or 24% of the original lawn area. This means that 918 square feet is 24% of the original, so: $918 = 0.24x$.

    $918 \div 0.24 = x$.

    $3825 = x$.

    The total back yard area is 3825 square feet, and we know from the problem that the width is 51 feet. Therefore, to find the length: $3825 \div 51 = 75$. The length then is 75 feet. Since 18 feet are taken up by the garden, then the lawn area is: 75 – 18 = 57 feet deep. The area of the lawn now measures 51' X 57'.

WORK WORD PROBLEMS

"Work" problems involve situations such as: two people working together to paint a house. You are usually told how long each person takes to paint a similarly-sized house, and then you are asked how long it will take the two of them to paint the house when they work together.

There is a "trick" to doing work problems: you have to think of the problem in terms of how much each person/machine/whatever does in a given unit of time.

Example:

Suppose one painter can paint the entire house in twelve hours, and the second painter takes eight hours. How long would it take the two painters together to paint the house?

> If the first painter can do the entire job in twelve hours, and the second painter can do it in eight hours, then (here is the trick!) the first painter can do 1/12 of the job per hour, and the second guy can do 1/8 per hour. How much then can they do per hour if they work together?

> To find out how much they can do together per hour, add together what they can do individually per hour: $1/12 + 1/8 = 5/24$. They can do 5/24 of the job per hour.

> Now let "t" stand for how long they take to do the job together. Then they can do $1/t$ per hour, so $5/24 = 1/t$. When for $t = 24/5$, $t = 4.8$ hours. That is:

Hours to complete job:

> First painter: 12.
> Second painter: 8.
> Together: t.

Work completed per hour:

> First painter: 1/12.
> Second painter: 1/8.
> Together: $1/t$.

Adding their labor:

> $1/12 + 1/8 = 1/t$.
> $5/24 = 1/t$.
> $24/5 = t$.
> $t = 4\ 4/5$ hours.

As you can see in the above example, "work" problems commonly create rational equations. But the equations themselves are usually pretty simple.

More Examples:

1. One pipe can fill a pool 1.25 times faster than a second pipe. When both pipes are opened, they fill the pool in five hours. How long would it take to fill the pool if only the slower pipe is used?

   Convert to rates.

   Hours to complete job:

   Fast pipe: f.
   Slow pipe: $1.25f$.
   Together: 5.

   Work completed per hour:

   Fast pipe: $1/f$.
   Slow pipe: $1/1.25f$.
   Together: $1/5$.

   Adding their labor:

   $1/f + 1/1.25f = 1/5$.

   Solve for f:

   $5 + 5/1.25 = f$.
   $5 + 4 = f$.
   $f = 9$.

   Then $1.25f = 11.25$, so the slower pipe takes 11.25 hours.

   If you're not sure how I derived the rate for the slow pipe, think about it this way: if someone goes twice as fast as you, then you take twice as long as he does; if he goes three times as fast, then you take three times as long. In this case, one pipe goes 1.25 times as fast, so the other takes 1.25 times as long.

This next one is a bit different:

2. Ben takes 2 hours to wash 500 dishes, and Frank takes 3 hours to wash 450 dishes. How long will they take, working together, to wash 1000 dishes?

   For this exercise, you are given *how many* can be done in one time unit, rather than *how much* of a job can be completed. But the thinking process is otherwise the same.

   Ben can do 250 dishes per hour, and Frank can do 150 dishes per hour. Working together, they can do $250 + 150 = 400$ dishes an hour. That is:

Ben: 500 dishes / 2 hours = 250 dishes / hour.

Frank: 450 dishes / 3 hours = 150 dishes / hour.

Together: (250 + 150) dishes / hour = 400 dishes / hour.

Next find the number of hours that it takes to wash 1000 dishes. Set things up so **units cancel** and you're left with "hours":

(1000 dishes) * (1 hour / 400 dishes).

(1000 / 400) hours.

2.5 hours.

It will take two and a half hours for the two of them to wash 1000 dishes.

3. If six men can do a job in fourteen days, how many would it take to do the job in twenty-one days?

Convert this to man-hours, or, in this case, man-days. If it takes six guys fourteen days, then: (6 men) * (14 days) = 84 man-days.

That is, the entire job requires 84 man-days. This exercise asks you to expand the time allowed from fourteen days to twenty-one days. Obviously, if they're giving you more time, then you'll need fewer guys. But how many guys, exactly? (x men) * (21 days) = 84 man-days.

...or, in algebra: $21x = 84$. $x = 4$. So, only four guys are needed to do the job in twenty-one days.

You may have noticed that each of these problems used some form of the "how much can be done per time unit" construction, but aside from that each problem was done differently. That's how "work" problems are; but, as you saw above, if you label things neatly and do your work orderly, you should find your way to the solution.

DISTANCE WORD PROBLEMS

"Distance" word problems, often also called "uniform rate" problems, involve something travelling at a fixed and steady ("uniform") pace ("rate" or "speed"), or else moving at some average speed. Whenever you read a problem that involves "how fast", "how far, or "for how long," you should think of the distance equation, $d = rt$, where d stands for distance, r stands for the (constant or average) rate of speed, and t stands for time. It is easier to solve these types of problems using a grid and filling in the information given in the problem.

Warning: Make sure that the units for time and distance agree with the units for the rate. For instance, if they give you a rate of feet per second, then your time must be in seconds and your distance must be in feet. Sometimes they try to trick you by using two different units, and you have to catch this and convert to the correct units.

1. An executive drove from his home at an average speed of 30 mph to an airport where a helicopter was waiting. The executive boarded the helicopter and flew to the corporate offices at an average speed of 60 mph. The entire distance was 150 miles; the entire trip took three hours. Find the distance from the airport to the corporate offices.

	d	r	t
driving	d	30	t
flying	$150-d$	60	$3-t$
total	150	---	3

The first row gives me the equation $d = 30t$.

Since the first part of his trip accounted for d miles of the total 150-mile distance and t hours of the total 3-hour time, you are left with $150 - d$ miles and $3 - t$ hours for the second part. The second row gives the equation: $150 - d$. $d = 60(3 - t)$.

This now becomes a system of equations problem.

Add the two "distance" expressions and setting their sum equal to the given total distance: $150 - d = 60(3 - t)$. $d = 30t$. $150 = 30t + 60(3 - t)$.

Solve for t: $150 = 30t + 180 - 60t$. $150 = 180 - 30t$. $-30 = -30t$. $1 = t$.

It is important to note that you are not finished when you have solved for the first variable. This is where it is important to pay attention to what the problem asked for. It does not ask for time, but the time is needed to solve the problem.

So now insert the value for t into the first equation: $d = 30$.

Subtract from total distance: $150 - 30 = 120$.

The distance to the corporate offices is 120 miles.

2. Two cyclists start at the same time from opposite ends of a course that is 45 miles long. One cyclist is riding at 14 mph and the second cyclist is riding at 16 mph. How long after they begin will they meet?

	d	r	t
slow guy	d	14	t
fast guy	$45-d$	16	t
total	45	---	---

Why is t the same for both cyclists? Because you are measuring from the time they both started to the time they meet somewhere in the middle.

Why "d" and "$45 - d$" for the distances? Because I assigned the slower cyclist as having covered d miles, which left $45 - d$ miles for the faster cyclist to cover: the two cyclists *together* covered the whole 45 miles.

Using "$d = rt$," you get $d = 14t$ from the first row, and $45 - d = 16t$ from the second row. Since these distances add up to 45, add the distance expressions and set equal to the given total: $45 = 14t + 16t$.

Solve for t, place it back into the equation, to solve for what the question asked. $45 = 30t$. $t = 45 \div 30 = 1\ ½$. They will meet 1 ½ hours after they begin.

RATIO PROBLEMS

To solve a ratio, simply find the equivalent fraction. To distribute a whole across a ratio:

1. Total all parts.

2. Divide the whole by the total number of parts.

3. Multiply quotient by corresponding part of ratio.

Example: There are 81 voters in a room, all either Democrat or Republican. The ratio of Democrats to Republicans is 5:4. How many republicans are there?

1) $5 + 4 = 9$.

2) $81 \div 9 = 9$.

3) $9 * 4 = 36$. 36 Republicans.

PROPORTIONS

Direct proportions: Corresponding ratio parts change in the same direction (increase/decrease).

Indirect proportions: Corresponding ratio parts change in opposite directions; as one part increases the other decreases.

Example (Indirect Proportion): A train traveling 120 miles takes 3 hours to get to its destination. How long will it take if the train travels 180 miles?

120 miles : 180 miles
        is to
x hours : 3 hours

Write as a fraction and cross multiply: $3 * 180 = 120x$.

$540 = 120x$. $x = 4.5$ hours. It will take the train 4.5 hours to reach its destination.

Chapter 2: English and Language Arts

The first step in getting ready for this section of the test consists of reviewing the basic techniques used to determine the meanings of words you are not familiar with. The good news is that you have been using various degrees of these techniques since you first began to speak. Sharpening these skills will also help you with the ELA subtest.

Parts of Speech

Nouns: Nouns are people, places, or things. They are typically the subject of a sentence. For example, "The hospital was very clean." The noun is "hospital;" it is the "place."

Pronouns: Pronouns essentially "replace" nouns. This allows a sentence to not sound repetitive. Take the sentence: "Sam stayed home from school because Sam was not feeling well." The word "Sam" appears twice in the same sentence. Instead, you can use a pronoun and say, "Sam stayed at home because *he* did not feel well." Sounds much better, right?

Most Common Pronouns:

- I, me, mine, my.

- You, your, yours.

- He, him, his.

- She, her, hers.

- It, its.

- We, us, our, ours.

- They, them, their, theirs.

Verbs: Remember the old commercial, "Verb: It's what you do"? That sums up verbs in a nutshell! Verbs are the "action" of a sentence; verbs "do" things.

They can, however, be quite tricky. Depending on the subject of a sentence, the tense of the word (past, present, future, etc.), and whether or not they are regular or irregular, verbs have many variations.

Example: "He runs to second base." The verb is "runs." This is a "regular verb."

Example: "I am 7 years old." The verb in this case is "am." This is an "irregular verb."

As mentioned, verbs must use the correct tense – and that tense must remain the same throughout the sentence. "I was baking cookies and eat some dough." That sounded strange, didn't it? That's because the two verbs "baking" and "eat" are presented in different tenses. "Was baking" occurred in the past; "eat," on the other hand, occurs in the present. Instead, it should be "**ate** some dough."

Adjectives: Adjectives are words that describe a noun and give more information. Take the sentence: "The boy hit the ball." If you want to know more about the noun "boy," then you could use an adjective to describe it. "The **little** boy hit the ball." An adjective simply provides more information about a noun or subject in a sentence.

Adverbs: For some reason, many people have a difficult time with adverbs – but don't worry! They are really quite simple. Adverbs are similar to adjectives in that they provide more information; however, they describe verbs, adjectives, and even other adverbs. They do **not** describe nouns – that's an adjective's job.

Take the sentence: "The doctor said she hired a new employee."

It would give more information to say: "The doctor said she **recently** hired a new employee." Now we know more about *how* the action was executed. Adverbs typically describe when or how something has happened, how it looks, how it feels, etc.

Prepositions: Prepositions express the location of a noun or pronoun in relation to other words and phrases in a sentence.

Example: "The nurse parked her car in a parking garage."

The preposition "in" is describing the location of the nurse's car. A prepositional phrase is a phrase that starts with a preposition and ends with a noun. The prepositional phrase is "in a parking garage." Here, "in" is the preposition and "garage is the noun."

Conjunctions: Conjunctions connect words, phrases, and clauses. Some common conjunctions include *and*, *but*, and *or*.

Example: "The nurse prepared the patient for surgery, and the doctor performed the surgery."

Here, the two independent clauses "The nurse prepared the patient for surgery" and "The doctor performed the surgery" are joined by the conjunction "and."

Interjections: Interjections express emotion.

Example: "Gee, that race was close!"

"Gee" is the interjection. It shows how excited this particular person is about the race.

The Parts of Words

Although you are not expected to know every word in the English language for your test, you will need to have the ability to use deductive reasoning to find the choice that is the best match for the word in question, which is why we are going to explain how to break a word into its parts of meaning

prefix – root – suffix

One trick in dividing a word into its parts is to first divide the word into its **syllables**. To show how syllables can help you find roots and affixes, we'll use the word **descendant,** which means one who comes from an ancestor. Start by dividing the word into its individual syllables; this word has three: **de-scend-ant**. The next step is to look at the beginning and end of the word, and then determine if these syllables are prefixes, suffixes, or possible roots. You can then use the meanings of each part to guide you in defining the word. When you divide words into their specific parts, they do not always add up to an exact definition, but you will see a relationship between their parts.

> **Note:** This trick won't always work in every situation, because not all prefixes, roots, and suffixes have only one syllable. For example, take the word **monosyllabic** (which ironically means "one syllable"). There are five syllables in that word, but only three parts. The prefix is "mono," meaning "one." The root "syllab" refers to "syllable," while the suffix "ic" means "pertaining to." Therefore, we have one very long word which means "pertaining to one syllable."

The more familiar you become with these fundamental word parts, the easier it will be to define unfamiliar words. Although the words found on the Word Knowledge subtest are considered vocabulary words learned by the tenth grade level of high school, some are still less likely to be found in an individual's everyday vocabulary. The root and affixes list in this chapter uses more common words as examples to help you learn them more easily. Don't forget that you use word roots and affixes every day, without even realizing it. Don't feel intimidated by the long list of roots and affixes (prefixes and suffixes) at the end of this chapter, because you already know and use them every time you communicate with some else, verbally and in writing. If you take the time to read through the list just once a day for two weeks, you will be able to retain most of them and understand a high number of initially unfamiliar words.

Roots, Prefixes, and Suffixes

Roots
Roots are the building blocks of all words. Every word is either a root itself or has a root. Just as a plant cannot grow without roots, neither can vocabulary, because a word must have a root to give it meaning.

> **Example**: The test instructions were **unclear.**

The root is what is left when you strip away all the prefixes and suffixes from a word. In this case, take away the prefix "un-," and you have the root **clear**.

Roots are not always recognizable words, because they generally come from Latin or Greek words, such as **nat**, a Latin root meaning **born**. The word native, which means a person born of a referenced placed, comes from this root, so does the word prenatal, meaning before birth. Yet, if you used the prefix **nat** instead of born, just on its own, no one would know what you were talking about.
Words can also have more than one root. For example, the word **omnipotent** means all powerful. Omnipotent is a combination of the roots **omni-**, meaning all or every, and -**potent**, meaning power or strength. In this case, **omni** cannot be used on its own as a single word, but **potent** can.

Again, it is important to keep in mind that roots do not always match the exact definitions of words and they can have several different spellings, but breaking a word into its parts is still one of the best ways to determine its meaning.

Prefixes

Prefixes are syllables added to the beginning of a word and suffixes are syllables added to the end of the word. Both carry assigned meanings. The common name for prefixes and suffixes is **affixes**. Affixes do not have to be attached directly to a root and a word can often have more than one prefix and/or suffix. Prefixes and suffixes can be attached to a word to completely change the word's meaning or to enhance the word's original meaning. Although they don't mean much to us on their own, when attached to other words affixes can make a world of difference.

Let's use the word **prefix** itself as an example:

Fix means to place something securely.

Pre means before.

Prefix means to place something before or in front.

Suffixes

Suffixes come after the root of a word.

Example: Feminism

Femin is a root. It means female, woman.

-ism means act, practice or process.

Feminism is the defining and establishing of equal political, economic, and social rights for women.

Unlike prefixes, **suffixes** can be used to change a word's part of speech.

Example: "Randy raced to the finish line." VS "Shana's costume was very racy."

In the first sentence, raced is a verb. In the second sentence, racy is an adjective. By changing the suffix from **-ed** to **-y**, the word race changes from a verb into an adjective, which has an entirely different meaning.

Although you cannot determine the meaning of a word by a prefix or suffix alone, you *can* use your knowledge of what root words mean to eliminate answer choices; indicating if the word is positive or negative can give you a partial meaning of the word.

Context Clues

The most fundamental vocabulary skill is using the context of a word to determine its meaning. Your ability to observe sentences closely is extremely useful when it comes to understanding new vocabulary words.

Types of Context

There are two different types of context that can help you understand the meaning of unfamiliar words: **sentence context** and **situational context**. Regardless of which context is present, these types of questions are not really testing your knowledge of vocabulary; rather, they test your ability to comprehend the meaning of a word through its usage.

Situational context is context that comes from understanding the situation in which a word or phrase occurs.

Sentence context occurs within the sentence that contains the vocabulary word. To figure out words using sentence context clues, you should first determine the most important words in the sentence.

> **Example:** I had a hard time reading her <u>illegible</u> handwriting.
> a) Neat.
> b) Unsafe.
> c) Sloppy.
> d) Educated.

Already, you know that this sentence is discussing something that is hard to read. Look at the word that **illegible** is describing: **handwriting**. Based on context clues, you can tell that illegible means that her handwriting is hard to read.

Next, look at the answer choices. Choice **a) Neat** is obviously a wrong answer because neat handwriting would not be difficult to read. Choice **b) Unsafe** and **d) Educated** don't make sense. Therefore, choice **c) Sloppy** is the best answer choice.

Types of Clues
There are four types of clues that can help you understand context, and therefore the meaning of a word. They are **restatement**, **positive/negative**, **contrast**, and **specific detail**.

Restatement clues occur when the definition of the word is clearly stated in the sentence.

> **Example**: The dog was <u>dauntless</u> in the face of danger, braving the fire to save the girl.
> a) Difficult.
> b) Fearless.
> c) Imaginative.

Demonstrating **bravery** in the face of danger would be **fearless,** choice **b)**. In this case, the context clues tell you exactly what the word means.

Positive/negative clues can tell you whether a word has a positive or negative meaning.

> **Example**: The magazine gave a great review of the fashion show, stating the clothing was **sublime**.
> a) Horrible.
> b) Exotic.
> c) Bland
> d) Gorgeous.

The sentence tells us that the author liked the clothing enough to write a **great** review, so you know that the best answer choice is going to be a positive word. Therefore, you can immediately rule out choices **a)** and **c)** because they are negative words. **Exotic** is a neutral word; alone, it doesn't inspire a **great** review. The most positive word is gorgeous, which makes choice **d) Gorgeous** the best answer.

The following sentence uses both restatement and positive/negative clues:

"Janet suddenly found herself <u>destitute</u>, so poor she could barely afford to eat."

The second part of the sentence clearly indicates that destitute is a negative word; it also restates the meaning: very poor.

Contrast clues include the opposite meaning of a word. Words like **but, on the other hand**, and **however** are tip-offs that a sentence contains a contrast clue.

Example: Beth did not spend any time preparing for the test, but Tyron kept a <u>rigorous</u> study schedule.
   a) Strict.
   b) Loose.
   c) Boring.
   d) Strange.

In this case, the word **but** tells us that Tyron studied in a different way than Beth. If Beth did not study very hard, then Tyron did study hard for the test. The best answer here, therefore, is choice **a) Strict**.

Specific detail clues give a precise detail that can help you understand the meaning of the word.

Example: The box was heavier than he expected and it began to become <u>cumbersome</u>.
   a) Impossible.
   b) Burdensome.
   c) Obligated.
   d) Easier.

Start by looking at the specific details of the sentence. Choice **d)** can be eliminated right away because it is doubtful it would become **easier** to carry something that is **heavier**. There are also no clues in the sentence to indicate he was **obligated** to carry the box, so choice **c)** can also be disregarded. The sentence specifics, however, do tell you that the package was cumbersome because it was heavy to carry; something heavy to carry is a burden, which is **burdensome**, choice **b)**.

It is important to remember that more than one of these clues can be present in the same sentence. The more there are, the easier it will be to determine the meaning of the word, so look for them.

Denotation and Connotation

As you know, many English words have more than one meaning. For example, the word **quack** has two distinct definitions: the sound a duck makes; and a person who publicly pretends to have a skill, knowledge, education, or qualification which they do not possess.

The **denotations** of a word are the dictionary definitions.

The **connotations** of a word are the implied meaning(s) or emotion which the word makes you think.

Example: "Sure," Pam said excitedly, "I'd just love to join your club; it sounds so exciting!"

Now, read this sentence:

"Sure," Pam said sarcastically, "I'd just love to join your club; it sounds so exciting!"

Even though the two sentences only differ by one word, they have completely different meanings. The difference, of course, lies in the words "excitedly" and "sarcastically."

Subject-Verb Agreement

The subject must agree with the verb in number. A singular noun requires a singular verb, and a plural noun requires a plural verb. Often, this is quite easy to accomplish because the subject and verb are usually quite close to each other.

"The cat (singular noun) chases (singular verb) the ball."
"The cats (plural noun) play (plural verb) at the same time."

Sometimes, the subject and verb are separated by clauses or phrases. In these instances, ignore the clauses and phrases and make sure the subject and verb agree in number.

"The cars (plural noun) that had been recalled by the manufacturer were returned (plural verb) within a few months."

Sometimes, the subject of a sentence is a collective noun. A collective noun is singular, but reflects a group of people or items. This group can reflect a single entity or separate entities. When the group reflects a single unit, use a singular verb; when the group reflects separate items, use a plural verb.

"The deer hid in the trees."
"The deer are not all the same size."

Sometimes, the subject of a sentence is a compound subject. When the subject contains two or more words connected by *and*, the subject is plural and requires a plural verb. When the subject contains two or more singular words connected by *or, either/or, neither/nor*, or *not only/but also*, the subject is singular and requires a singular verb. When the subject contains singular and plural words connected by *or, either/or, neither/nor*, or *not only/but also*, select a verb that agrees with the subject closest to it.

"The doctor and nurse (plural noun) work (plural verb) in the hospital."
"Neither the employer (singular noun) nor the employee (singular noun) was (singular verb) scheduled to take a vacation."
"Either the parents (plural noun) or the son (singular noun) was responsible (singular verb) for the success."

Pronoun-Antecedent Agreement

A pronoun modifies a noun. An antecedent is the noun to which a pronoun refers. So, when you hear the word *antecedent* in the pronoun-antecedent context, it simply means a noun and a pronoun that replaces it. A pronoun must agree with its antecedent in number and person. It must also refer clearly to a specific noun.

If a noun is singular, the pronoun replacing it must also be singular. Sometimes when people speak, they use plural pronouns for singular nouns. This is incorrect. Likewise, plural nouns require plural pronouns, although errors with plural nouns and pronouns are far less common than with singular nouns and pronouns.

>   Example: If a student forgets their homework, it is considered incomplete.
>   Corrected: If a student forgets his/her homework, it is considered incomplete.

Student is a singular noun. *Their* is a plural pronoun. So, this first sentence is grammatically incorrect. To correct it, replace *their* with the singular pronoun *his* or *her*.

Another common mistake involves the words *anybody, everybody, anyone, someone, nobody*, etc. These are singular nouns, but often are referred to with plural pronouns.

>   Example: Everybody will receive their paychecks promptly.
>   Corrected: Everybody will receive his/her paycheck promptly.

Everybody is a singular noun. *Their* is a plural pronoun. So, this sentence is grammatically incorrect. To correct it, replace *their* with the singular pronoun *his* or *her*.

If a noun is written in first-person perspective, the pronoun must also be written in first-person perspective. The same holds true for second-person and third-person perspectives. It is incorrect to switch perspectives midway through a sentence.

>   Example: When a nurse begins work at a hospital, you should wash your hands.
>   Corrected: When a nurse begins work at a hospital, he/she should wash his/her hands.

This sentence begins in third-person perspective and finishes in second-person perspective. So, this sentence is grammatically incorrect. To correct it, ensure the sentence finishes with third-person perspective.

A pronoun must clearly reference a specific noun. Sometimes, a pronoun is too vague or ambiguous. This confuses the reader and makes the meaning of the sentence unclear.

>   Example: After the teacher spoke to the student, she realized her mistake.
>   Corrected: After Mrs. White spoke to her student Bryan, she realized her mistake.
>   Corrected: After speaking to the student, the teacher realized her own mistake.

This sentence refers to a teacher and a student. But who does *she* refer to, the teacher or the student? To improve clarity, use specific names or state more specifically who realized her mistake.

Using Dialogue

Using dialogue can have a tremendous effect on your speech or writing. Instead of simply paraphrasing someone's words, you directly quote that person's exact dialogue. This is the difference between indirect dialogue and direct dialogue. **Indirect dialogue** talks about what another person said. **Direct dialogue** indicates exactly what another person said.

> Indirect dialogue: David said that he doesn't feel ready to take the exam.
> Direct dialogue: "I don't feel ready to take the exam," David said.

Direct dialogue is much more effective because it is very specific. The reader doesn't need someone to discuss what was said. He/she can read it firsthand.

It is also important to correctly punctuate the dialogue. Direct dialogue is always placed inside quotation marks. If there is a quote within a quote, you place single quotation marks within the double quotation marks.

> "Martha was happy when her teacher told her she was 'an absolute delight' and wished her luck in the future," Daniel said.

> Daniel said, "Martha was happy when her teacher told her she was 'an absolute delight' and wished her luck in the future."

In the examples above, the attributive tag—the part of the sentence that reflects who said the dialogue—is accompanied by a comma. If the tag appears after the quote, the quote ends with a comma inside the ending quotation mark. If the tag appears before the quote, the tag is followed by a comma, and the quote ends with a period (or question mark or exclamation mark) inside the ending quotation mark. It is also important to note that if the direct dialogue appears in the middle of a sentence (with text before and after it), always end it with a comma inside the ending quotation mark.

Although we have been placing the ending punctuation inside the ending quotation mark, it is not always correct. If you are asking a question or making an exclamation that applies to the entire sentence, the question mark or exclamation mark is placed outside the ending quotation mark.

> Why do politicians ignore our Constitution even though they take an oath to "preserve, protect, and defend the Constitution of the United States"?

The example above is a question. Even though it contains direct quotation, the question mark is placed outside the ending quotation mark. It looks a bit odd, but it is grammatically correct.

A final note about dialogue is that when the statement within quotation marks is a complete sentence, the first word inside the opening quotation mark is capitalized.

Point of View

A sentence's point of view is the perspective from which it is written.

Person	Pronouns Used	Emphasis	Example
first	I, we	on the writer	I take my time when shopping for shoes.
second	You	on the reader	You prefer to shop online.
third	He, she, it, they	on the subject	She buys shoes from her cousin's store.

Using first person is best for writing in which the writer's personal experiences, feelings, and opinions are an important element. Second person is best for writing in which the writer needs to directly address the reader. Third person is most common in formal and academic writing; it creates distance between the writer and the reader. Compare the following sentences:

I underestimated the amount of time needed to complete the test.
You underestimated the amount of time needed to complete the test.
They underestimated the amount of time needed to complete the test.

In the first example, which uses first person, the writer is relating his or her own personal experience to the reader. In the second example, which uses second person, the writer is directly addressing the reader; the tone of the sentence can be interpreted as almost accusatory, or finger-pointing. In the third example, which uses third person, the writer is sharing information with the reader, but it's not about either the writer or the reader, so there is some distance between them due to the subject of the sentence.
A sentence's point of view has to remain consistent, or the same, throughout the sentence.

Inconsistent: If someone wants to be a professional athlete, you have to practice often.
Consistent: If you want to be a professional athlete, you have to practice often.
Consistent: If someone wants to be a professional athlete, he/she has to practice often.

Coordinating and Subordinating Conjunctions

Conjunctions join two parts of a sentence, although the two types produce two very different sentences. A coordinating conjunction is a word that joins two equally significant parts of a sentence. The acronym FANBOYS makes it easier to remember the coordinating conjunctions: *for, and, nor, but, or, yet*, and *so*. A subordinating conjunction is a word that joins two unequal parts of a sentence, usually a subordinate clause to a main clause. Some subordinating conjunctions are: *because, though, although, as, as if, when*, and *while*.

Coordinating: I went to the movies last night, and I played hockey earlier that day.
Subordinating: I went to the movies last night, although I played hockey earlier that day.

In the first sentence, the two parts of the sentence are equal. You can separate them into two sentences. In the second sentence, the two parts of the sentence are unequal. You can't separate them in two sentences; the second part is dependent on the first part.

Active and Passive Voice

Nominalization is the forming of a noun from another part of speech, such as a verb or adjective. For instance, the noun *conclusion* is a nominative of the verb *conclude*. Using nominatives has become common, but try to avoid this practice by using active voice.

Sentences can be written in active voice or passive voice. Active voice means that the subjects of the sentences are acting or are being described. Passive voice means that the subjects are being acted on.

Active: Justin wrecked my car.
Passive: My car was wrecked by Justin.

Sometimes, passive voice is the best choice for a sentence. If the writer of the example sentences above wanted to emphasize that he/she did not know or did not care who wrecked the car, the passive voice would be an appropriate choice.

My car was wrecked this morning.

However, if the writer wanted to emphasize the action, the active voice would be the best choice.

Someone wrecked my car this morning.

In most cases, the active voice is the best choice: it makes sentences more interesting for readers and provides a greater feeling of action and energy.

Active: He received his paycheck at the end of the work week.
Passive: The paycheck was received by him at the end of the work week.

The sentence using active voice is shorter and easier to understand, and it sounds less awkward than the sentence using passive voice.

Simple Sentences

A simple sentence consists of only one independent clause. A simple sentence cannot contain a dependent clause. Because there are no dependent clauses in a simple sentence, it can simply be a two-word sentence, with one word being the subject and the other word being the verb. However, a simple sentence can also contain prepositions, adjectives, and adverbs. Even though these additions can extend the length of a simple sentence, it is still considered a simple sentence as long as it doesn't contain any dependent clauses.

Example: I ran.
Example: I am vacationing on an extravagant, lengthy cruise.

The first sentence is a simple sentence that has only two words, a subject and a verb. The second sentence is also a simple sentence even though it contains a preposition and adjectives. Both of these sentences are simple sentences because they do not contain any dependent clauses.

Sentence Structures

A sentence can be classified as simple, compound, complex, or compound-complex. A sentence is classified based on the type and number of clauses it has.

- **Simple sentences** have one independent clause and no subordinate clauses.
  I'll meet you there.

You come and go.
Even though the second sentence uses the word "and," it's still a simple sentence because both verbs—"come" and "go"—share the same subject—"You."

- **Compound sentences** have two or more independent clauses and no subordinate clauses. Usually a comma and a coordinating conjunction (*and, or, but, or, nor, for, so,* and *yet*) join the independent clauses, though semicolons can be used as well.
  In time, their relationship could have been so much stronger, but there just wasn't enough time.
  I don't feel like doing anything today; I just want to lay in my bed.

- **Complex sentences** have one independent clause and at least one subordinate clause. In the examples below, the subordinate clauses are italicized.
  Those *who do not learn from history* will repeat it.
  If you lie down with dogs, you'll wake up with fleas.

- **Compound-complex sentences** have two or more independent clauses and at least one subordinate clause. In the example below, the subordinate clause is italicized.
  Even though David was a vegetarian, he still went with his friends to steakhouses, but he focused his attention on the conversation instead of the meal.

The chart below summarizes the requirements for each type of sentence.

Sentence Type	Number of Independent Clauses	Number of Subordinate Clauses
Simple	1	0
Compound	2+	0
Complex	1	1+
Compound-Complex	2+	1+

There are two other classifications of sentences you should know for the exam.

- In a **periodic sentence**, the main idea of the sentence is held until the end.

  "To believe your own thought, to believe that what is true for you in your private heart is true for all men, that is genius." Ralph Waldo Emerson, *Self-Reliance*

- In a **cumulative sentence**, the independent clause comes first, and any modifying words or clauses follow it.

  "We need the tonic of wildness,—to wade sometimes in marshes where the bittern and meadow-hen lurk, and hear the booming of the snipe; to smell the whispering sedge where only some wilder and more solitary fowl builds her nest, and the mink crawls with its belly close to the ground." Henry David Thoreau, *Walden*

Note that this type of classification—periodic or cumulative—is not used in place of the simple, compound, complex, or compound-complex classification. A sentence can be both cumulative and complex, for example.

The exam may ask you to classify sentences or to identify which sentences belong with which classification(s).

Homophones

Homophones are word pairs that sound alike but have different meanings and are spelled differently. Listed below are some common homophones and their meanings.

affect: to influence something
effect: a consequence of a cause or action

accept: to receive
except: to leave out or exclude

advice: a suggestion or opinion about what to do
advise: to give ideas, suggestions, or advice

ascent: an upward incline
assent: an agreement

all ready: every person or thing in a group is ready
already: up to a particular time

all together: every person or thing in a group
altogether: totally, completely

altar: an object used in religious worship
alter: to modify or change something

ball: a round or sphere-shaped object
bawl: to cry, sob, or weep loudly

boll: the pod or seed of a plant i.e., a cotton boll
bowl: a deepened, round dish that holds food

brake: a mechanism used to slow down a vehicle or the act of slowing down a vehicle
break: a pause or interruption in an activity or event or the act of separating into smaller pieces

bear: to support
bare: to expose or reveal

capital: the governmental center of a state or province
capitol: a government building for legislatures

chili: small peppers or a food made with peppers, meat, and sometimes beans
chilly: a feeling or temperature that is cooler than warm, but not freezing or cold

conscience: the awareness of right and wrong, good and evil, just and unjust
conscious: to be awake or aware of one's surroundings

cite: to reference something
site: the location of something

complement: one of several parts that completes a whole
compliment: a positive or flattering comment

council: a group of people that gives guidance and makes recommendations
counsel: a piece of advice

dear: a word that signifies affection or a salutation at the beginning of a letter
deer: a quadruped animal

descent: a downward incline
dissent: a disagreement

dying: to cease to exist
dyeing: to paint or tint something with color

forth: onward or forward in time or place
fourth: a number in a sequence after third and before fifth

hear: registering or perceiving sound by the ear
here: one's current place, point, or position

lead: a chemical element, an example for others to follow, or the act of exerting authority
led: past tense of *lead*

loose: not fitting tightly or the status of being free or liberated
lose: the inability to find an object or a person

passed: past tense of *pass*
past: a prior time period

personal: individual or private
personnel: persons or staff that are part of an organization or business

principal: the chief officer of an organization
principle: a value or belief about something

stationary: immobile or still
stationery: paper used to write correspondence

some: an indeterminate amount or number or an extent of something
sum: the result of adding two numbers or items

than: a word used to make comparisons
then: a word that can mean next or shortly thereafter

their: shows possession
they're: a contraction for *they are*
there: indicates location

threw: past tense of *throw*
through: to travel from one side to the other
thru: a shortened misspelling of *through*

to: indicates purpose, outcome, or relation
too: more than enough
two: a sum of two parts or components

we're: a contraction for *we are*
were: the plural form of *was*

where: indicates place or position
wear: to put on one's body, as in apparel, or to erode or damage

whose: shows possession
who's: a contraction for *who is*

your: shows possession
you're: a contraction for *you are*

Commonly Misspelled Words

Words can be misspelled because you don't use them often, because they sound different from how they are spelled, or because they are the exception to a certain spelling rule, among other reasons. Listed below are some commonly misspelled words.

accidentally	amateur	bachelor
accept	annual	barbarian
accommodate	anxiety	barbarous
accompanied	apparent	barren
achieved	appearance	beggar
across	appropriate	believe
address	arctic	beneficial
aggravate	argument	benefited
aisle	arrangement	biscuit
allot	association	brilliant
allotted	attendance	business
alright	auxiliary	cafeteria
all right	awkward	calendar

candidate	descent	fascinate
career	describe	February
carriage	description	fiery
ceiling	desirable	finally
cemetery	desperate	financial
changeable	device	forehead
changing	devise	foreign
characteristic	dictionary	foremost
chauffeur	diphtheria	forfeit
colonel	disappear	fraternity
column	disappoint	furniture
commit	disastrous	ghost
committed	discipline	government
committee	discuss	grammar
comparative	discussion	grandeur
comparatively	disease	grief
comparison	dissatisfied	grievous
compel	dissatisfy	guidance
compelled	dissipate	handkerchief
competent	distribute	height
competition	dormitories	hesitancy
completely	drudgery	hesitate
compulsion	ecstasy	hindrance
conceivable	efficiency	hoping
conceive	eighth	hurriedly
conception	eligible	hygiene
confident	eliminate	hypocrisy
conqueror	eminent	imaginary
conscience	emphasize	imitation
conscientious	enemy	imminent
conscious	environment	incidentally
contemptible	equip	incredible
convenient	equipment	indigestible
coolly	equipped	indispensable
course	equivalent	inevitable
courteous	especially	influential
courtesy	exaggerate	innocence
cruelty	exceed	instance
curiosity	excel	instant
cylinder	excellent	intellectual
deceit	except	intelligence
deceive	exercise	intelligent
deception	exhaust	intelligible
decide	exhilaration	intentionally
decision	existence	intercede
defer	explain	interest
deference	explanation	irresistible
deferred	extraordinary	legitimate
definite	familiar	leisure

liable
library
lightning
likely
literature
livelihood
loneliness
magazine
maintain
maintenance
manual
marriage
material
mathematics
mattress
medicine
messenger
miniature
minute
mischievous
misspell
momentous
mortgage
muscle
naturally
nickel
niece
ninetieth
ninety
ninth
noticeable
notoriety
nucleus
obedience
obligation
oblige
obliged
obstacle
occasion
occur
occurred
occurrence
omission
omit
omitted
operate
opinion
optimistic
organization

outrageous
pageant
pamphlet
parallel
parliament
pastime
permissible
perseverance
persistent
persuade
physically
physician
picnic
picnicking
piece
pleasant
politician
possess
possession
possible
practically
prairie
precede
precedence
preceding
prefer
preference
preferred
prejudice
presence
prevalent
procedure
proceed
processor
pronunciation
propeller
psychiatrist
psychology
quantity
rally
realize
recede
receive
recognize
recommend
refer
reference
referred
region

reign
relieve
religious
repeat
repetition
representative
reservoir
resistance
restaurant
rhetoric
rhythm
ridiculous
sacrifice
sacrilegious
safety
salary
scarcely
schedule
science
secretary
seize
sentinel
separate
severely
shriek
siege
similar
soliloquy
sophomore
strenuous
studying
suffrage
supersede
suppress
surprise
syllable
symmetry
temperament
temperature
tendency
tournament
tragedy
transfer
transferred
tried
tries
truly
try
twelfth

tyranny
unanimous
unusual
usage
valuable

vengeance
vigilance
villain
Wednesday
wholly

writing
written
yoke
yolk

Punctuation Marks

Below are some rules of capitalization, ellipses, commas, semicolons, colons, hyphens, parentheses, quotation marks, and apostrophes.

Capitalization:

- The first word of a sentence is capitalized regardless of its status or part of speech.

- The first letter of proper nouns is always capitalized

- The first letter of words that modify proper nouns must be capitalized. For instance, when we refer to someone's uncle, the word is not capitalized. When we refer to a specific uncle, i.e., Uncle Murray, we must capitalize "uncle."

- The first letter of each word in the title of a document, book, film, etc. must be capitalized. Rules vary within different academic styles, but in legal writing, each word must be capitalized with the exception of "a," "an," all prepositions and all coordinating conjunctions.

- Months are capitalized, but not the names of the seasons.

- Some names include words that are not capitalized, including Edward von Morrison and Oscar de la Hoya. It may be helpful for you to know that these words usually mean "of" or "of the," neither of which we would capitalize in the title of a book. If you think of a name as the "title" of a person, you won't forget this rule.

Apostrophes:

An apostrophe is used to form contractions and to show possession for all singular and indefinite pronouns. The first use is illustrated in the following manner: "You're really becoming an expert in legal research."

The word "you're" is a contraction for the words you are. The use of the apostrophe lets the reader know that the implied meaning is you are but that the "a" has been omitted.

Some common contractions include *aren't, can't, couldn't, didn't, doesn't, don't, hasn't, haven't, I'm, isn't, it's, let's, they're, wasn't, weren't, won't,* and *you're.*

The second use of an apostrophe is to show possession as is illustrated in the following manner: The attorney's office was a mess. The use of the apostrophe in this sentence indicates that the attorney owns the office. The apostrophe is also used to show possession for indefinite pronouns: "Everyone's eyes stung from the smoke."

There are three very important rules to remember when using apostrophes:

1. Do not use an apostrophe when writing a personal possessive pronoun. A common mistake is to write the word "yours" as your's.

2. Sentences that refer to amounts of money or time usually require an apostrophe. For instance: "I really do not want to hear your two cents' worth of advice." "It is all in a day's work."

3. Plural possessive nouns that end in "s" need an apostrophe at the end. "The Harris' trial lasted one month." However, an apostrophe and an "s" should be added to plural nouns that do not end in "s": example: The group's noise was excessive.

Brackets:

The bracket is generally used to help clarify the meaning of words, and is often used interchangeably with the parenthesis (depending on the academic style.) This clarification can be in the form of indicating a misspelling or typo i.e. [judgement] or it can be used to add emphasis or make an editorial comment i.e. "Her large [Antebellum] house looked like Tara's from *Gone With the Wind*." The bracket, used in pairs, can be used to add a prefix, suffix or explanatory word in order to adapt a quote to your sentence i.e.: "Music is [our] only love." Brackets can also be used to change the tense of a verb in a quote to make a writer's sentences parallel and balanced, i.e. eat[ing], drink[ing] and be[ing] merry are actions guaranteed to make one happy.

Colons and Semicolons:

The colon (:) and the semicolon (;) are two punctuation marks that are commonly confused in formal writing. Colons are used to indicate lists, series and examples. Colons are also used to link two main clauses if the second clause is an explanation or example of the first clause, i.e. "The office was a nightmare for the paralegal: law books were all over the floor, case files were strewn across the desk, and the chair was stacked with unopened mail."

The semicolon should be used to link two independent clauses provided that they are not joined by a coordinating conjunction, i.e. "Two hundred students applied for law school; only fifty of the students were accepted." Both of these phrases could stand alone as sentences, but for stylistic reasons, the author may choose to put them in the same sentence, perhaps in order to make the reader infer a connection between the phrases where it is not immediately apparent. Semicolons are not used to separate subordinate clauses – in those cases, a comma is appropriate.

Other Punctuation Marks:

- The period (.) is the punctuation mark used to denote the end of a sentence with no special cases.

- The question mark (?) is used at the end of an interrogative sentence or one that asks a direct question. It is not used in sentences that ask indirect questions. For example: "Did you read the brief?" is correct. "I am perplexed as to why he included her name on the witness list?" is not correct, because this sentence refers to an indirect question.

- The exclamation mark or point (!) is used after short sentences, phrases and even after single words to show strong feelings or emotions. For example: "Hallelujah!" "Oh my God, a snake!"

- The hyphen (-) is a punctuation mark that is used in compound words that have a combined meaning, and to divide or break a word at the end of a line. If a hyphen is used to divide a word, it should be divided at a break in the syllables. An example of a hyphen used in a compound word is "part-time." Hyphens are commonly used now in many proper names: Sharon Thomas-Webb, Esq. The rules for hyphens will change in the future when children born with hyphenated names start to marry other children with hyphenated names.

- Parenthesis () is a punctuation mark closely related to the bracket. They are used in pairs to include information that would not normally appear in the sentence. One rule to remember about parenthesis involves ending punctuation marks: If the text within the parenthesis is a complete sentence, then the ending punctuation mark goes inside the parenthesis. For example: I like to read opinions written by 19th century justices (John Marshall is my favorite Supreme Court Justice.) If the text within the parenthesis is not a complete sentence then the punctuation mark goes after the parentheses i.e.: I use Lexis (not Westlaw).

- Rules regarding quotation marks (") are a little more complicated than some of the other punctuation marks. Quotation marks are used to set aside or enclose direct quotations; they are not used in indirect quotations. For example, Patrick Henry said "Give me liberty or give me death." Another rule to remember is that periods and commas are placed inside quotation marks (Please see the above example.) However, colons and semi colons are placed outside of the quotation marks. Another important rule to remember is that a question mark goes inside quotation marks if the text is a question, but the quotation marks are outside the question mark if the quotation is not a question, even if the whole sentence is. Examples: The spoiled child asked, "Where is my candy?" The second part of the rule is exemplified by: Did the judge say "I am holding both parties in contempt."? Finally, if a quote within a quote is needed then the outside quotation is enclosed by double quotation marks and the inside quotation is enclosed by single quotation marks. For example: The professor asked "How does the Miranda Court interpret 'custodial interrogation' in relation to arrests?"

- The ellipsis (…) is a punctuation mark that is seen fairly often in legal writing, but the name is not familiar to a lot of the users of this mark. An ellipsis is comprised of three dots evenly spaced apart, used to let the reader know that part of a quotation has been left out or omitted. It used in legal writing when a direct quote needs to be used, but the writer only wants to reference part of the quote, not the entire section. The use of the ellipsis serves to maintain brevity and conciseness in legal writing. For example: The concept of separate but equal… was abolished in 1954.

- The most difficult punctuation mark is the comma (,) which accounts more punctuation errors than all other punctuation marks combined. The comma is used to join main clauses, parts of sentences, words in series, adjectives, adverbs, nouns, verbs and just about any part of speech. Commas are also used after introductory words and transitional expressions. Some common introductory words are: yes, no, indeed, next, first, however, additionally, therefore, nevertheless and similarly. Common transitional words include: in fact, for example, as a result, in other words, and on the other hand. Commas are used after all participial phrases and introductory infinitive phrases. Example: Deafened by the noise, the puppy hid beneath the bed. Entire books have been written about comma usage; therefore it is evident this punctuation mark requires your studious attention. When in doubt, always refer to the dictionary. No discussion of commas would be complete without proper homage to the bane of most writers' existence: the comma splice. A comma splice occurs when a punctuation mark is used to link together or splice two independent phrases that could stand on their own as complete sentences. An example of comma splice: Terry studied a long time for her exam, Carl partied all night before the test, and Travis forgot to show up for the test. The comma splice is between the text regarding Terry's actions and Carl's actions. "Terry studied a long time for her exam" and "Carl partied all night before the test" are both independent phrases that can stand on their own as complete sentences.

Key Terms

Adjective- a word that modifies a noun

Adverb- a word that modifies a verb

Article- a word that is used with a noun to reflect a certain type of reference; the two types of articles are *a/an* and *the*

Clause- a group of words that has a subject committing an action and a predicate

Direct object- a noun or pronoun that receives the action of the verb

Noun- a word that reflects a person, place, or thing

Object of the preposition- a phrase that follows a preposition and completes its meaning

Phrase- a group of words that does not have a subject committing an action

Possessive pronoun- a pronoun that refers to a person or thing that belongs to another person; possessive pronouns must agree in number (singular or plural), person (first, second, or third), and gender (male or female)

Preposition- a word that expresses the location of a noun or pronoun in relation to other words and phrases in a sentence

Pronoun- a word that refers to a noun

Subject- one of the two parts of a clause; is the main entity of the clause (person, place, idea, etc.)

Verb- a word that reflects action

Antecedent- a word to which a pronoun refers

Gendered language- a word or phrase that uses masculine nouns or pronouns to reference both males and females

Indirect dialogue- dialogue that reflects the thoughts or words of someone else, but does not attribute the words to that person

Direct dialogue- dialogue that reflects the thought or words of someone else and does attribute the words to that person, usually through quotations

Attributive tag- specifies who said a particular statement or question

Point of view- the perspective in which a text is given; can be first, second, or third-person

First-person perspective- a point of view in which the narrator speaks about himself/herself; this perspective is usually identified by use of the words *I* and/or *we*

Second-person perspective- a point of view in which the narrator speaks to the audience; this perspective is usually identified by use of the word *you*

Third-person perspective- a point of view in which the narrator tells a story as a stranger or bystander; this perspective is usually identified by use of the words *he*, *she*, and/or *they*

Coordinating conjunction- a word that joins two equally significant components of a sentence

Subordinating conjunction- a word that joins a subordinate clause to a main clause

Nominalization- a noun formed from another part of speech such as a verb or adjective (example: *conclusion* from the verb *conclude*)

Audience- the person or people for whom a text is written

Active verb- a word used when the subject of the sentence is doing the action

Passive verb- a word used when the subject of the sentence is receiving the action

Passive voice- a grammatical structure used to reflect the subject of the sentence as the receiver of the action

Active voice- a grammatical structure used to reflect the subject of the sentence as the doer of the action

Context clues- words that provide information to help the reader determine the meaning of a particular word; types of context clues include definition, description, example, synonym, antonym, comparison, contrast, and explanation clues

Word structure- the way that parts of words are organized

Etymology- the study of the origin of words and the change in meanings of words

Root word- the base unit of a word, which cannot be reduced further

Prefix-a group of letters added before a base word that changes it into another word

Suffix- a group of letters added after a base word that changes it into another word

Simple sentence- one of four types of sentence structures; a sentence with only one independent clause

Compound sentence- one of four types of sentence structures; a sentence with at least two independent clauses

Complex sentence- one of the four types of sentence structures; a sentence with an independent clause and at least one dependent clause

Independent clause- a clause that expresses a complete thought and can stand as its own sentence

Dependent clause- a clause that is an incomplete thought and cannot stand as its own sentence

Verbal- a verb that functions as a noun or modifier instead of as a verb; examples of a verbal include infinitives, gerunds, and participles

Paragraph- a group of sentences with a main idea and supporting details about a certain topic

Topic sentence- the main idea of a paragraph

Transition- an organizational device used to connect two groups of words (usually paragraphs) that provides cohesion and progression

Support sentence- a supporting detail of a main idea

Periodic sentence- a sentence with an independent clause at the end

Cumulative sentence- a sentence with an independent clause at the beginning and subordinate phrases or clauses afterwards

Homophone- a word that sounds like another word, but is spelled differently and has a different meaning

Nonrestrictive phrase- a phrase (which does not contain a subject and verb) that is not necessary to the meaning of a sentence; the phrase conveys additional information and is usually offset by commas

Nonrestrictive clause- a clause (which does contain a subject and verb) that is not necessary to the meaning of a sentence; the clause conveys additional information and is usually offset by commas

Study Tips for Improving Vocabulary and Grammar

1. You're probably pretty computer savvy and know the Internet very well. Visit the Online Writing Lab website, which is sponsored by Purdue University, at http://owl.english.purdue.edu. This site provides you with an excellent overview of syntax, writing style, and strategy. It also has helpful and lengthy review sections that include multiple-choice "Test Your Knowledge" quizzes, which provide immediate answers to the questions.

2. It's beneficial to read the entire passage first to determine its intended meaning BEFORE you attempt to answer any questions. Doing so provides you with key insight into a passage's syntax (especially verb tense, subject-verb agreement, modifier placement, writing style, and punctuation).

3. When you answer a question, use the "Process-of-Elimination Method" to determine the best answer. Try each of the four answers and determine which one BEST fits with the meaning of the paragraph. Find the BEST answer. Chances are that the BEST answer is the CORRECT answer.

Chapter 3: Reading

There are three types of questions that you can encounter in the Reading Comprehension section of the TEAS:

1. **About the Author**: The question will ask about the author's attitude, thoughts, opinions, etc. When encountering a question asking specifically about the author, pay attention to context clues in the article. The answer may not be explicitly stated, but instead conveyed in the overall message.

2. **Passage Facts**: You must distinguish between facts and opinions presented in the passage. Remember, a fact is something verifiable or proven, whereas an opinion is simply a belief that cannot be proven for sure. For example: "The sky is blue" is a fact that cannot be argued; "the sky is a prettier blue today than it was yesterday" is an opinion, since there is no scientific basis for what makes the sky "prettier" to a person.

3. **Additional Information**: These questions will have you look at what kind of information could be added to or was missing from the passage. They may also ask in what direction the passage was going. Questions may ask what statement could be added to strengthen the author's statement, or weaken it; they may also provide a fill-in-the-blank option to include a statement that is missing from, but fits with the rest of, the passage. When looking over answer choices, read them with the passage to see if they sound correct in context.

Strategies

Despite the different types of questions you will face, there are some strategies for Reading Comprehension which apply across the board:

- **Read the Answer Choices First**, then read the passage. This will save you time, as you will know what to look out for as you read.

- **Use the Process of Elimination**. Some answer choices are obviously incorrect, and are relatively easy to detect. After reading the passage, eliminate those blatantly-incorrect answer choices; this increases your chance of finding the correct answer much more quickly.

- **Avoid "Negatives."** Generally, test-makers will not make negatives statements about anyone or anything. Statements will be either neutral or positive; so if it seems like an answer choice is making a negative connotation, it is very likely that the answer is intentionally false.

Here are some examples of the kinds of questions you may encounter in the Reading Section. Each passage will have at least one of the above listed question types – try to answer them for yourself before reading the solution. If you run into trouble, don't worry. We'll provide more practice drills later in the book, as well.

Sample One:

Exercise is a critical aspect for healthy development in children. Today, there is an epidemic of unhealthy children in the United States who will face health problems in adulthood due to poor diet and lack of exercise as children. This is a problem for all Americans, especially with the rising cost of health care.

It is vital that school systems and parents encourage their children to engage in a minimum of 30 minutes of cardiovascular exercise each day, meaning their heart rate is mildly increased for sustained period. This is proven to decrease the likelihood of development diabetes, becoming obese, and a multitude of other health problems. Also, children need a proper diet rich in fruits and vegetables so that they can grow and development physically, as well as learn healthy eating habits early on.

1. Which of the following describes the author's use of the word "vital"?
   a) Debatable.
   b) Very important.
   c) Somewhat important.
   d) Not important.
   e) Indicator.

Answer: This is an example of an "About the Author" question. You can tell, from both the tone and the intention of the article, that the author feels very strongly about the health of children and that action should be taken. Therefore, answer **b)** is the correct choice.

2. Which of the following is a fact in the passage, not an opinion?
   a) Fruits and vegetables are the best-tasting foods.
   b) Children today are lazier than they were in previous generations.
   c) The risk of diabetes in children is reduced by physical activity.
   d) Health care costs too much.
   e) Soccer is a better physical activity than tennis.

Answer: A fact is typically presented as a direct statement, not a comparison, which makes answer choice **c)** the correct answer. Notice that many of the incorrect answers contain words that can hint at it being an opinion such as "best," "better," "too much," or other comparisons. Also keep an eye out for answer choices that may be facts, but which are not stated in the passage.

3. What other information might the author have provided to strengthen the argument?
   a) Example of fruits and vegetables children should eat.
   b) How much health insurance costs today vs. 10 years ago.
   c) How many people live in the United States today.
   d) The rules of baseball and soccer.
   e) How many calories the average person burns by running 1 mile.

Answer: All of the choices would provide additional information, but only one pertains specifically to the improvement of health in children: choice **a)**.

Sample Two:

My "office" measures a whopping 5 feet by 7 feet. A large desk is squeezed into one corner, leaving just enough room for a rickety chair between the desk and the wall. Yellow paint is peeling off the walls in dirty chunks. The ceiling is barely six feet tall; it's like a hat that I wear all day long. The window, a single 2 x 2 pane, looks out onto a solid brick wall just two feet away.

1. What is the main idea implied by this paragraph?
   a) This office is small but comfortable.
   b) This office is in need of repair.
   c) This office is old and claustrophobic.
   d) This office is large and luxurious.
   e) None of the above.

Answer: Notice that all of the sentences in the passage relate to the office feeling small and cramped. The correct answer is choice **c)**. While choice **b)** is tempting, since one would think the office could use some repair, it is not the main point of the passage.

2. Which of the following describes the structure of the passage?
   a) The passage asks a question, then explains the answer using supporting arguments.
   b) The passage presents a statement, then follows with more detailed information.
   c) The passage makes an argument, then provides three examples to support it.
   d) The passage introduces a hypothesis, then explores more questions about the hypothesis.
   e) The passage starts with an argument, which is countered with a different argument leaving the reader to make their own conclusion.

Answer: No questions, arguments, or hypothesis were provided anywhere in the passage. Simply a statement of the size of the office and then additional details were given afterward. The correct answer is choice **b)**.

3. What is the author's meaning of the use of the word "hat" in the passage?
   a) An expression of a style of clothing the author prefers.
   b) To illustrate how very close the ceiling is to the author's head.
   c) The author does not like to wear hats, especially all day.
   d) The author enjoys wearing hats.
   e) None of the above.

Answer: The author uses the word "hat" to describe how low the ceiling sits in the office: that it feels as though it envelopes their head, much like a hat. While it can be inferred that the author does not like their office, there is no indication of whether the author likes or dislikes hats. The correct answer is choice **b)**.

Sample Three

1. Using the below Index, on which page would you find information on Organic Chemistry?

    Science
    Geology: 110-124
    Astronomy: 126-137
    Physics: 140-159
    Chemistry: 161-170
    Biology: 171-179

    Math
    Geometry: 201-209
    Calculus: 210-222
    Graphing: 225-251

    a) 210-222
    b) 225-251
    c) 126-137
    d) 161-170
    e) None of the above

Answer: The correct answer is choice **d)**. Pretty simple, huh? These types of questions are the easiest that you will find on the TEAS. Simply look for key-words (in this case "Chemistry" is the only matching word), and then eliminate everything else that doesn't relate.

The Main Idea

Finding and understanding the main idea of a text is an essential reading skill. When you look past the facts and information and get to the heart of what the writer is trying to say, that's the **main idea**.

Imagine that you're at a friend's home for the evening:

"Here," he says, "Let's watch this movie."

"Sure," you reply. "What's it about?"

You'd like to know a little about what you'll be watching, but your question may not get you a satisfactory answer, because you've only asked about the subject of the film. The subject—what the movie is about—is only half the story. Think, for example, about all the alien invasion films ever been made. While these films may share the same general subject, what they have to say about the aliens or about humanity's theoretical response to invasion may be very different. Each film has different ideas it wants to convey about a subject, just as writers write because they have something they want to say about a particular subject. When you look beyond the facts and information to what the writer really wants to say about his or her subject, you're looking for the main idea.

One of the most common questions on reading comprehension exams is, "What is the main idea of this passage?" How would you answer this question for the paragraph below?

"Wilma Rudolph, the crippled child who became an Olympic running champion, is an inspiration for us all. Born prematurely in 1940, Wilma spent her childhood battling illness, including measles, scarlet fever, chicken pox, pneumonia, and polio, a crippling disease which at that time had no cure. At the age of four, she was told she would never walk again. But Wilma and her family refused to give up. After years of special treatment and physical therapy, 12-year-old Wilma was able to walk normally again. But walking wasn't enough for Wilma, who was determined to be an athlete. Before long, her talent earned her a spot in the 1956 Olympics, where she earned a bronze medal. In the 1960 Olympics, the height of her career, she won three gold medals."

What is the main idea of this paragraph? You might be tempted to answer, "Wilma Rudolph" or "Wilma Rudolph's life." Yes, Wilma Rudolph's life is the **subject** of the passage—who or what the passage is about—but the subject is not necessarily the main idea. The **main idea** is what the writer wants to say about this subject. What is the main thing the writer says about Wilma's life?

Which of the following statements is the main idea of the paragraph?

a) Wilma Rudolph was very sick as a child.
b) Wilma Rudolph was an Olympic champion.
c) Wilma Rudolph is someone to admire.

Main idea: The overall fact, feeling, or thought a writer wants to convey about his or her subject.

The best answer is **c)**: Wilma Rudolph is someone to admire. This is the idea the paragraph adds up to; it's what holds all of the information in the paragraph together. This example also shows two important characteristics of a main idea:

1. It is **general** enough to encompass all of the ideas in the passage.

2. It is an **assertion.** An assertion is a statement made by the writer.

The main idea of a passage must be general enough to encompass all of the ideas in the passage. It should be broad enough for all of the other sentences in that passage to fit underneath it, like people under an umbrella. Notice that the first two options, "Wilma Rudolph was very sick as a child" and "Wilma Rudolph was an Olympic champion", are too specific to be the main idea. They aren't broad enough to cover all of the ideas in the passage, because the passage talks about both her illnesses and her Olympic achievements. Only the third answer is general enough to be the main idea of the paragraph.

A main idea is also some kind of **assertion** about the subject. An assertion is a claim that something is true. Assertions can be facts or opinions, but in either case, an assertion should be supported by specific ideas, facts, and details. In other words, the main idea makes a general assertion that tells readers that something is true.

The supporting sentences, on the other hand, show readers that this assertion is true by providing specific facts and details. For example, in the Wilma Rudolph paragraph, the writer makes a general assertion: "Wilma Rudolph, the crippled child who became an Olympic running champion, is an inspiration for us all." The other sentences offer specific facts and details that prove why Wilma Rudolph is an inspirational person.

Writers often state their main ideas in one or two sentences so that readers can have a very clear understanding about the main point of the passage. A sentence that expresses the main idea of a paragraph is called a **topic sentence.**

Notice, for example, how the first sentence in the Wilma Rudolph paragraph states the main idea:

> "Wilma Rudolph, the crippled child who became an Olympic running champion, is an inspiration for us all."

This sentence is therefore the topic sentence for the paragraph. Topic sentences are often found at the beginning of paragraphs. Sometimes, though, writers begin with specific supporting details and lead up to the main idea, and in this case the topic sentence is often found at the end of the paragraph. Sometimes the topic sentence is even found somewhere in the middle, and other times there isn't a clear topic sentence at all—but that doesn't mean there isn't a main idea; the author has just chosen not to express it in a clear topic sentence. In this last case, you'll have to look carefully at the paragraph for clues about the main idea.

Main Ideas vs. Supporting Details

If you're not sure whether something is a main idea or a supporting detail, ask yourself the following question: is the sentence making a **general statement,** or is it providing **specific information?** In the Wilma Rudolph paragraph above, for example, all of the sentences except the first make specific statements. They are not general enough to serve as an umbrella or net for the whole paragraph.

Writers often provide clues that can help you distinguish between main ideas and their supporting details. Here are some of the most common words and phrases used to introduce specific examples:

1. **For example...**

2. **Specifically...**

3. **In addition...**

4. **Furthermore...**

5. **For instance...**

6. **Others...**

7. **In particular...**

8. Some...

These signal words tell you that a supporting fact or idea will follow. If you're having trouble finding the main idea of a paragraph, try eliminating sentences that begin with these phrases, because they will most likely be too specific to be a main ideas.

Implied Main Idea

When the main idea is **implied**, there's no topic sentence, which means that finding the main idea requires some detective work. But don't worry! You already know the importance of structure, word choice, style, and tone. Plus, you know how to read carefully to find clues, and you know that these clues will help you figure out the main idea.

For Example:

"One of my summer reading books was *The Windows of Time*. Though it's more than 100 pages long, I read it in one afternoon. I couldn't wait to see what happened to Evelyn, the main character. But by the time I got to the end, I wondered if I should have spent my afternoon doing something else. The ending was so awful that I completely forgot that I'd enjoyed most of the book."

There's no topic sentence here, but you should still be able to find the main idea. Look carefully at what the writer says and how she says it. What is she suggesting?

    a) *The Windows of Time* is a terrific novel.
    b) *The Windows of Time* is disappointing.
    c) *The Windows of Time* is full of suspense.
    d) *The Windows of Time* is a lousy novel.

The correct answer is **b)** – the novel is disappointing. How can you tell that this is the main idea? First, we can eliminate choice **c)**, because it's too specific to be a main idea. It deals only with one specific aspect of the novel (its suspense).

Sentences **a)**, **b)**, and **d)**, on the other hand, all express a larger idea – a general assertion about the quality of the novel. But only one of these statements can actually serve as a "net" for the whole paragraph. Notice that while the first few sentences praise the novel, the last two criticize it. Clearly, this is a mixed review.

Therefore, the best answer is **b)**. Sentence **a)** is too positive and doesn't account for the "awful" ending. Sentence **d)**, on the other hand, is too negative and doesn't account for the reader's sense of suspense and interest in the main character. But sentence **b)** allows for both positive and negative aspects – when a good thing turns bad, we often feel disappointed.

Now let's look at another example. Here, the word choice will be more important, so read carefully.

"Fortunately, none of Toby's friends had ever seen the apartment where Toby lived with his mother and sister. Sandwiched between two burnt-out buildings, his two-story apartment building was by far the ugliest one on the block. It was a real eyesore: peeling orange paint (orange!), broken windows, crooked steps, crooked everything. He could just imagine what his friends would say if they ever saw this poor excuse for a building."

Which of the following expresses the main idea of this paragraph?

    a) Toby wishes he could move to a nicer building.
    b) Toby wishes his dad still lived with them.
    c) Toby is glad none of his friends know where he lives.
    d) Toby is sad because he doesn't have any friends.

From the description, we can safely assume that Toby doesn't like his apartment building and wishes he could move to a nicer building **a)**. But that idea isn't general enough to cover the whole paragraph, because it's about his building.

Because the first sentence states that Toby has friends, the answer cannot be **d)**. We know that Toby lives only with his mother and little sister, so we might assume that he wishes his dad still lived with them, **b)**, but there's nothing in the paragraph to support that assumption, and this idea doesn't include the two main topics of the paragraph—Toby's building and Toby's friends.

What the paragraph adds up to is that Toby is terribly embarrassed about his building, and he's glad that none of his friends have seen it **c)**. This is the main idea. The paragraph opens with the word "fortunately," so we know that he thinks it's a good thing none of his friends have been to his house. Plus, notice how the building is described: "by far the ugliest on the block," which says a lot since it's stuck "between two burnt-out buildings." The writer calls it an "eyesore," and repeats "orange" with an exclamation point to emphasize how ugly the color is. Everything is "crooked" in this "poor excuse for a building." Toby is clearly ashamed of where he lives and worries about what his friends would think if they saw it.

Cause and Effect

Understanding cause and effect is important for reading success. Every event has at least one cause (what made it happen) and at least one effect (the result of what happened). Some events have more than one cause, and some have more than one effect. An event is also often part of a chain of causes and effects. Causes and effects are usually signaled by important transitional words and phrases.

Words Indicating Cause:

    1. Because (of)

    2. Created (by)

    3. Caused (by)

    4. Since

Words Indicating Effect:

1. **As a result**

2. **Since**

3. **Consequently**

4. **So**

5. **Hence**

6. **Therefore**

Sometimes, a writer will offer his or her opinion about why an event happened when the facts of the cause(s) aren't clear. Or a writer may predict what he or she thinks will happen because of a certain event (its effects). If this is the case, you need to consider how reasonable those opinions are. Are the writer's ideas logical? Does the writer offer support for the conclusions he or she offers?

Reading Between the Lines

Paying attention to word choice is particularly important when the main idea of a passage isn't clear. A writer's word choice doesn't just affect meaning; it also creates it. For example, look at the following description from a teacher's evaluation of a student applying to a special foreign language summer camp. There's no topic sentence, but if you use your powers of observation, you should be able to tell how the writer feels about her subject.

> "As a student, Jane usually completes her work on time and checks it carefully. She speaks French well and is learning to speak with less of an American accent. She has often been a big help to other students who are just beginning to learn the language."

What message does this passage send about Jane? Is she the best French student the writer has ever had? Is she one of the worst, or is she just average? To answer these questions, you have to make an inference, and you must support your inference with specific observations. What makes you come to the conclusion that you come to?

The **diction** of the paragraph above reveals that this is a positive evaluation, but not a glowing recommendation.

Here are some of the specific observations you might have made to support this conclusion:

- The writer uses the word "usually" in the first sentence. This means that Jane is good about meeting deadlines for work, but not great; she doesn't always hand in her work on time.

- The first sentence also says that Jane checks her work carefully. While Jane may sometimes hand in work late, at least she always makes sure it's quality work. She's not sloppy.

97

- The second sentence tells us she's "learning to speak with less of an American accent." This suggests that she has a strong accent and needs to improve in this area. It also suggests, though, that she is already making progress.

- The third sentence tells us that she "often" helps "students who are just beginning to learn the language." From this we can conclude that Jane has indeed mastered the basics. Otherwise, how could she be a big help to students who are just starting to learn? By looking at the passage carefully, then, you can see how the writer feels about her subject.

Primary Sources

When researching a topic, you can use several kinds of sources. Primary sources are a direct account of events, people, ideas, facts, etc. These sources can be books, documents, or recordings, but they must be current with the specific event or person they are chronicling or critiquing. Primary sources are quite helpful, but several obstacles are associated with them. They can be difficult to find (especially if you're researching an event that occurred in the distant past), are often incomplete, and can be inaccurate or biased.

Primary sources can also be found on the Internet. However, be vigilant when using primary sources found online, as these can be inaccurate or meant to persuade instead of inform. The most credible online sources are professional organization websites and educational institution websites.

Facts, Opinions, Biases, and Stereotypes

When reading a text, you must be able to tell the difference between fact and opinion. A fact is a statement or thought that can be proven to be true. Contrastingly, an opinion is an assumption that is not based on fact and cannot be proven to be true. Sometimes, it is easy to conclude whether a statement is a fact or opinion; other times, it can be difficult. This is why it is important that a reader draw his/her own conclusions, instead of simply believing what an author says in the text.

An example of a fact is "12 inches equals 1 foot." An example of an opinion is "television is more entertaining than feature films."

It's also important to not let biases and stereotypes affect your judgments. A bias is a prejudice or unwarranted support for or against something or someone. A stereotype is a belief or view of an entire group of people or things based on inaccurate information.

An example of a bias is claiming that your alma mater is better than other schools simply because you attended that university. An example of a stereotype is assuming that nurses are always female.

The reality of facts, opinions, biases, and stereotypes are why readers should be critical when reading a text. Critical thinking will help you judge whether a statement is a fact or an opinion and if it is biased or stereotypical, ensuring that you draw valid and credible conclusions from the text.

Characteristics of Different Passage Types

When reading a text, you can determine that it is one of several types of passages: narrative, expository, technical, or persuasive. A narrative text tells a sequence of events. An expository text objectively describes a topic and background information. A technical text conveys specialized information. A persuasive text attempts to influence or convince. A text can include only one of these or several of these types of passages.

Some examples of these types of passages are listed below:

- Narrative—a biography or a fictional novel
- Expository—a news story
- Technical—a computer manual
- Persuasive—a political campaign message

Informative, Persuasive, Entertaining, and Expressive Passages

Whenever an author writes a text, he/she always has a purpose. An author's purpose can be to inform, persuade, entertain, and/or express. An informative text informs or educates the reader about something. A newspaper column is an example of an informative text. A persuasive text persuades or convinces the reader about something. A dissertation is an example of a persuasive text. An entertaining text provides entertainment value and amuses the reader. A theatrical play manuscript is an example of an entertaining text. An expressive text stimulates feelings of emotion in the reader. A poem is an example of an expressive text.

Before you read any text, it is best to determine the author's purpose. Doing so allows you to better understand the information presented, better judge its credibility and effectiveness, and better draw your own conclusions.

Organized Paragraphs, Topic Sentences, and Summary Sentences

Almost always, a text is broken down into paragraphs. A paragraph is a group of sentences that discuss a specific topic or idea. Paragraphs break up large blocks of information into smaller, more understandable sections. This makes the information easier to read and comprehend. It is also important that paragraphs transition smoothly from one to another. A transition is a shift from one thought to another. Some words that indicate a transition include *first, then, next, but, however, similarly, in addition to, moreover, therefore,* and *in conclusion*.

Topic sentences and summary sentences also make the paragraph, and the text in general, easier to comprehend. Topic sentences usually appear at the start of a chapter or section of text and introduce a main topic or idea. Summary sentences usually appear at the end of a chapter or section of text and reiterate important details. Typically, you can read the topic sentences and summary sentences of a chapter or section of text and obtain a general, although imprecise, understanding of the information presented.

In the following paragraph, what are the topic and summary sentences?

> The Constitution of the United States establishes a series of limits to reign in centralized power. Separation of powers distributes federal authority among three competing branches: the executive, the legislature, and the judiciary. Checks and balances allow the branches to check the usurpation of power by any one branch. Federalism establishes state sovereignty against encroachment by the federal government. Enumeration of powers names the specific and few powers the federal government has. These four restrictions have helped sustain the American republic for over two centuries.

The topic sentence is the first sentence in the paragraph. It introduces the topic of discussion, in this case the Constitutional limits aimed at resisting centralized power. The summary sentence is the last sentence in the paragraph. It sums up the information that was just presented, in this case the Constitutional limits having helped sustain the United States of America for over 200 years.

Within each paragraph, after the topic sentence and before the summary sentences, should be several supporting sentences. Supporting sentences include evidence and details that reinforce the topic sentence.

Purpose and Intention

One of the most important tasks to complete when reading a text is to determine an author's purpose. If his/her purpose is to persuade instead of inform, the information can be conveyed drastically different and the credibility of the author and information come into question as well.

If an author has character, he/she will tell the reader what his/her intentions are. Other authors simply do not do this. For instance, a political commentator may not make known his/her political affiliation in order to keep the reader from forming an opinion before reading his/her information.

At times, it may be difficult to determine an author's purpose and intentions solely from the presented information. In these cases, it may be necessary to investigate the author. A quick online search will usually reveal biographical and background information that will help you determine an author's purpose and intentions.

Drawing Logical Conclusions

When reading a text, it is imperative that you be able to draw logical conclusions. A logical conclusion is a thought or idea that you conclude after reading and understanding a text. Note that logical does not mean factual. For instance, an author may write about how aliens are invading the planet. A logical conclusion may be that the author firmly believes in extraterrestrials. However, that does not mean that you do. You are simply acknowledging that the author has strong feeling about the subject. Conclusions must be supported by information in the text, but that doesn't mean you personally believe or support them.

After reading a text, the answers to certain questions will help you determine a logical conclusion. These questions include:

"If what I just read is accurate, what can I assume?"
"Based only on the information in the text, what is the author trying to say?"

Some conclusions are quite obvious, and others are more subtle. For instance, after reading an opinion article in favor of a candidate for public office, it is easy to draw a conclusion. The author believes the candidate should be elected to office. However, after reading a magazine article about a failed attempt at opening a restaurant in which the entrepreneurs didn't budget properly, it is a bit more difficult to draw a conclusion. The article could be expressing specifically that budgeting is essential for successfully managing a restaurant, or it could be expressing generally that starting any business is difficult and success is not always certain. Drawing the correct conclusion requires careful reading and analysis.

Making Inferences

When reading a text, it is useful to infer certain things. An inference is a thought that is not directly related to the information in the text. While reading a text, it is important to look for author biases and infer how that may affect the way the information is portrayed. You do not want to mistake opinion for fact. Likewise, if you are reading how to work with electrical wiring in a motor vehicle, you would infer that it is necessary to disconnect the battery for safety, even though the text may not say anything about that.

Inferences, unlike conclusions, are based on personal knowledge. Making inferences subjects the text to scrutiny and eventually bolsters or damages the author's argument. This active reading of a text will also help you determine what is opinion and what is fact.

Informative, Persuasive, Entertaining, and Expressive Passages

Whenever an author writes a text, he/she always has a purpose. An author's purpose can be to inform, persuade, entertain, and/or express. An informative text informs or educates the reader about something. A newspaper column is an example of an informative text. A persuasive text persuades or convinces the reader about something. A dissertation is an example of a persuasive text. An entertaining text provides entertainment value and amuses the reader. A theatrical play manuscript is an example of an entertaining text. An expressive text stimulates feelings of emotion in the reader. A poem is an example of an expressive text.

Before you read any text, it is best to determine the author's purpose. Doing so allows you to better understand the information presented, better judge its credibility and effectiveness, and better draw your own conclusions.

Text Structure

Text structure is an organizational pattern that improves readability and coherence of a text. The three major types of text structure are:

- Problem-solution: the author presents a problem and then discusses a solution
- Comparison-contrast: the author presents two situations and then discusses the similarities and differences
- Cause-effect: the author presents an action and then discusses the resulting effects

Formatting (such as bulleted or numbered lists and font styles) and description can also improve text structure.

Well-implemented text structure cannot be easily identified. The purpose of a text is to convey information, not overly emphasize how that information is laid out. The reader's only task should be to understand the information presented.

Informational Source Comprehension

On the TEAS V exam, you will encounter questions designed to test your comprehension of sources that convey all sorts of information. These informational sources are discussed below.

Sets of Directions: Completing certain tasks requires you to follow directions. These directions can be given in a paragraph format or list format. Usually, each step, or direction, includes specific instructions that must be remembered in order to complete the subsequent steps.

Use the examples below to answer the following questions.

You start with three red apples and one green apple in a basket. After following the directions below, how many apples are in the basket?
1. Remove one red apple
2. Add one green apple
3. Add one red apple
4. Add one green apple
5. Remove two red apples
6. Remove one green apple
7. Add three red apples
8. Add two green apples

Answer: After following these directions, you have four red apples and four green apples in the basket.

You have 12 gallons of fuel in your tank. After following the directions below, how many gallons of fuel are left in the tank?
1. Use one gallon to drive to work
2. Use one gallon to drive home
3. Use half a gallon to drive the kids to soccer practice
4. Use half a gallon to drive to the grocery store
5. Use two gallons to drive back home

Answer: After following these directions, you have seven gallons of fuel in your tank.

Labels' Ingredients and Directions: Reading a label is crucial for extracting critical information such as ingredients on a nutrition label or recipe or such as side effects and dosage requirements on a prescription label.

Use the image below to answer the following questions.

Nutrition Facts

Serving Size 172 g

Amount Per Serving

Calories 200	Calories from Fat 8

% Daily Value*

Total Fat 1g	1%
Saturated Fat 0g	1%
Trans Fat	
Cholesterol 0mg	0%
Sodium 7mg	0%
Total Carbohydrate 36g	12%
Dietary Fiber 11g	45%
Sugars 6g	
Protein 13g	

Vitamin A	1%	•	Vitamin C	1%
Calcium	4%	•	Iron	24%

*Percent Daily Values are based on a 2,000 calorie diet. Your daily values may be higher or lower depending on your calorie needs.

NutritionData.com

If a woman is monitoring her fat intake, would the above product be acceptable to consume?

Answer: Yes, as this product has only 200 calories and 1 gram of total fat per serving.

If a man wants to build muscle, would the above product help him achieve his goal?

Answer: Yes. Protein aids muscle production, and this product has 13 grams of protein per serving.

Definitions in Context: When reading a text, you may encounter a word that has more than one possible meaning. In these cases, you can determine the intended meaning by using the context of surrounding words and sentences. This process works for words with more than one meaning as well as words you may not know the meaning of at all.

Using context clues, guess the meaning of the underlined word in the following sentences.

"David's parents were ecstatic about his good grades."
  a) Pleased
  b) Disinterested
  c) Upset

Answer: You can observe the positive connotation of *good grades*. Naturally, this would make David's parents happy. So, you can infer that *ecstatic* means pleased.

"Lori excoriated her neighbor for accusing her of stealing."
   a) Congratulated
   b) Dismissed
   c) Criticized

Answer: You can observe the negative connotation of *stealing*. Of course, to be accused of stealing would be upsetting. So, you can infer that excoriated means criticized.

Printed Communications: Often, a printed communication contains quite a bit of information. It is good practice to read through the document once to understand the general purpose. Then, re-read the document to obtain specific information or to answer questions you may have.

Use the example below to answer the following questions.

MEMO

To: Human Resources Department
From: Corporate Management
Date: December 6, 2013
Subject: Personal Use of Computers

The corporate office has been conducting standard monitoring of computer usage, and we have been quite dismayed at the amount of personal use occurring during business hours. Employee computers are available for the sole purpose completing company business, nothing else. These rules must be respected. If not, steps will be taken to ensure maximum productivity. Personal use should occur only in emergency situations and should be limited to 30 minutes per day. Please communicate these requirements to lower management and personnel.

What is the general purpose and tone of this memo?

Answer: The purpose is to address personal use of company computers and to correct the misuse. The overall tone is negative, almost threatening.

What are the specific instructions given to the Human Resources Department?

Answer: The Human Resources Department is to communicate to lower management and personnel that personal use of company computers is to occur only in emergency situations and should be limited to 30 minutes per day.

Indexes and Tables of Contents: An index is an alphabetical list of topics, and their associated page numbers, covered in a text. A table of contents is an outline of a text that includes topics and page numbers. Both of these can be used to look up information, but each has a slightly different purpose. An index helps the reader find where in the text he/she can find specific details. A table of contents shows the reader the general arrangement of the text.

Use the examples below to answer the following questions.

Nursing, 189-296
    certification, 192-236
    code of ethics, 237-291
Procedure, 34-55

According to the index above, where might the reader find information about nursing code of ethics?

Answer: Pages 237-291

According to the table of contents above, in which chapter would the reader find information about the circumference of a circle?

Answer: The circumference of a circle is part of geometry, so that information would be found in Chapter 2.

Product Information: One Product is the More Economical Buy: When purchasing a product, you typically see an advertised base price. However, shipping and handling fees and taxes are also applied to the purchase. The sum of the base price, shipping and handling fees, and taxes equals the total cost of a product. When considering a purchase, be sure to compare the total cost, not simply the base price, at different retailers.

Use the example below to answer the following questions.

Retailer	Base Price	Shipping & Handling	Taxes
Wholesale Footwear	59.99	10.95	7.68
Bargain Sales	65.99	5.95	5.38
Famous Shoes	79.99	0.00	4.89

Rachel wants to buy shoes and can't spend more than $75. From which retailer can she not buy?

Answer: When you add the base price, shipping & handling fees, and taxes, Famous Shoes is the only retailer with a total cost for shoes above $75.

Donald needs shoes and has only $78 to spend. From which retailer can he buy without borrowing money?

Answer: When you add the base price, shipping & handling fees, and taxes, Bargain Sales is the only retailer with a total cost for shoes under $78.

Information from a Telephone Book: The phone book, often called the yellow pages, lists businesses according to industry. This list usually includes a company's name, phone number, and physical address. Aside from being included in the generic list, businesses can also pay for other options, including bolded or enlarged text and full-page advertisements. These advertisements can provide extra information, such as store hours and email addresses, and help you form an opinion of the business.

Use the image below to answer the following questions.

If a man needs his suit dry-cleaned for a job interview and is unable to do it himself, how many businesses are available to complete the task for him?

Answer: There are three businesses that can dry-clean the man's suit: *A+ Laundry & Cleaners, Daily Spin Quality Cleaners, Opal's Cleaners*. The other seemingly-able businesses are either laundry-only centers or self-service cleaners.

A woman wants to hire a landscaping company this winter to improve how her yard looks. Which company should she contact?

Answer: She should contact *All Season Lawn Maintenance* because that company specifically states that it works year-round in all seasons. Since the woman wants the work done in the winter, this company can accommodate her.

Sources for Locating Information: The Internet has made information more accessible than ever before, but it has also increased the difficulty of finding valid and appropriate information. To find suitable information, first locate a source that discusses specifically what or who you are investigating. Secondly, locate a source that is credible, or not directly related to what or who you are investigating.

Using information from the paragraph above, answer the following questions.

Daniel wants to look up horsepower figures for a brand new car he wants to buy. In terms of specificity, which source would be best to find this information?
   a) Eco-Auto newsletter
   b) Hot Rod Heaven magazine
   c) The manufacturer's website

Answer: All three sources are related to vehicles in one way or another, but the manufacturer's website is the only source in which you could find horsepower numbers for the vehicle Daniel wants to buy.

Cynthia wants to research the effectiveness of soap from different manufacturers. In terms of credibility, which source would be best to look up information?
   a) An online blog
   b) The manufacturer's website
   c) An independent research firm's report

Answer: All three sources might discuss different soaps, but an independent research firm is the most credible because it is a professional firm and isn't related to the manufacturer.

Sample Listings of Items and Costs: When making a purchase, you must contend with several factors that could possibly affect your decision. Before selecting a specific brand of a particular product, consider the following steps. First, identify the product features most important to you. Second, gather product information from three to five competitors. Third, sort through this information and select the product that best matches your preferred features.

Use the example below to answer the following questions.

Company	Price	Color	Size
Maximum Tees	15.99/dozen	Red	M
Wholesale Tees	12.99/dozen	Blue	L
Total Tees	19.99/dozen	Green	XL

Ben needs to buy shirts for his youth baseball team. The team color is red, the players all wear medium-sized shirts, and would prefer to spend less than $12. Which company best suits Ben's requirements?

Answer: Ben's requirements are best suited by Maximum Tees. Although the price is higher than desired, the color and size match Ben's needs exactly. Often, you won't find a company or product that matches your requirements exactly.

Sarah is buying shirts for her church group. She would like them to be green, large-sized, and $15 or less. Which company best suits Sarah's requirements?

Answer: Sarah's requirements do not have one company that best suits them. Wholesale Tees offers shirts that are blue (not green), large-sized, and $12.99. Total Tees offers shirts that are green, extra-large-sized (not large-sized), and $19.99 (not $15 or less). Because Wholesale Tees matches two of Sarah's three requirements, compared to Total Tees' one matching requirement, Wholesale Tees best suits Sarah's needs.

Graphic Representations of Information: Information is usually represented as text, but it can also be represented graphically. Types of graphic information include charts, maps, graphs, drawings, and photographs. Graphic representations are used to quickly visualize an idea or compare bits of information. They are typically accompanied by a legend or additional information that aids comprehension.

Use the chart below to answer the following questions.

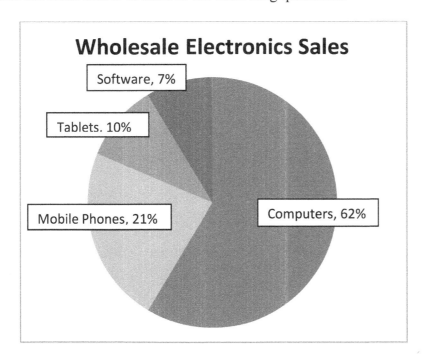

Which product accounts for most of Wholesale Electronics' total sales?

Answer: At 62%, computers account for most of Wholesale Electronics' total sales.

Mobile phones and tablets comprise what percentage of Wholesale Electronics' total sales?

Answer: Mobile phones and tablets comprise 31% of Wholesale Electronics' total sales.

Scale Readings: A scale reading is simply a numerical value collected from a scale, or measurement device, such as a weight scale or thermometer. To accurately interpret a scale reading, you must know the maximum and minimum values of the measurement device; otherwise, the measurement limits of the device can be misinterpreted as a genuine reading.

Use the image below to answer the following questions.

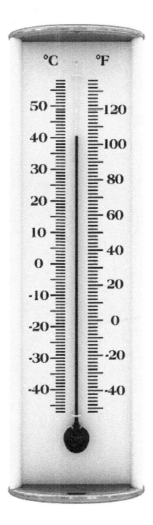

The current temperature is approximately 105° Fahrenheit. What is the approximate temperature in degrees Centigrade?

Answer: 105° F is approximately 40° C.

If the thermometer indicated a temperature of 15° C, what would the temperature be in degrees Fahrenheit?

Answer: 15° C is approximately 60° F.

Legends and Keys of Maps: The legend or key of a map explains the various symbols used on a map as well as their meanings and/or measurements. These symbols typically include a compass rose and a distance scale. A compass rose indicates the four cardinal directions (north, south, west, and east) and the four intermediate directions (northwest, northeast, southwest, and southeast). A distance scale is used to estimate distance, usually in miles or kilometers.

Use the map below to answer the following questions.

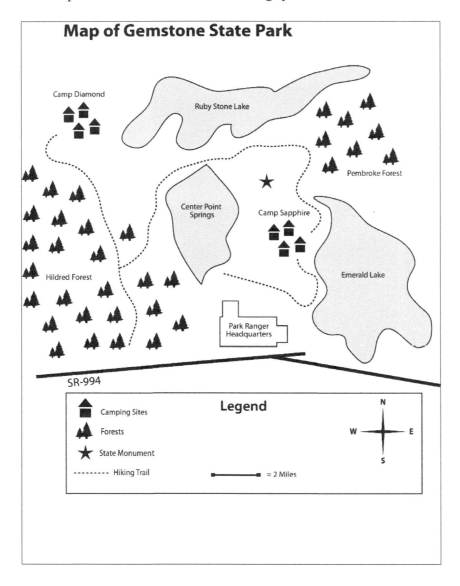

From Park Ranger Headquarters, which direction is Ruby Stone Lake?

Answer: Ruby Stone Lake is north of Park Ranger Headquarters.

Approximately how many miles is the state monument to the center of Pembroke Forest?

Answer: The center of Pembroke Forest is approximately 4 miles from the state monument.

Headings and Subheadings: A general topic or subject is usually divided into categories and sections so the text can be easily navigated and read. A heading is a subcategory of the subject, and a subheading is a subcategory of a heading. Both types of headings preview what will be covered in their respective sections, but a heading usually encompasses a broader range of information than a subheading. The font for headings is typically larger than the font for subheadings.

Use the example below to answer the following questions.

The Constitution of the United States of America

Article I
    Section I
    Section II
    Section III
    Section IV
    Section V

Is Article I a heading or subheading?

Answer: The subject is the Constitution of the United States of America. Since a heading is a subcategory of the subject, Article I is classified as a heading.

Is Section III a heading or subheading?

Answer: You already know that the subject is the Constitution of the United States of America. You also know that Article I is a heading. Since a subheading is a subcategory of a heading, Section III is classified as a subheading.

Text Features: Text features are stylistic elements used to clarify, add meaning, or differentiate. Examples of text features include bold, italicized, or underlined fonts and bulleted or numbered lists. The general rule of thumb for text features is to use them consistently. Inconsistency can confuse the reader and distort the intended purpose of a text feature.

Use the examples below to answer the following questions.

I'm glad you have accepted my invitation to meet with me. Directions to my office are below.

1. Head north on IH-10
2. Take the Woodview exit
3. Turn right onto Woodview
4. After 1.3 miles, turn left onto East Glen Street
5. Go 0.6 miles
6. The office will be on your right-hand side

What is the purpose of writing the directions as a numbered list?

Answer: Bulleted and numbered lists are quite helpful in identifying sequential items, especially travel directions.

> Steven: I'm so tired. *I should've completed my homework last night, instead of this morning.*
>
> Tina: I agree.

Why is the second sentence of Steven's dialogue written in italics?

Answer: Italics are often used to reflect someone's thoughts. Steven's first sentence was spoken; his second sentence was thought.

Key Terms

Primary source- a direct account of events, people, ideas, facts, etc.

Fact- a statement or thought that can be proven to be true

Opinion- an assumption that is not based on fact and cannot be proven to be true

Bias-prejudice; unwarranted support for or against something or someone

Stereotype- a belief or view of an entire group of people or things based on inaccurate information

Critical reading- a process in which the audience reads a text, analyzes it and the author, and draws conclusions instead of unquestioningly accepting the presented information as fact

Author's purpose- an author's reason or goal for writing a text

Narrative passage- a text that tells a story

Expository passage- a text intended to describe or inform; usually supported with background information and facts

Technical writing passage- a text intended to convey specialized information; usually presented in a specific way

Persuasive writing- a text intended to convince; usually advocates believing something, voting for someone, or purchasing something

Main idea- the central thesis of a text

Topic- a particular subject within the main idea of a text

Supporting detail- text that provides more information about a main topic or idea

Topic sentence- the opening sentence of a paragraph that hints at the upcoming information and ties it to the main idea of a text

Summary sentence- outlines the information that was just presented and highlights the important points

Logical conclusions- a conclusion derived from reasoning and critical analysis, not only from personal beliefs

Inference- a logical judgment made after reading a phrase or sentence in a text

Historical context- the historical setting in which a text is written

Text structure- a method of arranging text and emphasizing ideas and topics

Sequence of ideas- an arranged list of thoughts

Problem-solution structure- a text structure in which the author presents a problem and then discusses a solution

Comparison-contrast structure- a text structure in which the author presents two situations and then discusses the similarities and differences

Cause-effect structure- a text structure in which the author presents an action and then discusses the resulting effects

Context- text that surrounds a word or phrase and provides background information

Table of contents- an outline of a text that includes topics and page numbers

Index- an alphabetical list of topics, and their associated page numbers, covered in a text

Pie chart- a graphic representation of information in which the whole "pie" is divided into parts that reflect subcategories of the general topic

Scale- a measurement device, such as a weight scale or thermometer

Scale reading- a numerical value collected from a scale

Legend- explains the various symbols used on a map as well as their meanings and/or measurements

Compass rose- a symbol included in the legend of a map; used to indicate the four cardinal directions (north, south, west, and east) and the four intermediate directions (northwest, northeast, southwest, and southeast)

Distance scale- a symbol included in the legend of a map; used to estimate distance

Heading- a title of a section of text; a subcategory of a general subject

Subheading- a title of a section of text; a subcategory of a heading

Text features- stylistic elements used to clarify, add meaning, or differentiate

Chapter 4: Science

The Science section of the TEAS covers four major areas:

- Human Body Science
- Life Science
- Earth and Physical Science
- Scientific Reasoning

In plain English, those sections cover Anatomy and Physiology, Biology, Chemistry, and General Scientific Knowledge, all of which you should have learned in high school.

The approximate breakdown of question on the actual TEAS test is as follows:

- Human Body Science
  - 11 questions, which accoutns for 7% of the total exam
- Life Science
  - 15 questions, which accounts for 10% of the total exam
- Earth and Physical Science
  - 14 questions, which accounts for 9% of the total exam
- Scientific Reasoning
  - 8 questions, which accounts for 5% of the total exam

Based on the above information, you can see how many questions make up the quantity of questions, however, the amount of time each person must dedicate to each section will vary based on their previous experience and exposure to the concepts. For most people, Scientific Reasoning goes pretty quickly as the questions are relatively easy. Human Body Science on the other hand often requires a lot of time since most test-takers did not get as much exposure to anatomy and physiology courses in high school. Still others might have had no exposure at all, so with all the different aspects, the learning curve can be steep which means the time spent studying compared to the number of questions could be disproportionate. Typically Life Science and Earth & Physical Science falls somewhere in between for most students.

Scientific Reasoning

Statistical Measures

Though this typically only applies to experimental activities, there are different techniques and technologies that you can use to perform **statistical** measures and analyze the data. The following chart briefly summarizes some statistical tests. Analyze each situation to see when to best use a certain method – most likely, more than one method will be used at a time.

By utilizing the correct way to perform statistical measures, you increase the efficiency of the procedure, as well as its ease and accuracy.

Name of Statistical Method	Example(s)	When to Use
Graphing	Scatter plot, bar graphs, etc.	When comparing measurements
Descriptive Statistics	Mean, median, mode, SD, etc.	When summarizing measurements taken in an activity
Association Statistics	Linear regression	When trying to observe a correlation or regression between variables
Comparative Statistics	t-test and ANOVA	When comparing two or more sets of data
Frequency Statistics	X^2 -test of association	When counts are taken instead of measurements

The **International System of Units** (i.e., metric system) is the universal system of measurement that is utilized in the sciences. The chart below depicts the base units used in science.

Quantity	Base Unit
Length	Meter (m)
Mass	Gram (g)*
Temperature	Kelvin (K)
Time	Second (s)

Although gram is the base unit, kilogram is the most common unit used for mass.

118

Conversions for length and mass are simple with the metric system. Prefixes are used to stand for different amounts. The base unit alone is worth 1. To convert, simply divide the base unit by the corresponding amount based on the prefix. The basic prefixes are in the chart below:

Prefix	Amount
Mega (M-)	1 Million
Kilo- (K-)	1 Thousand
Hecto- (H-)	1 Hundred
Deka- (Da-)	1 Ten
Deci- (d-)	1 Tenth
Centi- (c-)	1 Hundredth
Milli – (m-)	1 Thousandth
Micro – (μ-)	1 Millionth

The Nature of Science

Science is the act of studying the physical and natural aspects of the world around us for more understanding. The interaction of science, math, and technology leads to many discoveries about the things that exist in our universe. Science allows us to not only understand our world, but also to make predictions about what is going to happen in our world.

Though science can help us to answer many questions, there are some **limitations** to science, such as **pseudosciences** which deal with the supernatural. For example, you cannot scientifically quantify astronomy and zodiacs (though scientific principles such as consistent measurements and graphs are often used). Science is also of no assistance in the areas of morals and values. It cannot tell us what is good versus bad or how pretty a color is.

> Science is limited to answering questions about the natural world. Science can answer the who, what, when, where, and why of the natural world. It can tell you how old an artifact is or who committed a crime. Science cannot answer questions of opinion or about emotion.

Scientific Investigations

Although limited, science does provide us a means to answering many questions about our natural world. Scientists use different types of investigations, each providing different types of results, based upon what they are trying to find. There are three main types of scientific investigations: descriptive, experimental, and comparative.

Descriptive Investigations

These types of investigations start by making observations. A model is then constructed to provide a visual of what was seen: a *description*. Descriptive investigations do not generally require hypotheses, as they usually attempt to find more information about a relatively unknown topic.

Experimental Investigations

These types of investigations are also referred to as **controlled** experiments because they are performed in a controlled environment. During experimental investigations, all variables are controlled except for one: the dependent variable, which will be the outcome of the experiment. Often, there are many tests involved in this process.

Comparative Investigations

These investigations involve manipulating different groups in order to compare them with each other. There is no control during comparative investigations. Once the investigations are complete, the data is thoroughly analyzed to check for the results or outcome of the manipulated variable.

In order to choose the appropriate type of investigation, scientists must first understand what type of outcome they require. To do this, background information about the topic or question must be collected. The **scientific method** can be used to design an **inquiry-based experiment**. Once that experiment is complete, scientists may communicate their results by writing scientific papers or reports or they participate in scientific presentations or conferences. During the communication phase, whether orally or verbally, scientists have a main goal of defending their points. This defense is built heavily around, not only the procedure and results of the investigation, but also the background research that was performed before the investigation began.

A theory and a hypothesis are both important aspects of science. There is a common misconception that they are one in the same, which is not true – though the two are very similar. A **hypothesis** is based upon background information and research, while a **theory** is formed based on the results of a tested hypothesis.

While testing a hypothesis by way of an investigation, observations are made and data is collected. When a scientist analyzes the data, they are looking for patterns that depict a relationship. If a test is performed multiple times with the same results, concepts can be explained and proven.

The Scientific Method

1. Observe and Ask Questions
2. Research, Collect, and Analyze Data
3. Construct Hypothesis
4. Experiment! Test your Hypothesis
5. Analyze Results and Draw Conclusions
   - Was your Hypothesis True? Report your Results!
   - Was your Hypothesis False? Return to Step 3 and Start Again!

Systems

A **system** is a whole unit with a main goal, or focus, to work toward; and the system's functions are based on the parts that make up the unit. Take the Respiratory System, for example. It's made up of many functions that all work towards effective respiration.

Each part of a system is interdependent and works together on a common task. All systems have three basic commonalities: structure, action, and interconnectivity.

Structure
All systems have a structure on which the foundation of the system is built. Systems in science have their own unique structure that serves as the systems' base.

Action
All systems perform actions. These actions consist of taking in information, internalizing it, and then giving some type of output.

Interconnectivity
The structures inside of a system all work together so that the system can meet its goals.

Systems can also work with other systems to perform an even bigger goal. The human body is an example of many systems working together for the common goal of keeping the body in equilibrium.

Systems are a part of all the science disciplines, and follow the same basic **model of systems**.

Interacting Parts
The body systems clearly illustrate how systems have interacting parts. Each system contains organs that cooperate in order to keep the whole system functioning.

Boundaries
There is a limit to what a system can do on its own without needing help from other systems. For example, the Earth is a part of the Solar System. The Earth is capable of spinning on its own axis; and this spinning is partly responsible for causing day, night, and season changes. But without the Sun, these processes would not be possible.

Input and Output
Systems must receive information in order to send out information. The input could be in the form of instructions, like when the nucleus of a cell gives instructions to the other organelles on when and what function they should be performing.

Feedback
Feedback occurs when a portion of the output is returned to the system and used to control or maintain the system. Nature, for instance, is constantly recycling itself in a great example of feedback.

Subsystems
Sometimes larger systems are made of smaller, independent systems. For example, a body cell is made of many organelles. There are some functions that are performed in conjunction with other organelles, but then there are certain tasks that an organelle can carry out on its own. In this way, the organelle serves as a subsystem to the cell as a whole.

Science is a highly-organized discipline. This organization stems on the fact that many parts of science share similar characteristics and are grouped accordingly. There are many sets of levels of organization that exists on Earth. These levels are based on large similarities and small differences. For example, all organisms are divided into one of the six kingdoms but are then further divided based on small differences from organisms in the main group. Concepts and investigations are also grouped in science. The results of an investigation can either be classified as evidence to a larger concept, a model of a system, or an explanation of a concept.

Parts of a system are grouped together because the parts work together on a common goal. Parts of science can also be grouped by its form or function. The definition of an organ is a group of tissues working together. For this reason, all organs can be grouped together because they all have the same basic make up. Of course they are very different and perform different functions, but their structure is the same.

There are many examples of systems and subsystems in the natural world. As previously mentioned a system can stand on its own and perform a function. Often there are smaller subsystems that make up a larger system. The subsystems perform a unique task on its own that is separate from the major system. Some of the subsystems interact with each other on common tasks as well.

History of Science

The development of science has been and will always be a collective effort. Individuals from all over the world with various backgrounds contribute to scientific developments. People have always wondered what makes up the world around us. Discoveries such as that of the atom and the cell have led to the discovery of many more elements on the periodic table and the structure of DNA.

Scientific theories and knowledge are constantly changing. As technology improves, current theories are tested under improved circumstances. An example of such an improvement surrounds the discovery of the atom.

> Dalton understood the basic concept of an atom, including atomic theory. However, scientists such as Thomson, Rutherford, and Bohr have made significant improvements to Dalton's original model. In fact, new discoveries have been made about atomic structure within the last ten years. Science is constantly evolving.

Science is a **subjective** area of study, largely based on the interests of those who are studying the concepts. It's largely a human endeavor influenced by societal, cultural, and personal views of the world. For example, a person's culture and background, as well as societal issues and biases, play key roles in determining scientific interests. Different countries have different focuses or areas they feel are important.

Ethics of Science

When conducting, analyzing, and publishing scientific investigations, there are certain ethics that must be followed. These ethical standards are accepted by the science community as a whole. The main standard is to always give credit when using someone else's work in your investigation.

The science community is very large and diverse, so it may be tempting to count someone's work as your own. However, this is never acceptable, and there are many ways of discovering and exposing plagiarism. Never risk your integrity – it's hard to ever come back from an incriminating event and regain creditability in the scientific community.

Applications of Science

One can apply scientific principles to analyze factors (e.g., diet, exercise, personal behavior) that influence personal and societal choices concerning fitness and health (e.g., physiological and psychological effects and risks associated with the use of substances and substance abuse). The scientific method can be used to solve almost any problem, concern, or wondering. These types of investigation rely heavily on observations.

Science makes logical conclusions, and therefore can help us make logical conclusions as well. One can apply scientific principles, the theory of probability, and risk/benefit analysis in order to analyze the advantages of, disadvantages of, or alternatives to a given decision or course of action.

Scientific principles such as Newton's Laws of Motion and the Bernoulli Principle are used constantly. The law of wearing safety belts, for example, is based upon Newton's First Law of Motion.

The Bernoulli Principle informs those who work in aeronautics the advantages and disadvantages of certain designs of aircrafts, and therefore ensures that aircrafts fly properly.

The scientific method can solve problems personal, societal, and global. You can increase your students' interest in science by giving examples of such problems. Take disease prevention, which is a huge concern. Researchers develop scientific experiments and field tests to determine the best method to controlling diseases. The West Nile Virus has proved to be a concern among many communities – but researchers have performed scientific investigations on how to control mosquitoes (and therefore the virus).

Natural Resources

Students may also be interested in understanding the role of science – and the role of humans – in affecting natural resources. There are two main groupings of natural resources: renewable and nonrenewable.

Renewable resources are those that can be replaced and managed. They are restored by nature and are therefore not in grave danger of depletion. Think of oxygen and water, for example. **Nonrenewable** resources, on the other hand, are lost once used. Examples include natural gas and other fossil fuels. Once these items are used up, there will be none left.

Human consumption of both renewable and nonrenewable resources is slowly becoming a problem. The renewable resources, although they replenish themselves, are being used faster than they can be replaced. As for nonrenewable resources, the dependency that has been developed on these materials is weighing heavy on society as a whole. Alternative methods and resources are being developed so that the consumption of nonrenewable products can decrease. Through scientific methods, solutions to these problems are being reached – showing once more how instrumental science is to the development and continuity of society.

Test Your Knowledge: Scientific Reasoning

1. Convert 3.5 meters to kilometers.

2. When handling live specimens, it is important to use proper _____ .

3. Which of the following numbers has the most significant figures?
   a) 3456
   b) 0.033
   c) 980
   d) 2010.0

4. Look at the following data table a student constructed during science class. What is wrong with his data?

Time	Distance	Speed
1 min	2 meters	2 meters/min
2 min	4 meters	2 meters/min
3 min	7 meters	2.33eters/min

5. Of the following answer choices, which ones can be answered by science?
   a) Why is the sky blue?
   b) Why does Sarah like blue better than pink?
   c) Why are my eyes blue instead of brown?
   d) Why does Jane like Michael?

6. True/False: There are no known variables in neither descriptive nor comparative investigations.

7. Briefly describe the characteristics of a system.

8. Choose a system in science that fits into the model of a system. Write out how the system fits into each of the five parts of the model.

9. What is the benefit of using a model?

10. Observe the following data. Which conclusion can be made based on this data?

Time	Distance	Speed
60 sec	2 meters	.03 meters/sec
120 sec	4 meters	.03 meters/sec
180 sec	7 meters	.039 meters/sec

a) As time increased, speed increased.
b) As distance increased, speed increased.
c) As distance and time increased, speed decreased.
d) As distance increased, speed remained about the same.

Science Reasoning - Answers

1. **0.0035 km**.

2. **"ethics."**

3. **d)** 2010.0 has five significant figures. Answer **a)** has four, and both **b)** and **c)** have two.

4. The **time** should be measured in **seconds, not minutes.**

5. Answers **a)** and **c)** can be answered by science, as there are scientific experiments that can be performed to answer them. Answers **b)** and **d)** are based on personal opinion and can therefore not be proven or answered by science.

6. **False**. Descriptive investigations do not have variables. Comparative investigations involve variables.

7. Answers will vary, but should include information about **structure, action,** and **interconnectivity.**

8. **Answer will vary but there are many science systems that fit this criteria.**

9. **Models allow you to study part of the natural world that cannot be studied in its natural state.**

10. **d)**

Human Body Science

Anatomy and Physiology are the studies of body parts and body systems. This section will cover all necessary medical terms, word parts and terminology, as well as the anatomy and physiology of each body system.

Structure Hierarchy of the Human Body

- Organsim
    - Organ Systems
        - Organs
            - Tissues
                - Cells
                    - Molecules
                        - Atoms

Directional Terms

Superior	Toward the head, or toward the upper body region
Inferior	Toward the lower body region
Anterior (Ventral)	On the belly or front side of the body
Posterior (Dorsal)	On the buttocks or back side of the body
Proximal	Near the trunk or middle part of the body
Distal	Furthest away from the point of reference
Medial	Close to the midline of the body
Lateral	Away from the midline of the body

Word Parts
A medical term often has three parts: the prefix, the root, and suffix.

- Prefix - Begins the word, modifies the root, and not a part of all medical terms.
  Example: hyperactive; hyper- modifies the word active.

- Root - Center part of the word, holds meaning, and is often referred to as the "body" of the word.
  Example: Tonsillectomy; tonsil is the root word.

- Suffix - Ends the word, modifies the root, refers to a procedure, action, or condition, and is not part of all medical terms.
  Example: Vasectomy; -ectomy modifies the root word vas.

Prefixes

epi-	on/upon
hyper-	over
hypo-	under
intra-	within
para-	beside
per-	through
peri-	surrounding
sub-	under

Suffixes

-coccus	spherical bacterium
-ia	condition
-ectomy	removal
-malacia	softening
-tome	an instrument to cut
-tomy	to cut
-rrhea	discharge
-plasty	surgical repair
-opsy	view of

Body Cavities

- Cranial cavity - Contains the brain
- Spinal cavity - Contains the spinal cord, and extends from the brainstem in the cranial cavity to the end of the spinal cord
- Thoracic cavity - Contains the lungs, heart, and large blood vessels, and is separated from the abdomen by the diaphragm
- Abdominal cavity - Contains the stomach, intestines, liver, gallbladder, pancreas, spleen, and kidneys, and is separated from the thoracic cavity by the diaphragm
- Pelvic cavity - Contains the urinary bladder, urinary structures, and reproductive organs

THE CIRCULATORY SYSTEM

The circulatory system is vital to human functioning. It is composed of the cardiovascular and pulmonary systems. The cardiovascular system includes the heart, blood, and blood vessels. This is where circulation begins, ends, and begins again. The pulmonary system is composed of the lungs and muscles that allow breathing.

The cardiovascular system plays a vital role in the functioning of humans, as it distributes oxygen, nutrients and hormones to the entire body. The whole system relies on the heart, a muscular organ that is no bigger than a closed fist. The heart must pump the blood low in oxygen to the lungs, and once the blood is in the lungs, it is oxygenated and returned to the heart. The heart then pumps the oxygenated blood through the whole body.

A. The Heart

The *heart* is the muscular organ located inside the rib cage. It can be found approximately between the second and the sixth rib from the bottom of the rib cage. The heart does not sit on the body's midline. Rather, two-thirds of it is located on the left side of the body. Other facts about the heart include:

- It is slightly cone shaped.

- The narrower part of the heart is called the *apex,* and it points downwards and to the left of the body.

- The broader part of the heart is called the *base,* and it points upwards.

The cavity that holds the heart is called the pericardial cavity. It is filled with serous fluid produced by the pericardium, which is the lining of the pericardial cavity. The serous fluid acts as a lubricant for the heart. It also keeps the heart in place and empties the space around the heart.

1. Three Layers of the Heart Wall

- *Epicardium* – This is the outermost layer of the heart, and is one of the two layers of the pericardium.

- *Myocardium* – This is the middle layer of the heart that contains the cardiac muscular tissue. It performs the function of pumping what is necessary for the circulation of blood. It is the most massive part of the heart.

- *Endocardium* – This is the smooth innermost layer that keeps the blood from sticking to the inside of the heart.

The heart wall is uneven because some parts of the heart – like the atria -- don't need a lot of muscle power to perform their duties. Other parts, like the ventricles, require a thicker muscle to pump the blood.

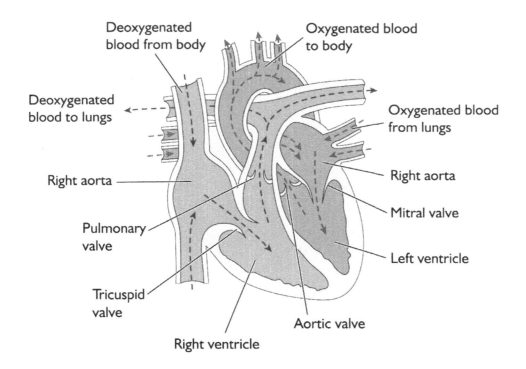

Deoxygenated blood from body

Oxygenated blood to body

Deoxygenated blood to lungs

Oxygenated blood from lungs

Right aorta

Right aorta

Pulmonary valve

Mitral valve

Left ventricle

Tricuspid valve

Aortic valve

Right ventricle

2. Four Chambers of the Heart

There are four chambers in the heart. These are:

- *Right atrium*
- *Left atrium*
- *Right ventricle*
- *Left ventricle*

The *atria* (plural for *atrium*) are smaller than the ventricles, and they have thin walls, as their function is to receive blood from the lungs and the body and pump it to the ventricles. The *ventricles* have to pump the blood to the lungs and the rest of the body, so they are larger and have a thicker wall. The left half of the heart, which is responsible for pumping the blood through the body, has a thicker wall than the right half, and this left ventricle pumps the blood to the lungs.

The blood vessels have one way valves allowing the blood to only flow in one direction. The valves that keep the blood from going back into the atria from the ventricles are called the *atrioventicular valves*, and the valves that keep the blood from going back from the arteries into the ventricles are called the *semilunar valves*.

132

The pumping function of the heart is made possible by two groups of cells that set the heart's pace and keep it well coordinated: the sinoatrial and the atrioventicular node.

- The *sinoatrial node* sets the pace and signals the atria to contract

- The *atrioventicular node* picks up the signal from the sinoatrial node, and this signal tells the ventricles to contract.

B. The Blood Vessels

The *blood vessels* carry the blood from the heart, to the body and then back. They vary in size depending on the amount of the blood that needs to flow through them. The hollow part in the middle, called the lumen, is where the blood actually flows. The vessels are lined with *endothelium,* which is made out of the same type of cells as the endocardium and serves the same purpose, to keep the blood from sticking to the walls and clotting.

1. Arteries

Arteries are blood vessels that transport the blood away from the heart. They work under a lot more pressure than the other types of blood vessels; hence, they have a thicker, more muscular wall, which is also highly elastic. The smaller arteries are usually more muscular, while the larger are more elastic.

The Aorta

The largest artery in the body is called the *aorta.* It ascends from the left ventricle of the heart, arches to the back left, and descends behind the heart. Narrower arteries that branch off of main arteries and carry blood to the capillaries are called *arterioles.* The descending part of the aorta carries blood to the lower parts of the body, except for the lungs. The lungs get blood through the *pulmonary artery* that comes out of the right ventricle.

The Aortic Arch

The arching part of the aorta (called the *aortic arch)* branches into three arteries: the brachiocephalic artery, the left common artery, and the left subclavian artery.

- The *brachiocephalic artery* carries blood to the brain and head. The brachiocephalic artery divides into the *right subclavian artery,* which brings the blood to the right arm.

- The *left common carotid artery* carries blood to the brain.

- The *left subclavian artery* carries blood to the left arm.

2. Veins

Veins are blood vessels that bring the blood from to the body and then back to the heart. As they don't work under the same pressure as the arteries, they are much thinner and not as muscular or elastic. The veins also have a number of one way valves that stops the blood from going back through them.

Veins use inertia, muscle work, and gravity to get the blood to the heart. Thin veins that connect to the capillaries are called *venules*. The lungs have their own set of veins: the left and right superior and inferior pulmonary veins. These vessels enter the heart through the left atrium.

Two Main Veins

The two main veins are called the superior vena cava and the inferior vena cava.

- *The superior vena cava* – This vein ascends from the right atrium and connects to the head and neck, delivering the blood supply to these structures. The superior vena cava also connects to the arms via both subclavian and brachiocephalic veins.

- *The inferior vena cava* – This vessel descends from the right atrium, carrying the blood from the lumbar veins, gonadal veins, hepatic veins, phrenic veins, and renal veins.

The lungs have their own set of veins: the left and right superior and inferior pulmonary veins. These vessels enter the heart through the left atrium.

3. Capillaries

Capillaries are the smallest blood vessels, and the most populous in the body. They can be found in almost every tissue. They connect to arterioles on one end and the venules on the other end. Also, capillaries carry the blood very close to the cells, and thus, enable cells to exchange gasses, nutrients, and cellular waste. The walls of capillaries have to be very thin for this exchange to happen.

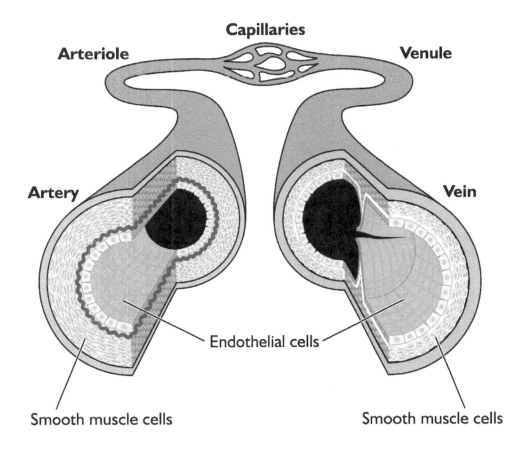

Arteriole

Capillaries

Venule

Artery

Vein

Endothelial cells

Smooth muscle cells

Smooth muscle cells

C. The Blood

The *blood* is the medium for the transport of substances throughout the body. There are 4 to 5 liters of this liquid connective tissue in the human body. The components of the blood are red blood cells, hemoglobin, white blood cells, platelets, and plasma.

1. Red Blood Cells (RBCs)

Also called erythrocytes, red blood cells (RBCs) are produced inside the red bone marrow and they serve to transport oxygen.

2. Hemoglobin (HGB)

Hemoglobin (HGB) is a red pigment found in the red blood cells, and HGB is rich in iron and proteins, which both allow these cells to transport the oxygen. Hemoglobin also has a biconcave shape, which means it is round and thinner in the middle. This shape gives them a larger surface area, making them more effective.

3. **White blood cells (WBCs)**
Also called leukocytes, white blood cells (WBCs) are important for the human immune system. There are two classes of white blood cells: granular and agranular leukocytes.

4. **Platelets** Also called thrombocytes, platelets are vital for blood clotting. They are formed in the red bone marrow and serve many functions in the body.

5. **Plasma** The plasma is the liquid part of the blood, and it forms 55 percent of the total blood volume. Plasma consists of up to 90 percent water, as well as proteins – Including antibodies and albumins. Other substances in plasma are circulating in the blood plasma, also, such as glucose, nutrients, cell waste, and various gasses.

- Granular leukocytes are divided into three types: the neutrophils that digest bacteria, the eosinophils that digest viruses, and the basophils that release histamine.

- Agranular leukocytes are divided into two classes: the lymphocytes, which fight off viral infections and produce antibodies for fighting pathogen-induced infection and the monocytes, which play a role in removing pathogens and dead cells from wounds.

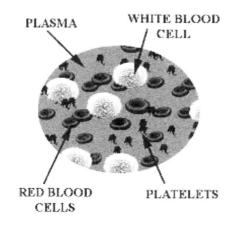

136

D. Physiology of the Heart and the Circulatory System

The heart works by shifting between two states: systole and diastole.

- Systole means the cardiac muscles are contracting and moving blood from any given chamber

- Diastole means the muscles are relaxing and the chamber is expanding to fill with blood.

The systole and diastole are responsible for the pressure in the major arteries. This is the blood pressure that is measured in a regular exam. The two values are systolic and diastolic pressures respectively, with the former being larger than the latter.

1. The Cardiac Cycle

A cardiac cycle is a series of events that happen during one heartbeat. These events include:

1. Atrial systole – The first phase of the cardiac cycle is atrial systole. With this, the blood is pushed by the atria through the valves into ventricles, which are in diastole during that event.

2. Ventricular systole – After atrial systole, ventricular systole occurs. This pushes the blood from the ventricles to the organs, which occurs while the atria are in diastole.

3. Relaxation phase – After ventricular systole, there is a pause called the relaxation phase. During this, all the chambers are in diastole, and the blood enters the atria through the veins.

4. Refilling phase – When atria are at about 75 percent of their capacity, the cycle starts again. With the refilling phase, the atria are fully filled before atrial systole occurs again.

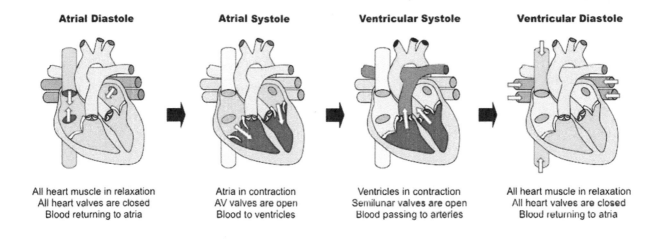

Atrial Diastole	Atrial Systole	Ventricular Systole	Ventricular Diastole
All heart muscle in relaxation	Atria in contraction	Ventricles in contraction	All heart muscle in relaxation
All heart valves are closed	AV valves are open	Semilunar valves are open	All heart valves are closed
Blood returning to atria	Blood to ventricles	Blood passing to arteries	Blood returning to atria

2. Oxygenating the Blood Cells

There are four steps to blood cell oxygenation. These include:

1. The poorly oxygenated blood comes into the right atrium through the superior and inferior vena cava.

2. The blood is then passed to the right ventricle, which sends it through the pulmonary artery into the lungs where oxygenation occurs.

3. The oxygen-rich blood then comes to the left atrium through the pulmonary veins, and gets moved from the left atrium to the left ventricle.

4. By way of blood pressure, the blood is then sent from the left ventricle through the aorta and the aortic arch into the arteries in the whole body.

Returning the Blood to the Heart

The blood passes from the arteries to the arterioles, and on from those vessels to the capillaries. The capillaries are where the exchange of gasses, nutrients, wastes, and hormones occur. The blood then passes into venules, and gets back to the heart through the veins. This way, a healthy resting heart can pump around 5 liters per minute.

The veins of the stomach and intestines don't carry the blood directly to the heart. Rather, they divert it to the liver first, through the hepatic portal vein, so that the liver can store sugar, remove toxins, and process the products of digestion. The blood then goes to the heart through the inferior vena cava.

These processes enable the circulatory system to perform its role of transportation, protection, and regulation. Using the cardiovascular and pulmonary systems, the body transports nutrients, gasses, cellular waste, and hormones. The blood also helps with temperature regulation and homeostasis.

Circulatory Questions:

A. At what rate does a healthy heart pump blood while resting?

    a) Around 3 liters per minute.
    b) Around 8 liters per minute.
    c) Around 5 liters per minute.

2. Which of the layers of the wall of the heart contains cardiac muscles?

    a) Myocardium
    b) Epicardium
    c) Endocardium

3. The heart chamber with the thickest wall is:

    a) The left ventricle
    b) The right ventricle
    c) The right atrium

4. The blood from the left ventricle goes to:

    a) The right ventricle
    b) The vena cava
    c) The aorta and aortic arch

5. The blood vessels that carry the blood from the heart are called:

    a) Veins
    b) Arteries
    c) Capillaries

THE RESPIRATORY SYSTEM

The human body needs oxygen in order to function. The system that is responsible for intake of the gas is called the respiratory system. It's also in charge of removing carbon dioxide from the body, which is equally important. The respiratory system can be divided into two sections: the upper respiratory tract and the lower respiratory tract.

A.   The Upper Respiratory Tract

The *upper respiratory tract* consists of the nose, nasal cavity, olfactory membranes, mouth, pharynx, epiglottis, and the larynx.

1. The Nose
The nose is the primary body part for air intake and removing carbon dioxide. The nose itself is made out of bone, cartilage, muscle, and skin, and it serves as a protector of the hollow space behind it called the nasal cavity.

2. The Nasal Cavity
The nasal cavity is covered with hair and mucus, which together serve an important function – they stop contaminants from the outside. Common contaminants include dust, mold, and other particles. The nasal cavity permits the contaminants from entering further into the respiratory system. The three important roles of the nasal cavity are:

- Moisturizing
- Warming
- Filtering the air

3. Olfactory Membranes
The nose and the nasal cavity also contain olfactory membranes, which are small organs responsible for our sense of smell. They are located on the top of the nasal cavity, just under the bridge of the nose.

4. The Mouth
We can also breathe through the mouth, although it is not the primary breathing opening. The mouth doesn't perform as well when it comes to the three functions of the primary opening: filtering, moisturizing, and warming of air. However, the mouth does have its advantages over the nose when it comes to breathing. These advantages include:

- It is larger than the nose and can take in a larger amount of air.
- It is physically closer to the lungs, making the passage of air shorter.
- That's why we breathe through the mouth when we need a lot of air fast.

5. The Pharynx (Throat)

The next part of the respiratory system is the throat, which is also called the pharynx. The pharynx is a smooth, muscular structure. It is lined with mucous that is divided into three regions:

- The nasopharynx
- The oropharynx
- The laryngopharynx

The air comes in through the nose, and then passes through the *nasopharynx,* which is also where the Eustachian tubes from the middle ears connect with the pharynx. The air continues through the rest of the throat and then comes in through the mouth. Once air enters the throat, it is in the oropharynx, which is the same passageway used for transporting food when eating. Both air and food also pass through the laryngopharynx, which is where these substances get diverted.

6. Epiglottis

The body part that is responsible for keeping air going into the trachea and the food going into the esophagus is called epiglottis. The epiglottis is a flap made of elastic cartilage, which covers the opening of one passage way to allow the air or food to go into the other one. When breathing, the opening of the esophagus is covered, and when swallowing, the opening of the trachea is covered.

7. The Larynx (Voice Box)

The larynx is the part of the airway that sits between the pharynx and the trachea. It is also called the voice box, because it contains mucous membrane folds that vibrate when air passes through them to produce vocal sounds – the vocal folds. The larynx is made out of several cartilage structures:

- The epiglottis
- The thyroid cartilage - Known as the Adam's apple
- The cricoid cartilage – Which is a ring-shaped structure that keeps the larynx open.

B. The Lower Respiratory Tract

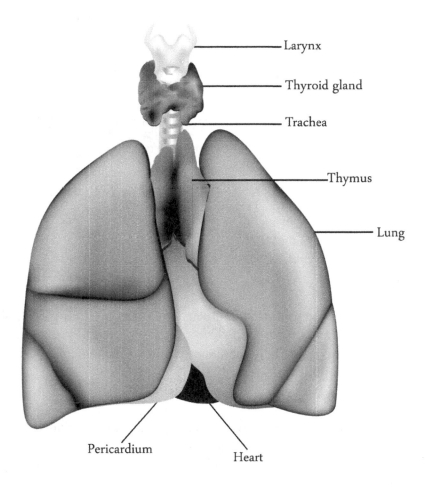

The *lower respiratory tract* – This consists of the trachea, bronchi, lungs, and the muscles that help with breathing.

1. Trachea (Windpipe)

The *lower respiratory tract* begins with the *trachea,* also known as the windpipe. The trachea is the part of the respiratory system between the larynx and the bronchi. As its name suggest, the windpipe resembles a pipe, and it's really flexible so it can follow various head and neck movements. The trachea is made out of fibrous and elastic tissues, smooth muscle, and about 20 cartilage rings.

The interior of the windpipe is lined with mucus-producing cells, as well as cells that have small fringes that resemble hair. These hair-like structures (cilia) allow the air to pass through the windpipe, where it is further filtered by the mucous. Also, the fringes help with moving the mucous up the airways and out, to keep the air passage free.

2. Bronchi

Connecting to the trachea are the *bronchi*, which branch to the left and the right of the primary bronchi to be precise. The primary bronchi are made out of many C-shaped cartilage rings, and they branch into the secondary bronchi. Two of them branch from the left primary bronchi, and three branch from the right, corresponding to the number of lobes in the lungs.

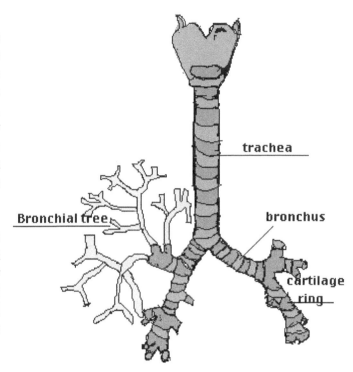

The secondary bronchi contain less cartilage and have more space between the rings. The same goes for the tertiary bronchi into which the secondary bronchi are divided in the lobes of the lungs. All of the bronchi are lined with *epithelium* that contains:

- The *goblet cells* – These produce the mucus that coats the lining of the bronchi and traps foreign particles and organisms, and
- The *cilia* – These are hair-like structures that move the mucus up and out of the lungs, keeping them clean and healthy.

3. Bronchioles

Bronchioles branch from the tertiary bronchi. They contain no cartilage at all; rather, they are made of smooth muscle and elastic fiber tissue, which allows them to be quite small and still able to change their diameter. Bronchioles end with terminal bronchioles, which connect them with alveoli. The changes that occur include:

- When the body needs more oxygen, they expand
- When there is a danger of pollutants entering the lungs, they constrict.

4. Alveoli

Alveoli are where the gas exchange happens. Alveoli are small cavities located in alveolar sacs and surrounded by capillaries. The inner surface of alveoli is coated with alveolar fluid, which plays a vital role in keep the alveoli moist, the lungs elastic, and the thin wall of alveoli stable.

The wall of the alveoli is made out of alveolar cells and the connective tissue which forms the respiratory membrane where it comes in contact with the wall of the capillaries.

5. The Lungs

The lungs themselves are two spongy organs that contain the bronchi, bronchioles, alveoli, and blood vessels. The lungs are contained in the rib cage, and are surrounded by the pleura, a double-layered membrane. The pleura consist of:

- The outer layer, called the parietal pleura.

144

- The inner layer, called the visceral pleura.

Between the layers of the pleura is a hollow space called the pleural cavity, which allows the lungs to expand. The lungs are wider at the top, which is referred to as the base, and they are narrower at the bottom part, which is called the apex. The lungs are divided into lobes, with the larger lung – the right one – consisting of three lobes, and the smaller lung – the left lung – consisting of two lobes.

6. The Muscles of Respiration

The muscles that play a major role in respiration are the diaphragm and the intercostal muscles. The diaphragm is a structure made of skeletal muscle, and it located under the lungs, forming the floor of the thorax. The intercostal muscles are located between the ribs. There are two types of intercostal muscles:

- The internal intercostal muscles – These help with breathing out (expiration) by depressing the ribs and compressing the thoracic cavity.
- The external intercostal muscles – These do the opposite and help with breathing in (inspiration).

C. Physiology of the Lungs and the Respiratory System

Breathing in and out is also called pulmonary ventilation. The two types of pulmonary ventilation are inhalation and exhalation.

1. Inhalation – Inspiration

- The diaphragm contracts and moves a few inches towards the stomach, making more space for the lungs to expand, and this movement pulls the air into the lungs.
- The external intercostal muscles also contract to expand the rib cage, and pull more air into the lungs.
- The lungs are naturally at a pressure lower than the atmosphere, or negative pressure, which also makes air come into to lungs until reaching a certain point. At this point, the pressure inside the lungs and the atmospheric pressure are the same.
- The diaphragm and the external intercostal muscles then expand the thoracic cavity to make the pressure in the lungs below that of the atmosphere, and this action continues to fill the lungs with air.

2. Exhalation – Expiration

- When breathing out, the diaphragm and the external intercostal muscles relax, and the internal intercostal muscles contract.
- The thoracic cavity becomes smaller, and the pressure in the lungs gets higher than the atmospheric pressure, which moves air out of the lungs.
- After this, the lungs return back to the negative pressure state by themselves.

3. Different Types of Breathing

Shallow breathing is one type of ventilation where air is moved at around half of a liter. This is called tidal volume. During deep breathing, a larger amount of air is moved (three to five liters), and this is known as vital capacity. The abdominal and other muscles are also involved in breathing in and out during deep breathing.

Eupnea is a term for the breathing our body does when resting, which consists of mostly shallow breaths, with an occasional deep breath. The lungs are never completely without air – around a liter of air is always present in the lungs.

Respiratory Questions:

1. The primary opening for breathing in and out is:
    a) The nose
    b) The mouth
    c) The skin pores

2. The air that we breathe in through the mouth enters the throat at the:
    a) Nasopharynx
    b) Oropharynx
    c) Laryngopharynx

3. For the air to go the lungs, the epiglottis needs to close:
    a) The esophagus
    b) The pharynx
    c) The larynx

4. How many lobes does the left lung have?
    a) 3
    b) 4
    c) 2

5. Bronchioles branch from the:
    a) Primary bronchi
    b) Secondary bronchi
    c) Tertiary Bronchi

THE SKELETAL SYSTEM

There are a number of roles the skeletal system plays in the body. The bones and joints that make the skeletal system are responsible for:

- Providing support and protection.
- Allowing movement.
- Blood cell genesis.
- Storing fat, iron, and calcium.
- Guiding the growth of the entire body.

Generally, the skeleton can be divided into two divisions: the axial skeleton and the appendicular skeleton.

- The axial skeleton - Consists of 80 bones, which are placed along the body's midline axis and grouped into the regions of skull, ribs, and sternum as well as the vertebral column.
- The appendicular skeleton - Consists of 126 bones grouped into the regions of upper and lower limbs, as well as the pelvic and the pectoral girdle.

A. Bone Components

1. Bone Parts

On the cellular level, the bone consists of two distinctively different parts: the matrix and living bone cells.

- The bone matrix – This is the non-living part of the bone, which is made out of water, collagen, protein, calcium phosphate, and calcium carbonate crystals.
- The living bone cells – These are found at the edges of the bones and throughout the bone matrix in small cavities. Bone cells play a vital part in the growth, development, and repair of bones, and can be used for the minerals they store.

2. Bone Layers

A cross section of a bone reveals that it is made out of layers. These include:

- Periosteum – This is the topmost layer of the bone, and it is a layer of connective tissue on the surface of the bones. The periosteum contains collagen fibers that serve to anchor the tendons and the muscles, as well as the stem and the osteoblast cells that are necessary for growth and repair of the bones. Nervous tissue, nerve endings, and blood vessels are also present in the periosteum.

- Compact bone – Under the periosteum is a layer of compact bone, which gives the bone its strength. Made out of mineral salts and collagen fibers, it also contains many cavities where the living bone cells - osteocytes - can be found.

- Trabeculae – Under the compact bone is a layer where the bone tissue grows in columns called trabeculae. The bone tissue forms space that contains the red bone marrow. The trabeculae give the bone structural strength by the way they grow, while keeping them light.

B. The Five Types of Bones

The five types of bones are:

- Long
- Short
- Flat
- Irregular
- Sesamoid

1. Long Bones
The long bones make up the major bones of the limbs. They are longer than they are wide, and they are responsible for the most of our height. The long bones can be divided in two regions: the epiphyses, located at the ends of the bone, and diaphysis, located in the middle. The middle of the diaphysis contains a hollow medullary cavity, which serves as a storage for bone marrow.

2. The Short Bones
The short bones are roughly as long as they are wide, and are generally cube-shaped or round. Short bones in the body include the carpal bones of the wrist and tarsal bones of the foot.

3. The Flat Bones
The flat bones do not have the medullary cavity because they are thin and usually thinner on one end regions. Flat bones in the body include the ribs, the hip bones, as well as the frontal, the parietal, and the occipital bones of the skull.

4. The Irregular Bones
The irregular bones are those bones that do not fit the criteria to be the long, the short, or the flat bones. The vertebrae and the sacrum, among others, are irregular bones.

5. The Sesamoid Bones
There are only two sesamoid bones that are actually counted as bones: the patella and the pisiform bone. Sesamoid bones are formed inside the tendons located across the joints, and apart from the two mentioned, they are not present in all people.

C. The Joints

The joints, also known as articulations, are where the bones come into contact with each other, the cartilage, or the tooth. There are three types of joints: synovial, fibrous, and cartilaginous joints.

1. Synovial Joints

The synovial joints feature a small gap between the bones that is filled with synovial fluid, which lubricates the joint. They are the most present type of joints in the body, and they allow the most of the movement.

2. Fibrous Joints

The fibrous joints enable little to no movement, as they are present where the bones fit tight together. These joints also hold the teeth in their sockets.

3. Cartilaginous Joints

The cartilaginous joints enable little movement, as they're present where there is a layer of cartilage between two bones. They also are present where the bones meet the cartilage.

D. The Skull

Made out of 22 bones, the skull protects the brain and the sense organs for vision, hearing, smell, taste and balance. The skull has only one movable joint that connects it with the mandible – the jaw bone, which is the only movable bone of the skull. The other 21 are fused together.

1. Cranium

The upper part of the skull is known as the cranium, which is the part that protects the brain, while the lower and frontal parts of the skull form the facial bones.

2. Hyoid

Located just under the mandible, and not a part of the skull, is the hyoid bone. The hyoid is the only bone in the body that is not attached to any other bone. It helps with keeping the trachea open, and is where the tongue muscles are anchored.

3. Auditory Ossicles

Another group of bones that are not a part of the skull, but are closely connected are the auditory ossicles: the malleus, incus and stapes. They play an important role in hearing.

E. The Vertebral Column

The vertebral column, or the spine, begins at the base of the skull and stretches through the trunk down the middle and to the back to the coccyx. It is made out of 24 vertebrae, plus the sacrum and the coccyx – the tailbone.

1. Three Vertebrae Groups

The 24 vertebrae are divided into three groups:

- The cervical, or the neck vertebrae – 7 of them
- The thoracic, or the chest vertebrae – 12 of them
- The lumbar, or the lower back vertebrae – 5 of them

Furthermore, each vertebra has its own name, which is devised from the first letter of the group it belongs (for example, L for lumbar vertebrae). The letter is placed in the group, followed by a number (the first of the lumbar vertebrae is thus called L1). The spine provides support for the weight of the upper body, allows for us to maintain posture and to move, and protects the spinal cord.

VERTEBRAL COLUMN

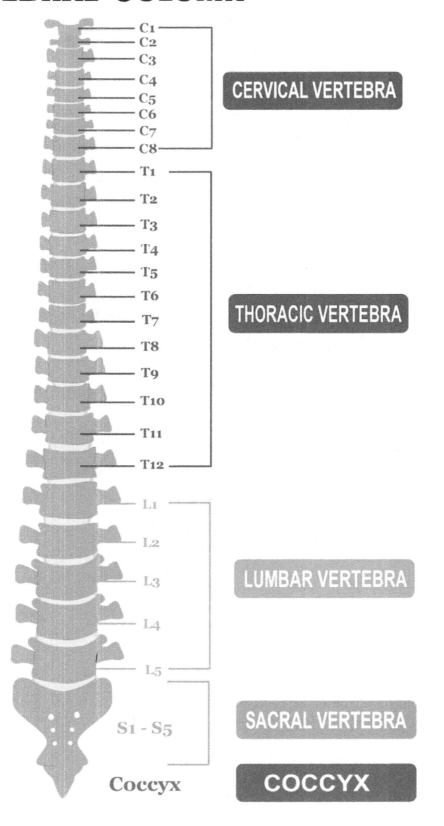

C1
C2
C3
C4
C5
C6
C7
C8

CERVICAL VERTEBRA

T1
T2
T3
T4
T5
T6
T7
T8
T9
T10
T11
T12

THORACIC VERTEBRA

L1
L2
L3
L4
L5

LUMBAR VERTEBRA

S1 - S5

SACRAL VERTEBRA

Coccyx

COCCYX

153

F. The Ribs and the Sternum

The ribs and the sternum are the bones that form the rib cage of the thoracic region. The sternum is also known as the breastbone. It is a thin bone that goes along the midline of the thoracic region, and most of the ribs are connected to this bone via the costal cartilage, a thin band of cartilage.

There are 12 ribs altogether. On the back side, they are attached to the thoracic vertebrae. On the front, first 7 of them attach directly to the sternum, the next 3 attach to the cartilage between the seventh rib and the sternum, and the remaining 2 do not attach to the sternum at all. Rather, they protect the kidneys, not the lungs and heart. The first 7 ribs are known as the true ribs, and the rest are known as false ribs.

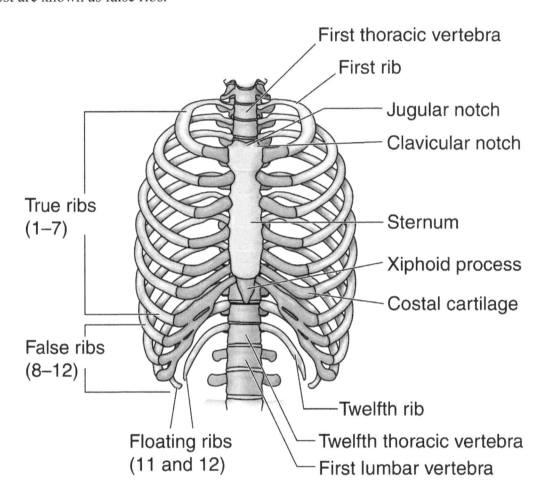

G. The Upper Limbs

The upper limbs, which belong to the appendicular skeleton, are connected with the axial skeleton by the pectoral girdle. The pectoral girdle is formed from the left and right clavicle and scapula. The scapula and the humerus, the bones of the upper arm, form the ball and socket of the shoulder joint. On its other end, the humerus forms the elbow joint.

1. **Two Forearm Bones**
   - The ulna – This bone forms the elbow joint with the humerus.
   - The radius – This bone allows the turning movement at the wrist.

2. **The Wrist Bones**

The wrist joint is formed out of the forearm bones and the 8 carpal bones, which themselves are connected with the 5 metacarpal bones. Together, these structures form the bones of the hand. The metacarpals connect with the fingers, each made out of 3 bones called phalanges, except the thumb which only has 2 phalanges.

H. The Lower Limbs

The lower limbs, which belong to the appendicular skeleton just like the upper limbs, are connected to the axial skeleton by the pelvic girdle. The pelvic girdle is made out of the left and right hip bone.

1. **The Hip Bones**

The hip joint is formed by the hip bone and the femur, which is the largest bone in the body. On its other end, the femur forms the knee joint with the patella – the kneecap – and the tibia, which is one of the bones of the lower leg.

2. **Leg Bones**

Out of the two lower leg bones, the tibia is the larger one, and it serves to carry to weight of the body. The fibula, the other one, serves mostly to anchor the muscle. Together, these two bones form the ankle joint with one of the 7 tarsal bones of the foot, called the talus.

3. **Foot Bones**

The tarsal bones form the back part of the foot and the heel. They connect to the 5 long metatarsals, which form the foot itself and connect to the toes. Each toe is made out of 3 phalanges, except the big toe, which has only 2 phalanges.

I. Physiology of the Skeletal System

The fact that the bones are connected by joints, and that they serve as anchor points for muscles, means these structures are vital for movement. The support and protection role of the skeletal system can be seen within every part group of bones:

- The skull protects and supports the brain and sensor organs.
- The thoracic cage supports and protects the lungs and heart.
- The vertebral column supports the upper body while protecting the spinal column.
- The limbs provide support and they serve as anchor points for muscles.

1. **Hematopoiesis and Calcification**

Inside the red bone marrow, which is located in the medullar cavity of the bones, a process called hematopoiesis occurs. In the process, white and red blood cells are made. The amount of the red bone marrow declines at the end of puberty, as a significant part of it is replaced by the yellow bone marrow.

When we are born, we have 300 bones. As we grow, the structure of the bones changes. The bones change their structure – from mostly hyaline cartilage and connective tissue to the osseous tissue – in the process called calcification. They also fuse together, which is why adults have 206 instead of 300 bones.

Skeletal System Questions:

1. How many bones do adults have?

   a) 201
   b) 300
   c) 206

2. The stem cells can be found in the:

   a) Red bone marrow
   b) Periosteum
   c) Compact bone

3. The long bones are the main bones of the:

   a) Limbs
   b) Thoracic cage
   c) Scull

4. The jaw bone is called the:

   a) Mandible
   b) Cranium
   c) Hyoid

5. The second vertebra in the chest region is called:

   a) L2
   b) T3
   c) T2

THE MUSCULAR SYSTEM

Movement is the main function of the muscular system. Muscles can be found attached to the bones in our bodies, but they are also present in the heart, the blood vessels, and digestive organs. The muscles also help movement, but not of the body itself. Instead, they facilitate movement of substances through the body.

There are three types of muscle:
- Visceral muscle
- Cardiac muscle
- Skeletal muscle

A. Visceral Muscle

Visceral muscle, also known as smooth muscle, is the weakest type of muscle. It can be found in the stomach, intestines, and blood vessels, where it helps contract and move substances through them. We cannot consciously control visceral muscles – they are controlled by the unconscious part of the brain. That's why it's sometimes referred to as involuntary muscle.

The term smooth muscle is given to visceral muscle because of its appearance under the microscope. The cells of the visceral muscle form a smooth surface, which is not the case with the other two types of muscle.

B. Cardiac Muscle

Cardiac muscle is only found in the heart, where it makes the heart contract and pump blood through the body. Although the heart is not controlled by the unconscious part of the brain, like visceral muscle, it is still an involuntary muscle. This is because the impulse to contract comes from the heart itself, and it's not consciously controllable.

Unlike the visceral muscle, the cardiac muscle is very strong, and when observed under a microscope, it looks like light and dark stripes. This is caused by the arrangement of protein inside the cells, which has a lot to do with its strength.

The cardiac muscle cells have to be very resistant to deal with the blood pressure, and they work constantly to pump the blood. These cells are shaped like the letters X and Y, and these branches become intertwined and form structures called intercalated disks. They keep the cells strongly bonded together, which helps with their endurance.

C. Skeletal Muscle

Skeletal muscle is the only type of muscle that contracts and relaxes by voluntary action. Skeletal muscle is attached to the bone by tendons or at least one end. Tendons are formed out of connective tissue rich in collagen fibers.

Skeletal muscle is made out of cells that are lumped together to form fiber structures. These fibers are covered by a cell membrane called the sarcolemma, which serves as a conductor for electrochemical signals that tell the muscle to contract or expand. The transverse tubes, which are connected to the sarcolemma, transfer the signals deeper, into the middle of the muscle fiber.

Calcium ions, which are necessary for contraction of the muscle, are stored in the sarcoplasmic reticulum. The fibers are also rich in mitochondria, which act as power stations fueled by sugars and providing the energy necessary for the muscle to work. Muscle fibers are mostly made out of myofibrils, which do the actual contraction, and are made out of protein fibers arranged into small subunits called sarcomeres.

1. Two Types of Skeletal Muscle Fibers

Skeletal muscle can be divided into two types, according to the way they produce and use energy. These include:

- Type I – These are slow contracting, fatigue-resistant fibers that are used for stamina and posture. They owe their fatigue resistance to the fact they produce energy from sugar using aerobic respiration.
- Type II – These are stronger but less enduring muscles. Type II A are mostly found in legs and are less strong and more enduring than Type II B, which are found mostly in the arms.

2. How Skeletal Muscles Work

Skeletal muscles work by contracting. This shortens the length in their middle part, called the muscle belly, which in turn pulls one bone closer to another. The place of the bone that is not actually moving – that remains stationary – is called the origin. The insertion is the place of the other bone, the one that is actually moving towards the other.

Skeletal muscles rarely work alone. They usually work in groups, in which the main muscle responsible for the action is called the agonist, and it's always paired with another muscle that does the opposite action, called antagonist. If the two were to contract together at the same time, they would cancel each other out and produce no movement. Other muscles that support the agonist are:

- Synergists – Usually found near the agonist and attached to the same bones, stabilize the movement and reduce unnecessary movement.
- Fixators – Which keep the origin stable.

3. Naming the Skeletal Muscles

With more than 600 skeletal muscles in the human body, naming them is done in several different ways. A lot of skeletal muscles are named by the region of body they can be found in, like transverse abdominis, which can be found in the region of the abdomen. They can also be named by the part of the bone they are anchored to – like the tibialis anterior.

Skeletal muscles are also named by the number of origins, since skeletal muscles that connect to more than one bone, or to more places on a single bone, have a larger number of origins. These are called:

- Biceps – They have two origins.
- Triceps – Which have three origins.
- Quadriceps – With four origins.

The easiest way to find muscles is by origin and insertion, because they get their name from the bones they are attached. For instance, the occipitofrontalis is attached to the occipital and the frontal bones.

Skeletal muscles can also be named by their function, like the flexor muscles of the forearm, which flex the wrist and fingers. Also, the deltoid muscle is named by its shape. Some muscles are named by the direction of the muscle fiber that makes them. Obliques are thus named because their muscle fiber runs at an angle.

When there are a number of similar muscles in the same region that vary in size, the largest is called the maximus, the middle one is called the medius, and the smallest is named the minimus. For example, the gluteus group: the gluteus maximus, gluteus medius, and gluteus minimus.

D. Physiology of the Muscular System

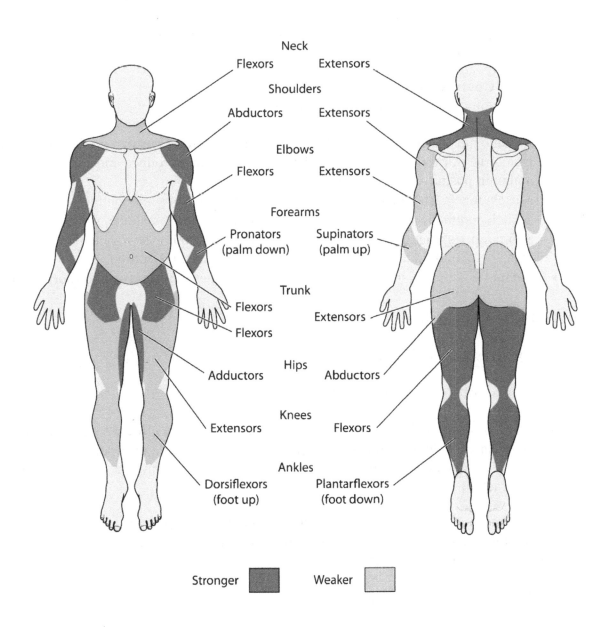

| Neck |
| Flexors | Extensors |
| Shoulders |
| Abductors | Extensors |
| Elbows |
| Flexors | Extensors |
| Forearms |
| Pronators (palm down) | Supinators (palm up) |
| Trunk |
| Flexors |
| Flexors | Extensors |
| Hips |
| Adductors | Abductors |
| Knees |
| Extensors | Flexors |
| Ankles |
| Dorsiflexors (foot up) | Plantarflexors (foot down) |

Stronger � Weaker ▢

The muscular system has four functions:

- Movement – It enables us to move.
- Maintaining the posture – It enables us to stand still or in a particular position.
- Substance movement through the body – this is the main role of the cardiac and visceral muscles.
- Body heat generation – When muscles work, they produce a lot of waste heat, which is responsible for our natural body temperature as well as the raised temperature after exertion.

161

1. Motor Neurons and Units

The neurons that control the muscles are called the motor neurons. These control a number of muscle cells that are called the motor unit. The number of cell in the motor unit is larger in large muscles that need more strength, like the muscles in the arms and legs. In small muscles that need precision more than strength, like the muscles in the fingers and around the eyes, the number of cells in motor units is smaller.

2. Types of Contractions

There are a number of different muscle contractions:

- Isotonic muscle contractions – These are muscle contractions that produce movement.
- Isometric muscle contractions – This type does not produce movement; rather, they maintain posture and keep us still.
- Muscle tone – This involves naturally occurring constant semi contraction of the muscle.
- Twitch contraction – This is a short contraction caused by a single, short nerve impulse.
- Temporal summation – This is a phenomenon in which a few short impulses delivered over time build up the muscle contraction in strength and duration.
- Tetanus – This is a state of constant contraction caused by many rapid short impulses.

3. Muscle Metabolism

Two Ways Muscles Get Energy

There are two ways for the muscle to get energy:

- Using oxygen from aerobic respiration, which is the more effective way to get energy.
- Using lactic acid fermentation, which is a type of anaerobic respiration. It's less effective and it only happens when the blood cannot get into the muscle due to the very strong contraction.

Both of these methods are aimed at producing adenosine tri-phosphate (ATP) from glucose. ATP is the most important energy molecule for our bodies. During its conversion adenosine di-phosphate (ADP), energy is released.

Molecules for Energy Production

Muscles also use other molecules to help in the production of energy:

- Myoglobin works similarly as hemoglobin – It stores oxygen, giving the muscles an amount of time of aerobic respiration even when there is no blood coming into the muscles.
- Creatine phosphate – Which gives its phosphate group to the energy-depleted adenosine di-phosphate and turns in back into the energy rich ATP.
- Glycogen – A large molecule made out of a number of glucose molecules. Muscles use the glucose to get ATP.

When it runs out of energy, a muscle goes into a state of muscle fatigue. This means it contains little to no oxygen, ATP, or glucose, and a lot of lactic acid and ADP. When a muscle is fatigued, it needs a lot of oxygen to replace the oxygen used from myoglobin, and to rebuild the other energy supplies.

Muscular System Questions:

1. Which type of muscle is found in the blood vessels?
   a) Cardiac muscle
   b) Skeletal muscle
   c) Visceral muscle

2. Cardiac muscle is:
   a) Involuntary muscle
   b) Voluntary muscle
   c) Both

3. Tendons attach the skeletal muscle at:
   a) Only one end always
   b) Both ends always
   c) At least one end

4. Myofibrils form:
   a) The layer around the muscle
   b) The muscle fiber
   c) The tendons

5. Which is the strongest type of skeletal muscle?
   a) Type II A
   b) Type II B
   c) Type I

THE NERVOUS SYSTEM

The nervous system is made out of the brain, the spinal cord, the nerves, and the sensory organs. This system is responsible for gathering, processing, and reacting to information from both within and outside of the body. It is divided into two parts: the central nervous system and the peripheral nervous system. The nervous system is mostly made out of nervous tissue, which is in turn made out of two classes of cells: the neurons and the neuralgia.

The central nervous system (CNS) is made of the brain and spinal cord and is responsible for processing and storing information, as well as deciding on the appropriate action and issuing commands.

The peripheral nervous system (PNS) is responsible for gathering information, transporting it to the CNS, and then transporting the commands from the CNS to the appropriate organs. Sensory organs and nerves do the gathering and transporting of information, while the efferent nerves transport the commands.

A. The Neurons

Neurons are the nerve cells. They can be divided into several different parts:

- The soma – This is the body of the neuron, and it contains most of the cellular organelles.
- The dendrites – These are small treelike structures that extend from the soma. Their main responsibility is to carry information to the soma, and sometimes away from it.
- The axon – This is a long, thin projection that also extends from the soma. There is usually one axon per soma, but it can branch out further down its length. It is responsible for sending information from the soma and rarely to it.
- Synapses – The places where two neurons meet, or where they meet other types of cells, are called synapses.

1. The Three Classes of Neurons

Neurons can be divided into three classes. These include:

- Efferent neurons – The motor neurons responsible for transmitting signals from the CNS to the effectors in the body.
- Afferent neurons – The sensory neurons responsible for transmitting signals from the receptors in the body to the CNS.
- Interneurons – The neurons that form the complex networks in the CNS. They are responsible for the integration of the signals received from the afferent neurons, and controlling the body by sending signals through the efferent neurons.

2. The Neuralgia

Neuralgia are the maintenance cells for the neurons. Neurons are so specialized for their task that they almost never reproduce. Therefore, they need the neuralgia cells, a number of which surrounds every neuron, to protect and feed them. Neuralgia are also called the glial cells.

165

B. The Central Nervous System

The CNS consists out of:

- The brain
- The spinal cord

Both the brain and the spinal cord are placed within cavities in protective skeletal structures. The brain is housed in the cranial cavity of the skull, and the spinal cord ins enclosed in the vertebral cavity in the spine.

Since the organs that form the CINS are very vital to our survival, they are also protected by two other important structures:

- The meninges
- The cerebrospinal fluid (CSF)

1. The Meninges

The meninges are a protective covering of the CNS that consists of three distinct layers:

- The dura mater – As its name suggests, is the most durable, outer part of the meninges. It is made out of collagen fibers-rich thick connective tissue, and it forms a space for the cerebrospinal fluid around the CNS.
- The arachnoid mater – This is the thin lining on the inner side of the dura mater. It forms many tiny fibers that connect the dura mater with the next layer – the pia mater.
- The pia mater – This is separated from the arachnoid mater by the subarachnoid space – a space filled with cerebrospinal fluid. The pia mater directly covers the surface of the brain and spinal cord, and it provides sustenance to the nervous tissue through its many blood vessels.

2. The Cerebrospinal Fluid

Found in the subarachnoid space, the cerebrospinal fluid is a clear fluid formed from blood plasma. It can be found in:

- The subarachnoid space.
- In the ventricles, the hollow spaces in the brain.
- In the central canal, a cavity found in the middle of the spinal cord.

As the CNS floats in the cerebrospinal fluid, it appears lighter than it really is. This is especially important for the brain, because the fluid keeps it from being crushed by its own weight. The floating also protects the brain and the spinal cord from shock – like sudden movements and trauma. Additionally, the CSF contains the necessary chemical substance for the normal functioning of the nervous tissue, and it serves to remove the cellular waste form the neurons.

3. The Brain And Nervous Tissue

The nervous tissue that makes up the brain is divided into two classes:

- The gray matter - Which consists mostly of interneurons that are unmyelinated, and is the tissue where the actual processing of signals happens. It is also where the connections between neurons are made.

166

- The white matter - Which consists mostly of myelinated neurons, and is the tissue that conducts signals to, from, and between the gray matter regions.

The brain can be divided into three distinct parts:

- The forebrain – Prosencephalon
- The midbrain – Mesencephalon
- The hindbrain – Rhombencephalon

The Prosencephalon
The forebrain consists out of two regions:
- The cerebrum
- The diencephalon

The Cerebrum
The outermost and the largest part of the brain, the cerebrum is divided through the middle by the longitudinal fissure into the left and the right hemisphere, which are further divided into four lobes each:
- Frontal
- Parietal
- Temporal
- Occipital

The surface of the cerebrum, called the cerebral cortex is made out of gray matter with characteristic grooves (sulci) and bulges (gyri). The cerebral cortex is where the actual processing happens in the cerebrum – it's responsible for the higher brain functions like thinking and using language. Under the cerebral cortex, there is a layer of white matter, which connects the regions of the cerebrum with one another, and the cerebrum itself with the rest of the body. It contains a special band of white matter that connects the two hemispheres, which is called the corpus callosum.

The several regions located under the white matter are divided into two groups:
- The basal nuclei, which help control and regulate the movement of muscles.
- The limbic system, which play a role in memory, emotions and survival.

The Diencephalon
The diencephalon is a structure formed by:

- The thalamus – Made out of two gray matter masses, the thalamus is located around the third ventricle of the brain. Its role is to route the sensory signals to the correct parts of the cerebral cortex.
- The hypothalamus – Located under the thalamus, the hypothalamus plays a role in regulating hunger, thirst, blood pressure and body temperature changes, as well as the heart rate and the production of hormones.
- The pineal gland – Located beneath the hypothalamus, and directly controlled by it, the pineal gland produces the hormone melatonin, which plays a vital role in sleep.

167

The Mesencephalon

The midbrain is the topmost part of the brain stem. It is divided into two regions:

- The tectum, which plays a role in reflex reactions to visual and auditory information
- The cerebral peduncules, which connect the cerebrum and thalamus with the lower parts of the brain stem, and the spinal cord. It also contains substantia nigra, which is involved in muscle movements by inhibiting their movements.

The Rhombencephalon

The hindbrain is made out of the brain stem and the cerebellum. The two parts of the brain stem that form the hindbrain are:

- The medulla oblongata connects the spinal cord with another part of the brainstem, called the pons. It is mostly made out of white matter, but it also contains gray matter that processes involuntary body functions like blood pressure, level of oxygen in the blood, and reflexes like sneezing, coughing, vomiting and swallowing.

- The pons are located between the medulla oblongata and the midbrain, and in front of the cerebellum. It is in charge of transporting signals to and from the cerebellum, and the between the upper regions of the brain, the medulla and the spinal cord.

The cerebellum looks like a smaller version of the cerebrum – it has two spheres and it's wrinkled. Its outer layer consists of gray matter, and it's called the cerebellar cortex, while the inner part consists of white matter which transports signals between the cerebellum and the rest of the body, and it's called the arbor vitae. The cerebellum's role is to control and coordinate complex muscle activities. It also helps us maintain posture and keep balance.

4. The Spinal Cord

The spinal cord, located inside the vertebral cavity, is made out of both white and gray matter. It serves to both carry signals and to process some reflexes to stimuli. The spinal nerves stretch out from it.

C. The Peripheral Nervous System

The nerves that form the peripheral nervous system are made out of bundled axons. Their role is to carry signals to and from the spinal cord and the brain. A single axon, covered with a layer of connective tissue called the endoneurium, bundles with other axons to form fascicles. These are covered with another sheath of connective tissue – the perineurium. Also, a lot of fascicles wrapped together in another layer of connective tissue – the epineurium – form a whole nerve.

1. The Five Types of Peripheral Nerves

There are five types of peripheral nerves:

- The afferent, efferent and mixed nerves, which are formed out of the neurons that share the same name, and they perform the same role.
- The spinal nerves – 31 pairs of them extend from the side of the spinal cord. They exit the spinal cord between the vertebrae, and they carry information to and from the spinal cord and the neck, the arms, the legs and the trunk. They are grouped and named according to the region they originate from: 8 pairs of cervical, 12 pairs of thoracic, 5 pairs of lumbar, 5 pairs of sacral, and 1 pair coccygeal nerves.

- The cranial nerves – 12 pairs of these nerves extend from the lower side of the brain. They are identified by their number, and they serve to conect the brain with the sense organs, head muscles, neck and shoulders muscle, the heart and the gastrointestinal track.

2. The Sense Organs

The sense organs include both the specialized sense organs, which are responsible for the specialized senses: the hearing, sight, balance, smell and taste. Sense organs also have sensory receptors for general senses: touch, pain and temperature. These senses are part of the PNS, and their role is to detect the stimuli and send the signal to the CNS when the detection occurs.

3. The Physiology of the Nervous System

The nervous system has three main functions:

- Sensory function is related to the intake of information from inside and outside of the body through the sensory organs and receptors, and then sending that information to the CNS.
- Integration is a process that happens in the CNS. When the signal from the sensory organs and receptors come to the CNS, the information it carries is evaluated, compared to previously stored information, stored or discarded, and used to make a decision.
- Motor function occurs once the integration is done, and the CNS may send a signal through the efferent nerves to the effector cells. These cells are located in all types of muscles and the glands, which then form a reaction to the stimuli.

The Different Divisions of the PNS

According to our ability to consciously control the PNS, it is divided into the:

- Somatic nervous system (SNS) - Which is the only part of the PNS we can consciously control. It stimulates the skeletal muscles.
- Autonomic nervous system (ANS) - Which is the part of the PNS we cannot consciously control, and which stimulates the visceral and cardiac muscle, as well as the glandular tissue.

The ANS itself is further divided into:

- The sympathctic division – Which forms the fight or flight reaction to stimuli like emotion, danger and exercise. It increases respiration and hearth rate, decreases digestion and releases stress hormones.
- The parasympathetic division – Which does the opposite of the sympathetic division after the stimuli subsides.
- Enteric nervous system (ENS) – Which is responsible for the digestive system and the processes that go on in it. This system works mostly independently from the CNS, although it can be regulated through the sympathetic and parasympathetic division.

Nervous System Questions

1. Which of the following form the CNS with the brain?
    a) The nerves
    b) The sensory organs
    c) The spinal cord

2. The part of the neuron that transports information from the cell is called:
    a) The soma
    b) The axon
    c) The dendrites

3. The motor neurons is another name for:
    a) Efferent neurons
    b) Afferent neurons
    c) Interneurons

4. The space outside the CNS filled with cerebrospinal fluid can be found:
    a) Between the dura mater and the arachnoid mater
    b) Outside the dura mater
    c) Between the arachnoid mater and the pia mater

5. The hypothalamus is located:
    a) In the mesencephalon
    b) In the rhombencephalon
    c) In the prosencephalon

THE DIGESTIVE SYSTEM

The digestive system is a system of organs in the body that is responsible for the intake and processing of food, as well as discarding the waste products of feeding. The digestive system ensures that the body has the necessary nutrients and the energy it needs to function.

The digestive system consists of the gastrointestinal (GI) tract, which is formed by the following organs through which the food passes on its way through the body:

- The oral cavity
- The pharynx
- The esophagus
- The stomach
- The small intestines
- The large intestines

Along with the GI tract, the digestive system also contains organs that have a role in processing food, but they do not food pass through them. These include:

- The teeth
- The tongue
- The salivary glands
- The liver
- The gallbladder
- The pancreas

DIGESTIVE SYSTEM

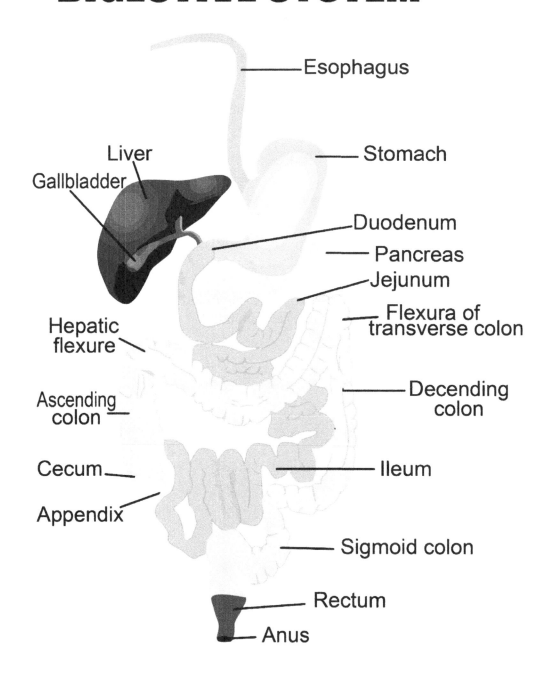

Esophagus

Liver

Gallbladder

Stomach

Duodenum

Pancreas

Jejunum

Flexura of transverse colon

Hepatic flexure

Ascending colon

Decending colon

Cecum

Ileum

Appendix

Sigmoid colon

Rectum

Anus

A. The Mouth

The digestive system begins with the mouth. Also known as the oral cavity, the mouth contains other organs that play a role in digestion:

- The teeth – Small organs that cut and grind food. They are located on the edges of the mouth, and are made out of dentin, which is a substance that resembles bone, and are covered by enamel. The teeth are very hard organs, and each of them has its own blood vessels and nerves, which are located in the matter that fills the tooth, called the pulp.

- The tongue – A muscle that is located in the oral cavity beneath and behind the teeth. The tongue contains the taste buds, and it plays a role in moving food around the mouth as it's being processed by the teeth and to move it towards the pharynx when it's time to swallow.
- The salivary glands – Charged with producing the saliva, these glands are located around the mouth. There are three pairs of salivary glands, and the saliva they produce serves to lubricate and digest carbohydrates.

B. The Pharynx

The pharynx is a tube that enables the passage of food and air further into the body. This structure performs two functions. The pharynx needs the help of a small flap called the epiglottis, which allows the food to pass to the esophagus by covering the opening of the larynx, a structure that carries air into the lungs. When we need to breathe in, the esophagus is closed, so the air passes only into the larynx.

C. The Esophagus

The esophagus begins at the pharynx and continues to carry food all the way to the stomach. The esophagus is a muscular tube, and the muscles in its wall help to push the food down. When throwing up, it pushes the food up.

The esophagus has two rings of muscle, called sphincters. These sphincters close at the top and the bottom ends when the food is not passing. The bottom one, when it cannot close entirely and allow the contents of the stomach to enter the esophagus, is responsible for heartburn.

D. The Stomach

The stomach is a round-shaped organ located on the left side of the body, just beneath the diaphragm. It can be divided into four different regions:

- The cardia – The region that connects with the esophagus. It is a transit from the tube-like shape of the esophagus into the sack shape of the rest of the stomach. The cardia is also where the lower sphincter of the esophagus is located.
- The body of the stomach – The largest part of the stomach.
- The fundus – Located above the body of the stomach.
- The pylorus – A funnel shaped region located beneath the body of the stomach. It controls the passage of the partially digested food further down the GI tract using the pyloric sphincter.

1. The Four Layers of Tissue in the Stomach

The stomach is made out of four layers of tissue:

- The mucosa – This is the innermost layer, which contains the mucous membrane that has a large number of cells which secrete digestive enzymes and hydrochloric acid. These cells are located within the small pores called the gastric pits. The mucous membrane also secretes a mucous that protects the stomach from its own digestive enzymes. The mucosa also contains some smooth muscle.

- The submucosa – This layer is located around the mucosa, it is made out of connective tissue and it contains the nerves and the blood vessels.
- The muscularis layer - Which as its name says, this structure is made out of three layers of smooth muscle. This layer enables the movement of the stomach.
- The serosa – This mucosa is the outermost layer. It secretes serous fluid which keeps it wet, and reduces friction between the stomach and the surrounding organs.

E. The Small Intestine

The small intestine continues from the stomach, and it takes up most of the space in the abdomen. It is around 22 feet long and looped, and it's attached to the wall of the abdomen to be kept in place.

The small intestine can be divided into three parts:
- The duodenum, which is the part of the small intestine that receives the food and chemicals from the stomach.
- The jejunum, which continues from the duodenum and is where most of the nutrients are absorbed into the blood.
- The ileum, which continues from the jejunum and where the rest of the nutrients are absorbed.

The absorption which happens in the small intestine is much helped by the villi. The villi are made out of smaller microvilli, and the villi are where the blood vessels that absorb the nutrients can be found.

F. The Liver

The liver is not a part of the GI tract. However, it performs roles that are vital for digestion and life itself. The liver is located just beneath the diaphragm, and it's the largest organ in the body after the skin. It's triangular in shape, and extends across the whole width of the abdomen.

The liver can be divided into four lobes:
- The left lobe
- The right lobe
- The caudate lobe, which wraps around the inferior vena cava
- The quadrate lobe that wraps around the gallbladder

The liver is connected to the peritoneum by four ligaments:
- The coronary ligament
- The left triangular ligament
- The right triangular ligament
- The falciform ligament

The liver is responsible for a number of different functions – from detoxification of the blood, to the storage of nutrients and production of components of blood plasma. However, for the digestive system, the role of the liver is to produce the bile, which is then carried through the bile ducts to the gallbladder.

G. The Gallbladder

Located just behind the liver, the gallbladder is a small muscular pair shaped organ. Its main role is to store bile produced by the liver and to release it into the duodenum when fat enters. This process facilitates the digestion of fat.

H. The Pancreas

The pancreas is another organ that is not a part of the GI tract, but plays a role in the digestion. It's located under the stomach and to the left. The pancreas' purpose is to secrete both the enzymes that digest the food and the hormones insulin and glucagon, which control blood sugar levels.

The pancreas is what is known as a heterocrine gland, which means it contains both the endocrine tissue, that produces insulin and glucagon, and exocrine tissue. Exocrine tissue produces:

- Pancreatic amylase - Which breaks large polysaccharides into smaller sugars
- Trypsin, chymotrypsin, and carboxypeptidase - Which break down proteins into amino acid subunits
- Pancreatic lipase - Which breaks down large fat molecules into fatty acids and monoglyceride
- Ribonuclease and deoxyribonuclease - Which digest nucleic acids.

I. The Large Intestine

The large intestine continues from the small intestine, and it surrounds its looped form. No digestion actually takes part in the large intestine. Rather, it only absorbs water and some leftover vitamins. The large intestine carries the waste (the feces) to the rectum, where it's stored until it's expelled through the anus.

J. The Digestive System Physiology

The roles of the digestive system are to:

- Ingest food
- Secrete fluids and enzymes
- Mix and move the food through the body
- Digest the food
- Absorb the food
- Remove the waste

Digestive System Questions:

1. The GI tract consists of:
    a) Organs of the digestive system through which the food passes
    b) Organs of the digestive system through which the food does not pass
    c) All of the organs in the digestive system
    d) None of the above

2. How many pair of salivary glands is there?
    a) 4
    b) 1
    c) 3
    d) None of the above

3. Where is the lower sphincter of the esophagus located?
    a) The body of the stomach
    b) The cardia
    c) The fundus
    d) None of the above

4. Which layer of the stomach contains the blood vessels and the nerves?
    a) The mucosa
    b) The submucosa
    c) The serosa
    d) None of the above

5. Bile is stored in:
    a) The liver
    b) The duodenum
    c) The gallbladder
    d) None of the above

Answers

The Circulatory System
1. C)
2. A)
3. A)
4. C)
5. B)

The Respiratory System
1. A)
2. B)
3. A)
4. C)
5. C)

The Skeletal System
1. C)
2. B)
3. A)
4. A)
5. C)

The Muscular System
1. C)
2. A)
3. C)
4. B)
5. B)

The Nervous System
1. C)
2. B)
3. A)
4. C)
5. C)

The Digestive System
1. A)
2. C)
3. B)
4. B)
5. C)

Earth and Physical Science

ELEMENTS, COMPOUNDS, AND MIXTURES

Matter

Matter is commonly defined as anything that takes up space and has mass. **Mass** is the quantity of matter something possesses, and usually has a unit of weight associated with it.

Matter can undergo two types of change: chemical and physical.

> A **chemical change** occurs when an original substance is transformed into a new substance with different properties. An example would be the burning of wood, which produces ash and smoke.

> Transformations that do not produce new substances, such as stretching a rubber band or melting ice, are called **physical changes**.

The fundamental properties which we use to measure matter are mass, weight, volume, density and specific gravity.

Extrinsic properties are directly related to the amount of material being measured, such as weight and volume.

Intrinsic properties are those which are independent of the quantity of matter present, such as density and specific gravity.

Atom

An atom is the ultimate particle of matter; it is the smallest particle of an element that still is a part of that element. All atoms of the same element have the same mass. Atomic chemical changes involve the transfer of whole atoms from one substance to another; but atoms are not created or destroyed in ordinary chemical changes.

An atom is made up of several parts. The center is called the **nucleus**, and is made up of two particles: a positively-charged particle, called a **proton**, and a particle that does not have a charge, called a **neutron**. The masses of a proton and neutron are about the same.

The nucleus of the atom is surrounded by negatively-charged particles called **electrons**, which move in orbits around the nucleus. The nucleus is only a small portion of the total amount of space an atom takes up, even though most of an atom's mass is contained in the nucleus.

Molecular Weight

A **mole** is the amount of substance that contains 6.02×10^{23} basic particles. This is referred to as **Avogadro's number** and is based on the number of atoms in C_{12} (Carbon 12). For example, a mole of copper is the amount of copper that contains exactly 6.02×10^{23} atoms, and one mole of water contains 6.02×10^{23} H_2O molecules. The weight of one mole of an element is called its **atomic weight**. The atomic weight of an element with isotopes, which are explained further on the next page, is the average of the isotopes' individual atomic weights.

The negatively-charged electrons are very light in mass. An atom is described as neutral if it has an equal number of protons and electrons, or if the number of electrons is the same as the atomic number of the atom. You may have already assumed – correctly! – from that information that the atomic number of an atom equals the number of protons in that atom. The **atomic weight** or **mass** of the atom is the total number of protons and neutrons in the atom's nucleus.

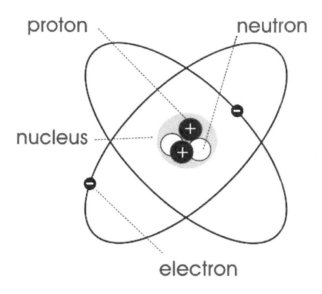

Elements
An element is a substance which cannot be broken down by chemical means; they are composed of atoms that have the same **atomic number** and are defined by the number of protons and neutrons they have. Some elements have more than one form, such as carbon; these alternate forms are called **isotopes.** There are approximately 109 known elements. Eighty-eight of these occur naturally on earth, while the others are **synthesized** (manufactured).

Hydrogen is the most abundant element in the Universe. It is found in 75% of all matter known to exist. **Helium** is the second most abundant element, found in approximately 25% of all known matter. The Earth is composed mostly of iron, oxygen, silicon, and magnesium, though these elements are not evenly distributed. 90% of the human body's mass consists of oxygen, carbon, hydrogen, nitrogen, calcium, and phosphorus. 75% of elements are metals, and eleven are gases in their natural state. We'll cover this more in-depth when we view the periodic table.

Molecules
A molecule is the smallest part of a substance that isn't chemically bonded to another atom. **Chemical formulas** are used to represent the atomic composition of a molecule. For example, one molecule of water contains 2 atoms of Hydrogen and 1 atom of Oxygen; its chemical formula is $2H + O = H_2O$.

Compounds and Mixtures
Substances that contain more than one type of element are called **compounds.** Compounds that are made up of molecules which are all identical are called **pure substances**. A **mixture** consists of two or more substances that are not chemically bonded. Mixtures are generally placed in one of two categories:

Homogeneous Mixture: Components that make up the mixture are uniformly distributed; examples are water and air.

Heterogeneous Mixture: Components of the mixture are not uniform; they sometimes have localized regions with different properties. For example: the different components of soup make it a heterogeneous mixture. Rocks, as well, are not uniform and have localized regions with different properties.

A uniform, or homogenous, mixture of different molecules is called a **solution**. If the solution is a liquid, the material being dissolved is the **solute** and the liquid it is being dissolved in is called the **solvent.** Both solids and gases can dissolve in liquids. A **saturated** has reached a point of maximum concentration; in it, no more solute will dissolve.

Practice Drill: Elements, Compounds, and Mixtures

1. Which statement best describes the density of an atom's nucleus?
   a) The nucleus occupies most of the atom's volume, but contains little of its mass.
   b) The nucleus occupies very little of the atom's volume, and contains little of its mass.
   c) The nucleus occupies most of the atom's volume, and contains most of its mass.
   d) The nucleus occupies very little of the atom's volume, but contains most of its mass.

2. Which of the following is not a physical change?
   a) Melting of aspirin.
   b) Lighting a match.
   c) Putting sugar in tea.
   d) Boiling of antifreeze.

3. A solid melts gradually between 85°C and 95°C to give a milky, oily liquid. When a laser beam shines through the liquid, the path of the beam is clearly visible. The milky liquid is likely to be:
   a) A heterogeneous mixture.
   b) An element.
   c) A compound.
   d) A solution.

4. The identity of an element is determined by:
   a) The number of its protons and neutrons.
   b) The number of its neutrons.
   c) The number of its electrons.
   d) Its atomic mass.

5. True or False? When a match burns, some matter is destroyed.
   a) True.
   b) False.

6. What is the reason for your answer to question 5?
   a) This chemical reaction destroys matter.
   b) Matter is consumed by the flame.
   c) The mass of ash is less than the match it came from.
   d) The atoms are not destroyed, they are only rearranged.
   e) The match weighs less after burning.

7. An unsaturated solution:
   a) Hasn't dissolved as much solute as is theoretically possible.
   b) Has dissolved exactly as much solute as is theoretically possible.
   c) Is unstable because it has dissolved more solute than would be expected.
   d) None of the above.

8. A teaspoon of dry coffee crystals dissolves when mixed in a cup of hot water. This process produces a coffee solution. The original crystals are classified as a:
   a) Solute.
   b) Solvent.

c) Reactant.
d) Product.

Practice Drill: Elements, Compounds, and Mixtures – Answers

1. **d)**
2. **b)**
3. **c)**
4. **a)**
5. **b)**
6. **d)**
7. **a)**
8. **a)**

STATES OF MATTER
The physical states of matter are generally grouped into three main categories:

1. **Solids**: Rigid; they maintain their shape and have strong intermolecular forces. Typical solids are rigid at room temperature. In solids, the molecules are closely packed together, and solid materials usually have a high density. In the majority of solids, called crystalline solids, the ions or molecules are packed into a crystal structure that is highly ordered.

2. **Liquids**: Cannot maintain their own shape, conform to their containers, and contain forces strong enough to keep molecules from dispersing into spaces. Solids will generally become liquids when heated to a high enough temperature.

3. **Gases**: Have indefinite shape; disperse rapidly through space due to random movement and are able to occupy any volume. They are held together by weak forces. Gases are produced when liquids are heated enough, and have an additional energy associated with them called the enthalpy of vaporization. This is the energy required to break the liquid bonds, and allow the material to transfer to the gaseous phase.

Two specific states of matter are **liquid crystals**, which can maintain their shape as well as be made to flow, and **plasmas**, gases in which electrons are stripped from their nuclei.

Phase Diagrams
Phase diagrams are used to represent the state of matter depending on the temperature and pressure of the matter. Typically, as temperature drops, a substance is more likely to be a solid, and as pressure drops, a substance is more likely to be a gas. Seen below is an approximate phase diagram for water.

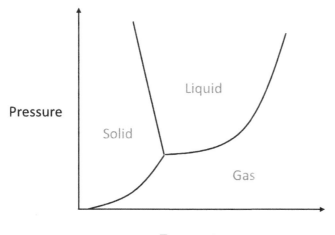

As can be seen, at high pressures and moderate temperatures, gas will be a solid. As temperature increases, water will slowly transition to becoming a liquid, and then a gas. The point at which the three lines meet is called the triple point, which is a state in which the material will exist in all three forms: solid, liquid, and gas. The triple point of water is at 0.01 °C and 0.006 atmospheres of pressure.

Gases

There are four physical properties of gases that are related to each other. If any one of these changes, a change will occur in at least one of the remaining three.

1. Volume of the gas.
2. Pressure of the gas.
3. Temperature of the gas.
4. The number of gas molecules.

The laws that relate these properties to each other are:

Boyle's Law: The volume of a given amount of gas at a constant temperature is inversely proportional to pressure. In other words; if the initial volume decreases by half, the pressure will double and vice versa. The representative equation is: $P_1V_1 = P_2V_2$.

Charles's Law: The volume of a given amount of gas at a constant pressure is directly proportional to absolute (Kelvin) temperature. If the temperature of the gas increases, the volume of the gas also increases and vice versa. The representative equation is: $V_1/T_1 = V_2/T_2$.

Avogadro's Law: Equal volumes of all gases under identical conditions of pressure and temperature contain the same number of molecules. The molar volume of all ideal gases at $0°$ C and a pressure of 1 atm. is 22.4 liters.

The **kinetic theory of gases** assumes that gas molecules are very small compared to the distance between the molecules. Gas molecules are in constant, random motion; they frequently collide with each other and with the walls of whatever container they are in.

Ideal Gas Law

The ideal gas law is an important equation that is used to estimate the properties of gas at different temperatures and pressures. It is called the ideal gas law because in order for it to be effective, the gas must be ideal, meaning that:

1. The gas consists of a large number of molecules that move randomly.
2. The volume that the molecules of the gas occupies is very small compared to the total volume of the gas.
3. There are no attractive or repulsive interactions between the gas molecules.

The Ideal Gas Law can be stated as:

$$PV = nRT$$

Where P is the pressure, V is the volume, n is the number of mols of gas, R is the ideal gas constant (8.314 J/mol K) and T is the temperature.

Practice Drill: States of Matter

1. Under the same conditions of pressure and temperature, a liquid differs from a gas because the molecules of the liquid:
   a) Have no regular arrangement.
   b) Are in constant motion.
   c) Have stronger forces of attraction between them.
   d) Take the shape of the container they are in.

2. Methane (CH4) gas diffuses through air because the molecules are:
   a) Moving randomly.
   b) Dissolving quickly.
   c) Traveling slowly.
   d) Expanding steadily.

3. Which of the following would not change if the number of gas molecules changed?
   a) Volume of the gas.
   b) Type of gas.
   c) Pressure of the gas.
   d) Temperature of gas.

4. When the pressure is increased on a can filled with gas, its volume _____ .
   a) Stays the same.
   b) Increases.
   c) Decreases.
   d) Turns to liquid.

5. Equal volumes of all gases at the same temperature and pressure contain the same number of molecules. This statement is known as:
   a) Kinetic theory of gases.
   b) Charles's Law.
   c) Boyle's Law.
   d) Avogadro's Law.

6. If the pressure of water is kept below its triple point, and the temperature is increased, ice will:
   a) Turn to liquid
   b) Turn to gas
   c) Remain the same
   d) Become more crystalline

7. Which of the following is true regarding molecules in water vapor at 100 °C?
   a) They have less energy than liquid water at 100 °C
   b) They have more energy than liquid water at 100 °C
   c) They will condense into liquid if the pressure is reduced.
   d) There will be both liquid and vapor if the temperature is increased slightly.

8. A scientist has 1 mol of a sample of gas at 0°C and 1 atm of pressure. How much volume will it occupy?
    a) 18.5 liters
    b) 19.9 liters
    c) 22.4 liters
    d) 25.2 liters

9. Which of the following is likely to have the most number of molecules?
    a) 1 liter of water vapor
    b) 1 liter of water
    c) 0.5 liters of ice
    d) 0.5 liters of an ice water mixture

10. Which of the following is *not* true about a liquid?
    a) A liquid can always be compressed.
    b) A liquid is fluid and can change shape.
    c) A liquid is higher in energy than a solid.
    d) Molecules in a liquid can have attractive interactions.

11. Which of these is not a solid?
    a) Hair
    b) A fork
    c) Orange juice
    d) A desk

12. The freezing point of a compound is:
    a) The same as the boiling point of the compound
    b) The same as melting point of the compound
    c) The same as the triple point of the compound
    d) The same as the critical point of the compound

13. Which of these is the only state of matter in which molecules are not typically moving?
    a) Gas
    b) Liquid
    c) Plasma
    d) Solid

14. When a liquid turns into a gas, it is known as vaporization. What is the opposite process?
    a) Condensation
    b) Sublimation
    c) Transmogrification
    d) Precipitation

15. Liquids that are highly viscous, such as grease or paint, are:
    a) Resistant to movement
    b) Highly flammable
    c) Able to become solid at high temperatures
    d) None of the above

Practice Drill: States of Matter – Answers

1. c)
2. a)
3. b)
4. c)
5. d)
6. b)
7. b)
8. c)
9. b)
10. a)
11. c)
12. b)
13. d)
14. a)
15. a)

PERIODIC TABLE AND CHEMICAL BONDS

The Periodic table

The Periodic Table is a chart which arranges the chemical elements in a useful, logical manner. Elements are listed in order of increasing atomic number, lined up so that elements which exhibit similar properties are arranged in the same row or column as each other.

hydrogen 1 **H** 1.0079																	helium 2 **He** 4.0026
lithium 3 **Li** 6.941	beryllium 4 **Be** 9.0122											boron 5 **B** 10.811	carbon 6 **C** 12.011	nitrogen 7 **N** 14.007	oxygen 8 **O** 15.999	fluorine 9 **F** 18.998	neon 10 **Ne** 20.180
sodium 11 **Na** 22.990	magnesium 12 **Mg** 24.305											aluminium 13 **Al** 26.982	silicon 14 **Si** 28.086	phosphorus 15 **P** 30.074	sulfur 16 **S** 32.005	chlorine 17 **Cl** 35.453	argon 18 **Ar** 39.948
potassium 19 **K** 39.098	calcium 20 **Ca** 40.078	scandium 21 **Sc** 44.956	titanium 22 **Ti** 47.867	vanadium 23 **V** 50.942	chromium 24 **Cr** 51.996	manganese 25 **Mn** 54.938	iron 26 **Fe** 55.845	cobalt 27 **Co** 58.933	nickel 28 **Ni** 58.693	copper 29 **Cu** 63.546	zinc 30 **Zn** 65.39	gallium 31 **Ga** 69.723	germanium 32 **Ge** 72.61	arsenic 33 **As** 74.922	selenium 34 **Se** 78.96	bromine 35 **Br** 79.904	krypton 36 **Kr** 83.80
rubidium 37 **Rb** 85.468	strontium 38 **Sr** 87.62	yttrium 39 **Y** 88.906	zirconium 40 **Zr** 91.224	niobium 41 **Nb** 92.906	molybdenum 42 **Mo** 95.94	technetium 43 **Tc** [98]	ruthenium 44 **Ru** 101.07	rhodium 45 **Rh** 102.91	palladium 46 **Pd** 106.42	silver 47 **Ag** 107.87	cadmium 48 **Cd** 112.41	indium 49 **In** 114.82	tin 50 **Sn** 118.71	antimony 51 **Sb** 121.76	tellurium 52 **Te** 127.60	iodine 53 **I** 126.90	xenon 54 **Xe** 131.29
caesium 55 **Cs** 132.91	barium 56 **Ba** 137.33	57-70 ✳	lutetium 71 **Lu** 174.97	hafnium 72 **Hf** 178.49	tantalum 73 **Ta** 180.95	tungsten 74 **W** 183.84	rhenium 75 **Re** 186.21	osmium 76 **Os** 190.23	iridium 77 **Ir** 192.22	platinum 78 **Pt** 195.08	gold 79 **Au** 196.97	mercury 80 **Hg** 200.59	thallium 81 **Tl** 204.38	lead 82 **Pb** 207.2	bismuth 83 **Bi** 208.98	polonium 84 **Po** [209]	astatine 85 **At** [210]	radon 86 **Rn** [222]
francium 87 **Fr** [223]	radium 88 **Ra** [226]	89-102 ✳✳	lawrencium 103 **Lr** [262]	rutherfordium 104 **Rf** [261]	dubnium 105 **Db** [262]	seaborgium 106 **Sg** [266]	bohrium 107 **Bh** [264]	hassium 108 **Hs** [269]	meitnerium 109 **Mt** [268]	ununnillium 110 **Uun** [271]	unununium 111 **Uuu** [272]	ununbium 112 **Uub** [277]		ununquadium 114 **Uuq** [289]			

*Lanthanide series

lanthanum 57 **La** 138.91	cerium 58 **Ce** 140.12	praseodymium 59 **Pr** 140.91	neodymium 60 **Nd** 144.24	promethium 61 **Pm** [145]	samarium 62 **Sm** 150.36	europium 63 **Eu** 151.96	gadolinium 64 **Gd** 157.25	terbium 65 **Tb** 158.93	dysprosium 66 **Dy** 162.50	holmium 67 **Ho** 164.93	erbium 68 **Er** 167.26	thulium 69 **Tm** 168.93	ytterbium 70 **Yb** 173.04

**Actinide series

actinium 89 **Ac** [227]	thorium 90 **Th** 232.04	protactinium 91 **Pa** 231.04	uranium 92 **U** 238.03	neptunium 93 **Np** [237]	plutonium 94 **Pu** [244]	americium 95 **Am** [243]	curium 96 **Cm** [247]	berkelium 97 **Bk** [247]	californium 98 **Cf** [251]	einsteinium 99 **Es** [252]	fermium 100 **Fm** [257]	mendelevium 101 **Md** [258]	nobelium 102 **No** [259]

Note the following characteristics:

Each box contains the symbol of the element, its atomic number, and its atomic weight.

The elements appear in increasing order according to their atomic numbers, except for the two separate rows.

The vertical columns are called **groups**. Elements within a group share several common properties and often have the same outer electron arrangement. There are two categories: the main group and the transition elements.

> The number of the main group corresponds to the number of valence electrons. Most of the transition elements contain 2 electrons in their valence shells.

The horizontal rows are called **periods** and correspond to the number of occupied electron shells of the atom.

The elements set below the main table are the **lanthanoids** (upper row) and **actinoids**. They also usually have two electrons in their outer shells.

Most of the elements on the periodic table are metals. The alkali metals, alkaline earths, basic metals, transition metals, lanthanides, and actinides are all groups of metals.

In general, the elements increase in mass from left to right and from top to bottom.

The main difference between the modern periodic table and the one Mendeleev (the periodic table's creator) came up with is that Mendeleev's original table arranged the elements in order of increasing atomic weight, while the modern table orders the elements by increasing atomic number.

Electronic Structure of Atoms
The electrons of an atom have fixed energy levels. Those in the principle energy levels are said to be in **electron shells**. Shells which correspond to the highest energy levels, called **valance shells**, include the electrons usually involved in chemical bonding. Chemical formulas of simple compounds can often be predicted from valences. The valence electrons increase in number as you go across the periodic table.

The electrons in the outer orbit can combine with other atoms by giving up electrons or taking on electrons. Atoms that give up electrons (**cations**) change from being neutral to having a *positive* charge. Atoms that gain electrons (**ions**) change from being neutral to having a *negative* charge. The **octet rule** is a chemical rule which states that atoms of a low atomic number will share, gain, or lose electrons in order to fill outer electron shells with eight electrons. This is achieved through different types of bonding.

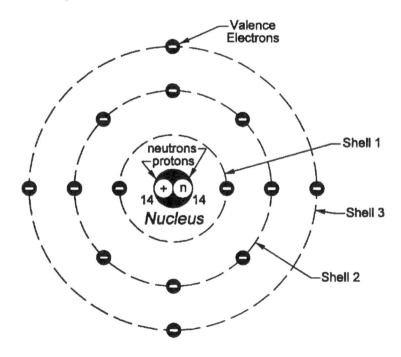

Chemical Bonds

Electromagnetism is involved in all chemical behavior, including the chemical bonds which hold atoms together to form molecules, as well as those holding molecules together to form all substances. **Electronegativity** measures the tendency of an atom to attract a bonding pair of electrons, and is affected by both the atomic number, and the distance between the valence electrons and the charged nucleus. The higher the assigned electronegativity number, the more an element or compound attracts electrons.

There are two main types of bonds formed between atoms: **Ionic** and **Covalent bonds.** Anions and cations, being negatively and positively charged respectively, exist because of the attraction of opposite charges, and usually form **ionic bonds**.

A covalent bond forms when atoms share valence electrons. However, atoms do not always share electrons equally, resulting in a **polar covalent bond**. Electrons shared by two metallic atoms, form a **metallic bond**. Those electrons participating in metallic bonds may be shared between any of the metal atoms in the region.

If the electronegativity values of two atoms are similar, then:
- Metallic bonds form between two metal atoms.
- Covalent bonds form between two non-metal atoms.
- Non-polar covalent bonds form when the electronegativity values are very similar.
- Polar covalent bonds form when the electronegativity values are a little further apart.

If the electronegativity values of two atoms are different, then ionic bonds are formed.

Most metals have less than 4 valence electrons, which allows them to either gain a few electrons or lose a few; they generally tend to lose electrons, which causes them to become more positive. (This means that metals tend to form cations.)

A **hydrogen bond** is not considered a chemical bond. Instead, in a hydrogen bond, the attractive force between hydrogen is attached to an electronegative atom of one molecule and an electronegative atom of a different molecule. Usually the electronegative atom is oxygen, nitrogen, or fluorine, which have partial negative charges. The hydrogen has the partial positive charge. Hydrogen bonds are much weaker than both ionic and covalent bonds.

Multiple Bonding Patterns

Depending on the electron structure of the atom, double or even triple bonds are possible between atoms. Double and triple bonds share 4 and 6 electrons between a pair of atoms, respectively. These types of bonds are usually quite stable. For example, O_2 possesses a double bond and N_2 possesses a triple bond. An example of a larger molecule with a double or triple bond is seen below:

$$\equiv (CH_3)_2C{=}CHCH_2C(CH_3)_3$$

2,5,5-trimethyl-2-hexene

The double bond structure is represented in chemistry by a pair of parallel lines, rather than the single line seen for a normal bond. In the molecule above, the double bond is located between the 2nd and 3rd carbon in the hexane molecule.

VSEPR Bonding Theory

VSEPR, short for Valence Shell Electron Pair Repulsion theory is a method that aids in understanding the three dimensional structure of a molecule. According to the repulsion of each pair of electrons in a bond, we can understand how a molecule's geometry will look like. The basic forms of geometry are:

- **Linear** – When there are 3 atoms in a molecule that have no high electronegativity differences, the molecule is linear:

$$X - A - X$$

- **Trigonal Planar** – Seen in molecules with four atoms that may have a lone pair on each end:

- **Tetrahedral** – The tetrahedral molecule is the standard shape for a single central atom surround by 4 bonds. The bond angles between the different atoms may be different due to electronegativity differences.

There are additional bonding structures, such as trigonal bipyrimidal (6 total atoms), octahedral, and pentagonal. However, these bonding structures are not common in day to day chemical reactions.

Practice Drill: Periodic Table and Chemical Bonds

1. When cations and anions join, they form what kind of chemical bond?
   a) Ionic.
   b) Hydrogen.
   c) Metallic.
   d) Covalent.

2. Generally, how do atomic masses vary throughout the periodic table of the elements?
    a) They decrease from left to right and increase from top to bottom.
    b) They increase from left to right and increase bottom to top.
    c) They increase from left to right and increase top to bottom.
    d) They increase from right to left and decrease bottom to top.

3. The force involved in all chemical behavior is:
    a) Electronegativity.
    b) Covalent bonds.
    c) Electromagnetism.
    d) Ionic bonds.

4. Which one of the following is not a form of chemical bonding?
    a) Covalent bonding.
    b) Hydrogen bonding.
    c) Ionic bonding.
    d) Metallic bonding.

5. Two atoms which do not share electrons equally will form what type of bond?
    a) Metallic bonds.
    b) Polar covalent.
    c) Ionic bonds.
    d) They cannot form bonds.

Practice Drill: Periodic Table and Chemical Bonds – Answers

1. a)
2. c)
3. c)
4. b)
5. b)

CHANGES IN STATE: VAPORIZATION/CONDENSATION

A material can change from one state, such as liquid, to another state, such as gas, depending on the surrounding temperature and pressure. In most conditions that we see, the pressure is atmospheric, and as a general rule, as temperature increases, the state will progress from solid to liquid to gas, and the opposite will occur as temperature decreases.

Terminology to know:

Boiling point: The boiling point is also the point of vaporization of a material. For example, the boiling point of water is 100 °C at normal atmospheric pressure. Thus, at 100 °C liquid water will turn into water vapor.

Freezing point: The freezing point is also the melting point of a solid. For example, the melting/freezing point of water is 0 °C.

Critical point: The critical point is the temperature and pressure at which defined states do not exist. For example, at the critical point of water, which happens at 374°C and 218 atmospheres, there is no defined state for water. It is considered "plasma", and behaves with different properties than either liquid or gas.

Latent heat: The latent heat of vaporization is the heat required for a liquid to turn into a gas. Below is a table showing example values of latent heat for some common substances.

Substance	Latent heat of Vaporization	Boiling Point (C)
Ethanol	855 kJ/kg	78.3
Water	2260 kJ/kg	100
Nitrogen	200 kJ/kg	-196

In these examples provided, we can understand the following:

The energy that is in 1 kilogram of water vapor is 2,260 kJ more than in 1 kilogram of liquid water.

Specific Heat

The specific heat of a substance is the amount of energy it requires to raise the substance by 1 unit of temperature. For example, the specific heat of water is about 4.19 J/g*K. This means that you need 4.19 Joules of energy to heat 1 gram of water by 1 degree centigrade. The specific heat is a useful property that can be used to predict the amount of energy needed to heat up a substance. For example, if you want to warm a 100 mL (100 g) cup of water from 25 °C to 50 °C, you would need about 10,450 joules of energy.

Practice Drill: Changes in State

1. What is the correct term for the energy required for a solid to become a liquid?
    a) Latent heat of vaporization
    b) Latent heat of fusion
    c) Latent heat of fission
    d) None of the above

2. A student wishes to boil 0.5 kg of water, about half a liter. After the water reaches 100 °C, how much more energy is required for it to boil?
    a) 760 kJ
    b) 960 kJ
    c) 1130 kJ
    d) 2240 kJ

3. Which of the following is not a state of matter?
    a) Plasma
    b) Liquid
    c) Solid
    d) All of the above are states of matter

4. A student has a cup of water at room temperature 25 °C and 1 atm. He notices the temperature in the room is rapidly increasing! How might he keep the water in liquid state and prevent it from vaporizing?
    a) Further increasing the temperature
    b) Increasing the pressure in the room
    c) Decreasing the pressure in the room
    d) Mixing the water very quickly

5. What is the best definition of a solution?
    a) A mixture of a solute dissolved in a solvent
    b) A combination of more than 3 elements in a liquid form
    c) Any pure, liquid, element
    d) None of the above can be classified as a solution

Practice Drill: Changes in State—Answers

1. b)
2. c)
3. d)
4. b)
5. a)

CHEMICAL REACTIONS

A chemical reaction occurs when there is a conversion of one set of chemical substances to another set. Chemical reactions are caused primarily by a change in bonding structure in these substances due to the exchange of electrons.

In a chemical reaction, the starting substances are called the reagents, and the ending substances are called the products. In the reaction below, sodium hydroxide reacts with iron sulfate to form sodium sulfate and iron hydroxide, the products.

$$2NaOH + FeSO_4 \rightarrow Na_2SO_4 + Fe(OH)_2$$

The above reaction is known as a double displacement reaction. In double displacement reactions, there are two reagents which interact to form two products. The ions from *both* reagents are displaced, hence the name double displacement. There are also 5 other primary types of chemical reactions:

1. Combustion reaction – A combustion reaction occurs when oxygen is reacted in the presence of heat to a combustible compound, usually an organic compound. The products of a combustion reaction are always water and carbon dioxide. For example, the reaction of methane with oxygen will proceed as follows:

$$CH_4 + 2\,O_2 \rightarrow CO_2 + 2H_2O$$

2. Synthesis reaction – This is the most simple reaction in the book. Two compounds, usually elements, combine to form a third compound, the product:

$$C + O_2 \rightarrow CO_2$$

3. Decomposition reaction – This is the opposite of a synthesis reaction, and is usually endothermic. In the decomposition reaction, a single compound decomposes to form two new compounds.

4. Single Displacement reaction – Similar to the double displacement reaction seen above, but only one reactive species changes. For example:

$$MgCl_2 + 2Na \rightarrow Mg + 2NaCl$$

5. Acid Base reaction – In an acid base reaction, one of two reactive species must be seen: a hydrogen ion (H+), or a hydroxide ion (OH-). Hydrogen ions are acidic in nature, and hydroxide ions are basic in nature. When combined, the two ions react to form water.

Energy States

Chemical reactions are influenced by the energy state of the reagents and the products, and a chemical reaction is much more likely to occur if the energy state of the products is *lower* than the energy state of the reactants. However, even if the energy state of the products is higher than that of the reactants, energy can be put into the chemical reaction in order to force it to occur. This highlights two primary types of reactions:

Endothermic reaction: Chemical reactions can be endothermic, meaning heat absorbing. An endothermic reaction requires an input of energy before the reaction can start. A majority of chemical reactions are endothermic. For example, although air will react with metal to form rust, the reaction is endothermic in nature, and will occur either slowly or not at all. This is why your table and chair don't fall apart in the air.

Exothermic reaction: A chemical reaction that is exothermic, or heat releasing, will release energy during its course, forming lower energy products. These reactions are spontaneous, and do not require added energy.

Reaction Stoichiometry

Stoichiometry is the ratio of different compounds taking part in a reaction. The reaction stoichiometry is the relative ratio of each of the reactants and products in a reaction. Stoichiometry is used to determine the amount of products that can be formed from a given set of reactants.

For example, in the single displacement reaction shown above:

$$MgCl_2 + 2Na \rightarrow Mg + 2NaCl$$

1 mol of magnesium chloride in addition to 2 mols of sodium are required in the reactants. This then creates 1 mol of magnesium and 2 mols of sodium chloride.

Reaction stoichiometry can be used to predict the amount of products formed. Given the reaction:

$$C_2H_8 + 4O_2 \rightarrow ?$$

This is a combustion reaction. How many mols of carbon dioxide and water are formed?

To answer this question, we can follow these steps:

1. Convert masses to mols (In this case, we already have mol values, so this is not necessary. In some problems, however, mass values will be given)
2. Write and balance the equation:

    We know that this is a combustion reaction, so the reaction should be:

$$C_2H_8 + 4O_2 \rightarrow CO_2 + H_2O$$

However, this is not balanced. There are more atoms on the left than the right. We see that we need to have 2 carbon dioxide molecules and 4 water molecules in order for the mass balance to be correct. This gives us:

$$C_2H_8 + 4O_2 \rightarrow 2CO_2 + 4H_2O$$

We can check and see that the reaction stoichiometry is correct. There are the same number of carbons, hydrogens, and oxygen on the left as there are on the right.

3. Convert mols back to mass if necessary.

Practice Drill: Chemical Reactions

1. In your home, natural gas (methane) is burned to produce heat to keep the house warm. What sort of reaction is this?
   a) Acid base reaction
   b) Combustion reaction
   c) Single displacement reaction
   d) Synthesis reaction

2. A student mixes two unknown chemicals into a beaker (don't do this at home!). He notices that the beaker gets really hot. What type of reaction is this?
   a) Exothermic
   b) Endothermic
   c) Combustion
   d) Reaction

3. Which of the following is a substance or compound that is entering into a reaction?
   a) Mol
   b) Reactant
   c) Product
   d) Chemical

4. Acid rain is produced from the interaction of water and sulfur trioxide. Sulfur trioxide (SO_3) is produced when sulfur is burned. Which of the following is the correct general reaction for this process?
   a) Sulfur + nitrogen → sulfur trioxide
   b) Sulfur + oxygen → sulfur dioxide
   c) Sulfur dioxide + oxygen → sulfur trioxide
   d) Sulfur + oxygen → sulfur trioxide

5. In a balanced equation:
   a) The mass of the reactants equals the mass of the products
   b) The number of mols of reactants equals the number of mols of the products
   c) The size of each molecule in the reaction remains the same
   d) None of the above are correct

Practice Drill: Chemical Reactions—Answers

1. b)
2. a)
3. b)
4. d)
5. a)

ACIDS AND BASES

Acids

Naturally-occurring **acid solutions**, in which the solvent is always water, have several characteristic properties in common. They have a sour taste; speed up the corrosion, or rusting, of metals; conduct electricity; and introduce H^+ cations into aqueous solutions.

These characteristic properties can be changed by the addition of a base.

Bases (Alkalis)

Bases don't occur in as many common materials as do acids. A few examples of bases are: lime, lye, and soap. Basic solutions, as opposed to acidic solutions, have a bitter taste; conduct electricity, when their solvent is water; and introduce OH^- ions into an aqueous solution.

The characteristic properties can be changed by the addition of an acid.

The acidity or basicity of a solution is expressed by **pH values**. A neutral solution is defined by the following: it has equal concentrations of H^+ cations and OH^- ions, and a pH of 7. Neutrality is based on the pH of pure water. The more acidic a solution, the lower the pH is below 7. The more basic the solution, the higher the pH is above 7. The pH scale is based on logarithms of base 10. (If one solution has a pH of 8 and another has a pH of 10, then there is a 10^2 or 100 fold difference between the two.)

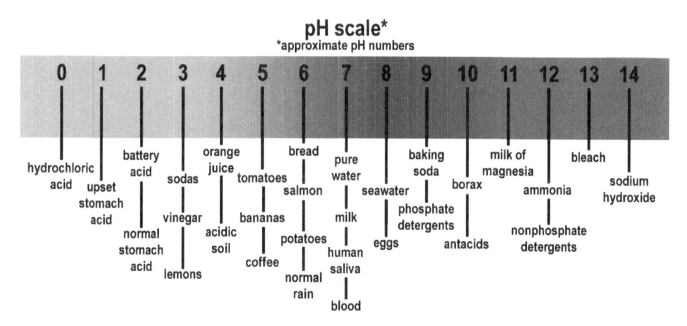

A **buffer** is used to make a solution which exhibits very little change in its pH when small amounts of an acid or base are added to it.

An acidic buffer solution is simply one which has a pH less than 7. Acidic buffer solutions are commonly made from a weak acid and one of its salts - often a sodium salt. A strong basic solution can be weakened by adding an acidic buffer.

An alkaline buffer solution has a pH greater than 7. Alkaline buffer solutions are commonly made from a weak base and one of its salts. A strong acid can be made weaker by adding an alkaline buffer.

The human body contains many enzymes that only function at a specific pH. Once outside of this range, the enzymes are either unable to catalyze reactions or, in some cases, will break down. Our bodies produce a buffer solution that is a mixture of carbonic acid and bicarbonate, in order to keep the pH of blood at 7.4.

Practice Drill: Acids and Bases

1. One of the characteristic properties of an acid is that they introduce:
   a) Hydrogen ions.
   b) Hydroxyl ions.
   c) Hydride ions.
   d) Oxide ions.

2. A solution with a pH of 12 is:
   a) Very acidic.
   b) Neutral.
   c) Very basic.
   d) You can't have a solution with a pH of 12.

3. Buffers keep the pH of a solution from changing by:
   a) Converting strong acids to weak ones.
   b) Converting weak acids to strong ones.
   c) Converting weak bases to strong ones.
   d) More than one of the above answers is correct.

4. Proper blood pH level for humans is:
   a) 7.0.
   b) 7.2.
   c) 7.6.
   d) 7.4.

5. All of the following are properties of alkalis except:
   a) Bitter taste.
   b) Basic solutions are high conductors of electricity.
   c) Introduce OH^- ions into an aqueous solution.
   d) The characteristic properties can be changed by the addition of an acid.

Practice Drill: Acids and Bases – Answers

1. a)
2. c)
3. a)
4. d)
5. b)

CATALYSTS & ENZYMES

A catalyst is a substance that is used to increase the rate of a chemical reaction. The rate of a chemical reaction is influenced by the following:

- Nature of the reactants – the electronegativity or electron structure of the reactants will affect how quickly they react.
- Concentration of the reactants – the more concentrated a reactive species is, the more likely they will come into contact with each other and react.
- Temperature – the temperature of the surrounding environment increases the internal energy of the reactants. This transfer of energy can help overcome the activation energy barrier before a reaction starts.

Of all the factors, the activation energy of a chemical reaction by far is the most important factor. Catalysts can aid a reaction in two ways: they can reduce the activation energy of a reaction, or they can bring two reactants closer together so that a reaction is more likely to occur.

Examples of catalytic metals include: Vanadium oxide, zeolites, platinum, chelated nickel.

Activation Energy

The activation energy of a chemical is an amount of energy that needs to be put into the reaction system before a reaction can begin. A diagram of activation energy is seen below:

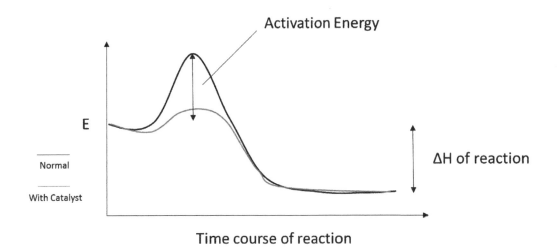

As seen in the diagram, a catalyst lowers the reaction activation energy, making it easier for a reaction to begin. In this manner, the rate of a reaction will begin faster. The activation energy of a reaction is governed by the Arrhenius equation, seen below:

$$k = Ae^{-E_a/RT}$$

k represents the rate of reaction, A is the Arrhenius constant, Ea is the activation energy, R is the universal gas constant, and T is the temperature in kelvin.

As can be seen, either increasing the temperature or reducing the activation energy will dramatically increase the value of k, thus speeding up the reaction.

Enzymes

Enzymes are best termed as "biological catalysts". Enzymes are proteins found in living organisms that catalyze biological reactions. Unlike traditional catalysts, enzymes are very specific to the reaction that they work on. For example, a platinum catalyst can be used in many different reactions, such as decomposition of unburned hydrocarbons in your car to dehydrogenation of vegetable oils. On the other hand, and enzyme such as cellulase is specifically active for only one reaction: the breaking of the glycosidic bond between two glucose molecules in a cellulose chain.

Enzymes are created by ribosomes which bind amino acids into a long chain, known as the primary structure of an enzyme. These chains of amino acids then interact through disulfide bonds and hydrogen bonds to form the secondary and tertiary structure of an enzyme. A quaternary structure of enzymes also exists, and is due to the interaction of a group of enzymes.

Practice Drill: Catalysts & Enzymes

1. Which of the following is true about an enzyme catalyzed reaction?
   a) It is usually slower than a metal catalyst
   b) The rate of a catalyzed reaction will decrease as temperature increases
   c) It is a linear function of concentration
   d) None of the above

2. A student runs a reaction and notices a kinetic rate of 1 $mol \cdot L^{-1} \cdot s^{-1}$. If he increases the temperature by a factor of 5, how much would he expect the reaction rate to increase?
   a) Roughly 5 times
   b) Roughly 4 times
   c) Roughly 2 times
   d) There will be no change

3. Which of the following reactions would you believe to have the highest activation energy?
   a) Conversion of H_2 into 2H
   b) Reaction of HCl with water
   c) Reaction of oxygen with metal to form rust
   d) Combustion of methane

4. A reaction with a positive ΔH value will:
   a) Require an energy input
   b) A catalyst for the reaction to occur
   c) Produce energy
   d) Have a very low activation energy

5. A company is trying to make ammonia from the reaction of nitrogen (N_2) and hydrogen (H_2), but the reaction is progressing very slowly. Which of the following would be effective in increasing the reaction rate?
   a) Increasing the temperature
   b) Increasing the pressure
   c) Adding a catalyst
   d) All of the above

Practice Drill: Enzymes & Catalysts—Answers

1. d)
2. c)
3. a)
4. a)
5. d)

PHYSICS

Physics is the science of matter and energy, and of interactions between the two, grouped in traditional fields such as acoustics, optics, mechanics, thermodynamics, and electromagnetism.

Motion

Speed is a scalar quantity and is defined as distance divided by time. (Ex: miles per hour.) **Velocity** is a vector quantity that describes speed and the direction of travel. **Magnitude of Acceleration** is defined as the change in velocity divided by the time interval. A **scalar quantity** is described only by its magnitude, whereas a **vector quantity** is described by magnitude and direction.

Acceleration is change in velocity divided by time; an object accelerates not only when it speeds up, but also when slowing down or turning. The **acceleration due to gravity** of a falling object near the Earth is a constant $9.8 m/s^2$; therefore an object's magnitude increases as it falls and decreases as it rises.

Newton's Three Laws of Motion

1. An object at rest will remain at rest unless acted on by an unbalanced force. An object in motion continues in motion with the same speed and in the same direction unless acted upon by an unbalanced force. This law is often called "**the law of inertia**".

2. Acceleration is produced when a force acts on a mass. The greater the mass (of the object being accelerated) the greater the amount of force needed (to accelerate the object). Think of it like this: it takes a greater amount of force to push a boulder, than it does to push a feather.

3. Every action requires an equal and opposite reaction. This means that for every force, there is a reacting force both equal in size and opposite in direction. (I.e. whenever an object pushes another object, it gets pushed back in the opposite direction with equal force.)

An object's **density** is its mass divided by its volume. **Frictional forces** arise when one object tries move over or around another; the frictional forces act in the opposite direction to oppose such a motion. **Pressure** is the force per unit area which acts upon a surface.

There are **Three Important Conservation Laws** which are embodied within Newton's Laws. They offer a different and sometimes more powerful way to consider motion:

1. **Conservation of Momentum**: Embodied in Newton's first law (Law of Inertia), this reiterates that the momentum of a system is constant if no external forces act upon the system.

2. **Conservation of Energy**: Energy is neither created nor destroyed; it can be converted from one form to another (i.e. potential energy converted to kinetic energy), but the total amount of energy within the domain remains fixed.

3. **Conservation of Angular Momentum**: If the system is subjected to no external force, then the total angular momentum of a system has constant magnitude and direction. This is the common physics behind figure-skating and planetary orbits.

Energy and Forces

The energy stored within an object is called its **potential energy** – it has the potential to do work. But where does that energy come from? When gravity pulls down on an object (**gravitational energy**) the object receives potential energy. **Kinetic energy**, the energy of motion, is the energy possessed because of an object's motion.

The sum of an object's kinetic and potential energies is called the total **mechanical energy** (or, **internal energy**).

Frictional forces convert kinetic energy and gravitational potential energy into **thermal energy**. **Power** is the energy converted from one form to another, divided by the time needed to make the conversion. A **simple machine** is a device that alters the magnitude or direction of an applied force. Example: an inclined plane or lever.

Objects that move in a curved path have acceleration towards the center of that path. That acceleration is called a **centripetal acceleration. Centripetal force** is the inward force causing that object to move in the curved path. If the centripetal force is the action, the (opposite) reaction is an outwardly-directed **centrifugal force**.

Thermal Physics

Temperature and Heat

Heat and temperature are two different things. **Heat** is a measure of the work required to change the speeds in a collection of atoms or molecules. **Temperature** is a measure of the average kinetic energy of the atoms or molecules of a substance.

A **calorie** is the amount of heat required to raise the temperature of 1 gram of water by 1 degree Celsius. The **specific heat** of a substance is the ratio of the amount of heat added to a substance, divided by the mass and the temperature change of the substance.

The change of a substance from solid to liquid, or liquid to gas, etc., is called a **phase change**.

> **Heat of Fusion:** The amount of heat required to change a unit mass of a substance from solid to liquid at the *melting point.*

> **Heat of Vaporization:** The amount of heat needed to change a unit mass of a substance from liquid to vapor at the *boiling point.*

Heat Transfer

Temperature Scales

There are three common temperature scales: **Celsius, Fahrenheit**, and **Kelvin**. Because it is based upon what we believe to be **absolute zero** (the lowest theoretical temperature possible before life ceases), the Kelvin scale is also known as the **absolute scale**.

Temperature Scale	Point at Which Water Freezes
Celsius	0° C
Fahrenheit	32° F
Kelvin	273K

The Two Mechanisms of Heat Transfer

Conduction: Heat transfer via conduction can occur in a substance of any phase (solid, liquid, or gas), but is mostly seen in solids.

Convection: Convection heat transfer occurs only in fluids (liquids and gases).

Both types of heat transfer are caused by molecular movement in the substance of interest.

Practice Drill: Physics

1. An object that has kinetic energy must be:
   a) Moving.
   b) Falling.
   c) At an elevated position.
   d) At rest.

2. A moving object has
   a) Velocity.
   b) Momentum.
   c) Energy.
   d) All of these.

3. _____ increases, decreases, or changes the direction of a force.
   a) A simple machine.
   b) Energy.
   c) Momentum.
   d) Inertia.

4. _____ is a measure of the average kinetic energy of the atoms or molecules of a substance.
   a) Specific Heat
   b) Temperature
   c) Heat
   d) Force

5. Average speed is:
   a) A measure of how fast something is moving.
   b) The distance covered per unit of time.
   c) Always measured in terms of a unit of distance divided by a unit of time.
   d) All of the above.

6. Which of the following controls can change a car's velocity?
   a) The steering wheel.
   b) The brake pedal.
   c) Both A and B.
   d) None of the above.

Practice Drill: Physics – Answers

1. a)
2. d)
3. a)
4. b)
5. d)
6. c)

Life Science

BASICS OF LIFE

We began learning the difference between living (**animate**) beings and nonliving (**inanimate**) objects from an early age. Living organisms and inanimate objects are all composed of **atoms** from elements. Those atoms are arranged into groups called **molecules**, which serve as the building blocks of everything in existence (as we know it). Molecular interactions are what determine whether something is classified as animate or inanimate. The following is a list of the most commonly-found elements found in the molecules of animate beings:

- Oxygen
- Chlorine
- Carbon
- Nitrogen
- Sodium
- Calcium
- Magnesium
- Phosphorous
- Iodine
- Iron
- Sulfur
- Hydrogen
- Potassium

Another way to describe living and nonliving things is through the terms **organic** and **inorganic.**

- **Organic molecules** are from living organisms. Organic molecules contain **carbon-hydrogen bonds**.
- **Inorganic molecules** come from non-living resources. They do not contain carbon-hydrogen bonds.

There are four major classes of organic molecules:

1. **Carbohydrates**
2. **Lipids**
3. **Proteins**
4. **Nucleic acids**.

Carbohydrates

Carbohydrates consist of only hydrogen, oxygen, and carbon atoms. They are the most abundant single class of organic substances found in nature. Carbohydrate molecules provide many basic necessities such as: fiber, vitamins, and minerals; structural components for organisms, especially plants; and, perhaps most importantly, energy. Our bodies break down carbohydrates to make **glucose**: a sugar used to produce that energy which our bodies need in order to operate. Brain cells are exclusively dependent upon a constant source of glucose molecules.

There are two kinds of carbohydrates: simple and complex.

> **Simple carbohydrates** can be absorbed directly through the cell, and therefore enter the blood stream very quickly. We consume simple carbohydrates in dairy products, fruits, and other sugary foods.

> **Complex carbohydrates** consist of a chain of simple sugars which, over time, our bodies break down into simple sugars (which are also referred to as stored energy.) **Glycogen** is the storage form of glucose in human and animal cells. Complex carbohydrates come from starches like cereal, bread, beans, potatoes, and starchy vegetables.

Lipids

Lipids, commonly known as fats, are molecules with two functions:

1. They are stored as an energy reserve.
2. They provide a protective cushion for vital organs.

In addition to those two functions, lipids also combine with other molecules to form essential compounds, such as **phospholipids,** which form the membranes around cells. Lipids also combine with other molecules to create naturally-occurring **steroid** hormones, like the hormones estrogen and testosterone.

Proteins

Proteins are large molecules which our bodies' cells need in order to function properly. Consisting of **amino acids,** proteins aid in maintaining and creating many aspects of our cells: cellular structure, function, and regulation, to name a few. Proteins also work as neurotransmitters and carriers of oxygen in the blood (hemoglobin).

Without protein, our tissues and organs could not exist. Our muscles bones, skin, and many other parts of the body contain significant amounts of protein. **Enzymes**, hormones, and antibodies are proteins.

Enzymes

When heat is applied, chemical reactions are typically sped up. However, the amount of heat required to speed up reactions could be potentially harmful (even fatal) to living organisms. Instead, our bodies use molecules called enzymes to bring reactants closer together, causing them to form a new compound. Thus, the whole reaction rate is increased without heat. Even better – the enzymes are not consumed during the reaction process, and can therefore be used reused. This makes them an important biochemical part of both photosynthesis and respiration.

Nucleic Acid

Nucleic acids are large molecules made up of smaller molecules called **nucleotides. DNA** (deoxyribonucleic acid) transports and transmits genetic information. As you can tell from the name, DNA is a nucleic acid. Since nucleotides make up nucleic acids, they are considered the basis of reproduction and progression.

Test Your Knowledge: Basics of Life

1. Life depends upon:
   a) The bond energy in molecules.
   b) The energy of protons.
   c) The energy of electrons.
   d) The energy of neutrons.

2. Which of the following elements is **NOT** found in carbohydrates?
   a) Carbon.
   b) Hydrogen.
   c) Oxygen.
   d) Sulfur.

3. Which of the following is a carbohydrate molecule?
   a) Amino acid.
   b) Glycogen.
   c) Sugar.
   d) Lipid.

4. Lipids are commonly known as:
   a) Fat.
   b) Sugar.
   c) Enzymes.
   d) Protein.

5. Proteins are composed of:
   a) Nucleic acids.
   b) Amino acids.
   c) Hormones.
   d) Lipids.

Test Your Knowledge: Basics of Life – Answers

1. **a)**
2. **d)**
3. **c)**
4. **a)**
5. **b)**

CELLULAR RESPIRATION

As you can imagine, there are a great deal of processes which require energy: breathing, blood circulation, body temperature control, muscle usage, digestion, brain and nerve functioning are all only a few examples. You can refer to all of the body's physical and chemical processes which convert or use energy as **metabolism**.

All living things in the world, including plants, require energy in order to maintain their metabolisms. Initially, that energy is consumed through food. That energy is processed in plants and animals through **photosynthesis** (for plants) and **respiration** (for animals). **Cellular respiration** produces the actual energy molecules known as **ATP** (Adenosine Tri-Phosphate) molecules.

Plants use ATP during **photosynthesis** for producing glucose, which is then broken down during cellular respiration. This cycle continuously repeats itself throughout the life of the plant.

Photosynthesis: Plants, as well as some Protists and Monerans, can use light energy to bind together small molecules from the environment. These newly-bound molecules are then used as fuel to make more energy. This process is called photosynthesis, and one of its byproducts is none other than oxygen. Most organisms, including plants, require oxygen to fuel the biochemical reactions of metabolism.

You can see in the following equation that plants use the energy taken from light to turn carbon dioxide and water – the small molecules from their environment – into glucose and oxygen.

The photosynthesis equation:

$$CO_2 + H_2O \xrightarrow{\text{Light}} C_6H_{12}O_6 + O_2$$

$$\begin{array}{llll} \text{Carbon} & \text{Water} & \text{Glucose} & \text{Oxygen} \\ \text{Dioxide} & & \text{(sugar)} & \end{array}$$

Chlorophyll

In order for photosynthesis to occur, however, plants require a specific molecule to capture sunlight. This molecule is called **chlorophyll**. When chlorophyll absorbs sunlight, one of its electrons is stimulated into a higher energy state. This higher-energy electron then passes that energy onto other electrons in other molecules, creating a chain that eventually results in glucose. Chlorophyll absorbs red and blue light, but not green; green light is reflected off of plants, which is why plants appear green to us. It's important to note that chlorophyll is absolutely necessary to the photosynthesis process in plants –if it photosynthesizes, it will have chlorophyll.

The really fascinating aspect of photosynthesis is that raw sunlight energy is a very nonliving thing; however, it is still absorbed by plants to form the chemical bonds between simple inanimate compounds. This produces organic sugar, which is the chemical basis for the formation of all living compounds. Isn't it amazing? Something nonliving is essential to the creation of all living things!

Respiration

Respiration is the metabolic opposite of photosynthesis. There are two types of respiration: **aerobic** (which uses oxygen) and **anaerobic** (which occurs without the use of oxygen).

You may be confused at thinking of the word "respiration" in this way, since many people use respiration to refer to the process of breathing. However, in biology, breathing is thought of as **inspiration** (inhaling) and **expiration** (exhalation); whereas **respiration** is the metabolic, chemical reaction supporting these processes. Both plants and animals produce carbon dioxide through respiration.

Aerobic respiration is the reaction which uses enzymes to combine oxygen with organic matter (food). This yields carbon dioxide, water, and energy.

The respiration equation looks like this:

$$\text{C6H12O6} + \text{6O2} \xrightarrow{\textbf{Enzymes}} 7\ \text{6CO2} + \text{6H2O} + \text{energy}$$

If you look back the equation for photosynthesis, you will see that respiration is almost the same equation, only it goes in the opposite direction. (Photosynthesis uses carbon dioxide and water, with the help of energy, to create oxygen and glucose. Respiration uses oxygen and glucose, with the help of enzymes, to create carbon dioxide, water, and energy.)

Anaerobic respiration is respiration that occurs WITHOUT the use of oxygen. It produces less energy than aerobic respiration produces, yielding only two molecules of ATP per glucose molecule Aerobic respiration produces 38 ATP per glucose molecule.

So, plants convert energy into matter and release oxygen gas – animals then absorb this oxygen gas in order to run their own metabolic reaction and, in the process, release carbon dioxide. That carbon dioxide is then absorbed by plants in the photosynthetic conversion of energy into matter. Everything comes full circle! This is called a **metabolic cycle.**

Test Your Knowledge: Cellular Respiration

1. Which of the following is **NOT** true of enzymes?
   a) Enzymes are lipid molecules.
   b) Enzymes are not consumed in a biochemical reaction.
   c) Enzymes are important in photosynthesis and respiration.
   d) Enzymes speed up reactions and make them more efficient.

2. Plants appear green because chlorophyll:
   a) Absorbs green light.
   b) Reflects red light.
   c) Absorbs blue light.
   d) Reflects green light.

3. Photosynthesis is the opposite of:
   a) Enzymatic hydrolysis.
   b) Protein synthesis.
   c) Respiration.
   d) Reproduction.

4. The compound that absorbs light energy during photosynthesis is:
   a) Chloroform.
   b) Chlorofluorocarbon.
   c) Chlorinated biphenyls.
   d) Chlorophyll.

5. What is the name of the sugar molecule produced during photosynthesis?
   a) Chlorophyll.
   b) Glycogen.
   c) Glucose.
   d) Fructose.

Test Your Knowledge: Cellular Respiration – Answers

1. a)
2. d)
3. c)
4. d)
5. c)

CLASSIFICATION OF ORGANISMS

All of Earth's organisms have characteristics which distinguish them from one another. Scientists have developed systems to organize and classify all of Earth's organisms based on those characteristics.

Kingdoms

Through the process of evolution, organisms on Earth have developed into many diverse forms, which have complex relationships. Scientists have organized life into five large groups called **kingdoms**. Each kingdom contains those organisms that share significant characteristics distinguishing them from organisms in other kingdoms. These five kingdoms are named as follows:

1. **Animalia**
2. **Plantae**
3. **Fungi**
4. **Protista**
5. **Monera**

Kingdom Animalia

This kingdom contains multicellular organisms multicellular, or those known as complex organisms. These organisms are generically called **heterotrophs**, which means that they must eat preexisting organic matter (either plants or other animals) in order to sustain themselves.

Those heterotrophs which eat only plants are called **herbivores** (from "herbo," meaning "herb" or "plant"); those that kill and eat other animals for food are called **carnivores** (from "carno," meaning "flesh" or "meat"); and still other animals eat both plants *and* other animals – they are called **omnivores** (from "omnis," which means "all").

Those organisms in the Animal Kingdom have nervous tissue which has developed into nervous systems and brains; they are also able to move from place to place using muscular systems. The Animal Kingdom is divided into two groups: **vertebrates** (with backbones) and **invertebrates** (without backbones).

Kingdom Plantae

As you can guess from its name, the Plant Kingdom contains all plant-based life. Plants are multicellular organisms that use chlorophyll, which is held in specialized cellular structures called **chloroplasts,** to capture sunlight energy. Remember: photosynthesis! They then convert that sunlight energy into organic matter: their food. Because of this, most plants are referred to as **autotrophs** (self-feeders). There are a few organisms included in the Plant Kingdom which are not multicellular – certain types of algae which, while not multicellular, have cells with a nucleus. These algae also contain chlorophyll.

Except for algae, most plants are divided into one of two groups: **vascular plants** (most crops, trees, and flowering plants) and **nonvascular plants** (mosses). Vascular plants have specialized tissue that allows them to transport water and nutrients from their roots, to their leaves, and back again – even when the plant is several hundred feet tall. Nonvascular plants cannot do this, and therefore remain very small in size. Vascular plants are able to grow in both wet and dry environments; whereas nonvascular plants, since they are unable to transport water, are usually found only in wet, marshy areas.

Kingdom Fungi

The Fungi Kingdom contains organisms that share some similarities with plants, but also have other characteristics that make them more animal-like. For example, they resemble animals in that they lack chlorophyll – so they can't perform photosynthesis. This means that they don't produce their own food and are therefore heterotrophs.

However, they resemble plants in that they reproduce by spores; they also resemble plants in appearance. The bodies of fungi are made of filaments called **hyphae**, which in turn create the tissue **mycelium.** The most well-known examples of organisms in this Kingdom are mushrooms, yeasts, and molds. Fungi are very common and benefit other organisms, including humans.

Kingdom Protista

This kingdom includes single-celled organisms that contain a nucleus as part of their structure. They are considered a simple cell, but still contain multiple structures and accomplish many functions. This Kingdom includes organisms such as paramecium, amoeba, and slime molds. They often move around using hair-like structures called *cilia* or *flagellums.*

Kingdom Monera

This kingdom contains only bacteria. All of these organisms are single-celled and do not have a nucleus. They have only one chromosome, which is used to transfer genetic information. Sometimes they can also transmit genetic information using small structures called **plasmids.** Like organisms in the Protista Kingdom, they use flagella to move. Bacteria usually reproduce asexually.

There are more forms of bacteria than any other organism on Earth. Some bacteria are beneficial to us, like the ones found in yogurt; others can cause us to get sick such as the bacteria *E. coli.*

KINGDOM	DESCRIPTION	EXAMPLES
Animalia	Multi-celled; parasites; prey; consumers; can be herbivorous, carnivorous, or omnivorous	Sponges, worms, insects, fish, mammals, reptiles, birds, humans
Plantae	Multi-celled; autotrophs; mostly producers	Ferns, angiosperms, gymnosperms, mosses
Fungi	Can be single or multi-celled; decomposers; parasites; absorb food; asexual; consumers	Mushrooms, mildew, molds, yeast
Protista	Single or multi-celled; absorb food; both producers and consumers	Plankton, algae, amoeba, protozoans
Monera	Single-celled or a colony of single-cells; decomposers and parasites; move in water; are both producers and consumers	Bacteria, blue-green algae

Levels of Classification

Kingdom groupings are not very specific. They contain organisms defined by broad characteristics, and which may not seem similar at all. For example, worms belong in Kingdom Animalia – but then, so do birds. These two organisms are very different, despite sharing the necessary traits to make it into the animal kingdom. Therefore, to further distinguish different organisms, we have multiple levels of classification, which gradually become more specific until we finally reach the actual organism.

We generally start out by grouping organisms into the appropriate kingdom. Within each kingdom, we have other subdivisions: **Phylum, Class, Order, Family, Genus, and Species.** (In some cases, "Species" can be further narrowed down into "Sub-Species.")

As we move down the chain, characteristics become more specific, and the number of organisms in each group decreases. For an example, let's try to classify a grizzly bear. The chart would go as follows:

Kingdom - insect, fish, bird, pig, dog, bear

Phylum - fish, bird, pig, dog, bear

Class - pig, dog, bear

Order - dog, bear

Family - panda, brown, grizzly

Genus -
brown, grizzly

Species -
grizzly

Here is an easy way to remember the order of terms used in this classification scheme:

Kings **P**lay **C**ards **O**n **F**riday, **G**enerally **S**peaking.

Kingdom, **P**hylum, **C**lass, **O**rder, **F**amily, **G**enus, **S**pecies

Binomial Nomenclature

Organisms can be positively identified by two Latin words. Therefore, the organism naming system is referred to as a binomial nomenclature ("binomial" referring to the number two, and "nomenclature" referring to a title or name). Previously-used words help illustrate where the organism fits into the whole scheme, but it is only the last two, the genus and species, that specifically name an organism. Both are written in italics. The genus is always capitalized, but the species name is written lowercase.

Grizzly bears fall underneath the genus *Ursus*, species *arctos*, and sub-species *horribilis*. Therefore, the scientific name of the grizzly bear would be *Ursus arctos horribilis*. *Canis familiaris* is the scientific name for a common dog, *Felis domesticus* is a common cat, and humans are *Homo sapiens*.

Test Your Knowledge: Classification of Organisms

1. Which feature distinguishes those organisms in Kingdom Monera from those in other kingdoms? Organisms in Kingdom Monera:
   a) Contain specialized organelles.
   b) Contain a nucleus.
   c) Contain chloroplasts.
   d) Lack a nucleus.

2. Which of the following has the classification levels in the correct order, from most general to most specific?
   a) Kingdom, Phylum, Class, Order, Family, Genus, Species.
   b) Order, Family, Genus, Species, Class, Phylum, Kingdom.
   c) Species, Genus, Family, Order, Class, Phylum, Kingdom.
   d) Kingdom, Phylum, Class, Species, Genus, Family, Order.

3. The _____ contains organisms with both plant-and-animal-like characteristics?
   a) Animal Kingdom.
   b) Plant Kingdom.
   c) Fungi Kingdom.
   d) Monera Kingdom.

4. Which of the following statements is true about the binomial nomenclature system of classification?
   a) The genus and species names describe a specific organism.
   b) The category of kingdom is very specific.
   c) The category of species is very broad.
   d) Three names are needed to correctly specify a particular organism.

5. Which of the following kingdom's members are multicellular AND autotrophic?
   a) Fungi.
   b) Animalia.
   c) Protista.
   d) Plantae.

6. Which of the following kingdom's members have tissue called hyphae?
   a) Fungi.
   b) Animalia.
   c) Protista.
   d) Plantae.

Test Your Knowledge: Classification of Organisms – Answers

1. d)
2. a)
3. c)
4. a)
5. d)
6. a)

CELLS, TISSUES, AND ORGANS

All organisms are composed of microscopic cells, although the type and number of cells may vary. A cell is the minimum amount of organized living matter that is complex enough to carry out the functions of life. This section will briefly review both animal and plant cells, noting their basic similarities and differences.

Cell Structure

Around the cell is the **cell membrane**, which separates the living cell from the rest of the environment and regulates the comings and goings of molecules within the cell. Because the cell membrane allows some molecules to pass through while blocking others, it is considered **semipermeable**. Each cell's membrane communicates and interacts with the membranes of other cells. In additional to a cell membrane, *plants* also have a **cell wall** which is necessary for structural support and protection. Animal cells do not contain a cell wall.

Organelle

Cells are filled with a gelatin-like substance called **protoplasm** which contains various structures called **organelles**; called so because they act like small versions of organs. The diagram on the next page illustrates the basic organelles of both a plant and an animal cell. Pay attention to the differences and similarities between the two.

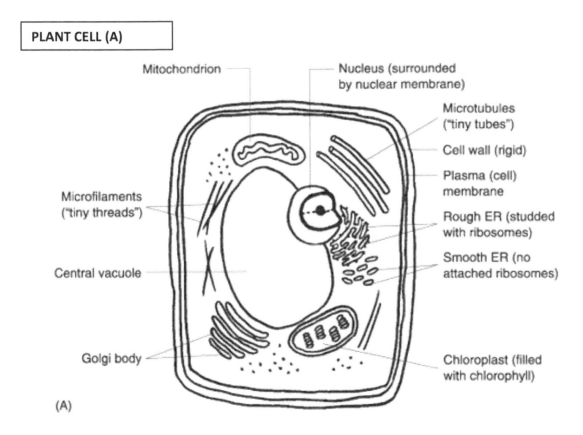

PLANT CELL (A)

Mitochondrion

Nucleus (surrounded by nuclear membrane)

Microtubules ("tiny tubes")

Cell wall (rigid)

Plasma (cell) membrane

Rough ER (studded with ribosomes)

Smooth ER (no attached ribosomes)

Microfilaments ("tiny threads")

Central vacuole

Golgi body

Chloroplast (filled with chlorophyll)

(A)

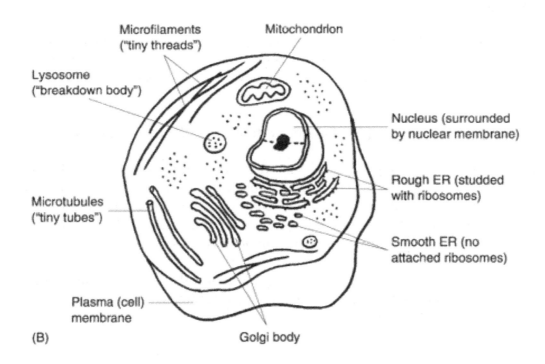

Microfilaments ("tiny threads")
Mitochondrion
Lysosome ("breakdown body")
Nucleus (surrounded by nuclear membrane)
Rough ER (studded with ribosomes)
Microtubules ("tiny tubes")
Smooth ER (no attached ribosomes)
Plasma (cell) membrane
(B)
Golgi body

Organelles (Defined)

Mitochondria are spherical or rod-shaped organelles which carry out the reactions of aerobic respiration. They are the power generators of both plant and animal cells, because they convert oxygen and nutrients into ATP, the chemical energy that powers the cell's metabolic activities.

Ribosomes are extremely tiny spheres that make proteins. These proteins are used either as enzymes or as support for other cell functions.

The **Golgi Apparatus** is essential to the production of polysaccharides (carbohydrates), and made up of a layered stack of flattened sacs.

The **Endoplasmic Reticulum** is important in the synthesis and packaging of proteins. It is a complex system of internal membranes, and is called either rough (when ribosomes are attached), or smooth (no ribosomes attached).

Chloroplasts are only found in plants. They contain the chlorophyll molecule necessary for photosynthesis.

---

[1] Graphics from: http://www.education.com

The **Nucleus** controls all of the cell's functions, and contains the all-important genetic information, or DNA, of a cell.

Cellular Differentiation

Single-celled organisms have only one cell to carry out all of their required biochemical and structural functions. On the other hand, multi-celled organisms – except for very primitive ones (i.e. sponges) – have various groups of cells called **tissues** that each perform specific functions (**differentiation**).

There are four main types of tissues: **epithelial, connective, muscular,** and **nervous**.

Epithelial tissue is made up groups of flattened cells which are grouped tightly together to form a solid surface. Those cells are arranged in one or many layer(s) to form an external or internal covering of the body or organs. Epithelial tissue protects the body from injury and allows for the exchange of gases in the lungs and bronchial tubes. There's even a form of epithelial tissue that produces eggs and sperm, an organism's sex cells.

Connective tissue is made of cells which are surrounded by non-cellular material. For example, bones contain some cells, but they are also surrounded by a considerable amount of non-cellular, extracellular material.

Muscular tissue has the ability to contract. There are three types:

1. **Cardiac** tissue, found in the heart.

2. **Smooth** tissue, located in the walls of hollow internal structures such as blood vessels, the stomach, intestines, and urinary bladder.

3. **Skeletal** (or striated) tissue, found in the muscles.

Nervous tissue consists of cells called **neurons.** Neurons specialize in making many connections with and transmitting electrical impulses to each other. The brain, spinal cord, and peripheral nerves are all made of nervous tissue.

Organs and Organ Systems

As living organisms go through their life cycle, they grow and/or develop. Single-celled organisms grow and develop very rapidly; whereas complex, multi-celled organisms take much longer to progress. All organisms go through changes as they age. These changes involve the development of more complex functions, which in turn require groups of tissues to form larger units called **organs.** Here are some examples of organs:

1. **The heart** - Made of cardiac muscle and conjunctive tissue (conjunctive tissue makes up the valves), the heart pumps blood first to the lungs in order to pick up oxygen, then through the rest of the body to deliver the oxygen, and finally back to the lungs to start again.

2. **Roots** - A tree's are covered by an epidermis which is in turn made up of a protective tissue. They are also *composed* of tissue, which allows them to grow. The root organ also contains **conductive tissue** to absorb and transport water and nutrients to the rest of the plant.

Generally, in complex organisms like plants and animals, many organs are grouped together into **systems.** For example, many combinations of tissues make up the many organs which create the digestive system in animals. The organs in the digestive system consist of the mouth, the esophagus, the stomach, small and large intestines, the liver, the pancreas, and the gall bladder.

Test Your Knowledge: Cells, Tissues, and Organs

1. Which statement is true about Earth's organisms?
   a) All organisms are based on the cell as the basic unit of life.
   b) Protists are an exception to the cell theory and are not based on cells.
   c) Only single-celled organisms are based on cells.
   d) All organisms are based on tissues as the basic unit of life.

2. What organelle produces the cell's energy source?
   a) Chloroplast.
   b) Nucleus.
   c) Mitochondrion.
   d) Endoplasmic reticulum.

3. The formation of tissue depends upon:
   a) Cell differentiation.
   b) Cell membranes.
   c) Cell death.
   d) Cell organelles.

4. Cardiac muscle is an example of what tissue?
   a) Smooth muscle.
   b) Nervous.
   c) Contractile.
   d) Connective.

5. Which organelle has two forms: rough and smooth?
   a) Mitochondrion.
   b) Golgi apparatus.
   c) Nucleus.
   d) Endoplasmic reticulum.

6. Which organelle is important in the production of polysaccharides (carbohydrates)?
   a) Mitochondrion.
   b) Golgi apparatus.
   c) Nucleus
   d) Endoplasmic reticulum.

Test Your Knowledge: Cells, Tissues, and Organs – Answers

1. a)
2. c)
3. a)
4. c)
5. d)
6. b)

HEREDITY

A duck's webbed feet, a tree whose leaves change color in the fall, and humans having backbones are all characteristics inherited from parent organisms. These inheritable characteristics are transmitted through **genes** and **chromosomes**. In sexual reproduction, each parent contributes half of his or her genes to the offspring.

Genes

Genes influence both what we look like on the outside and how we work on the inside. They contain the information that our bodies need to make the proteins in our bodies. Genes are made of DNA: a double helix (spiral) molecule that consists of two long, twisted strands of nucleic acids. Each of these strands are made of sugar and phosphate molecules, and are connected by pairs of chemicals called **nitrogenous bases** (just bases, for short). There are four types of bases:

1. **Adenine (A)**
2. **Thymine (T)**
3. **Guanine (G)**
4. **Cytosine (C)**

These bases link in a very specific way: **A** always pairs with **T**, and **C** always pairs with **G**.

A gene is a piece of DNA that codes for a specific protein. Each gene contains the information necessary to produce a single trait in an organism, and each gene is different from any other. For example, one gene will code for the protein insulin, and another will code for hair. For any trait, we inherit one gene from our father and one from our mother. Human beings have 20,000 to 25,000 genes, yet those genes only account for about 3% of our DNA.

Alternate forms of the same gene are called **alleles**. When the alleles are identical, the individual is **homozygous** for that trait. When the alleles are different, the individual is **heterozygous** for that trait.

For example, a child may have red hair because she inherited two identical red color genes from each parent; that would make her homozygous for red hair. However, a second child may have brown hair because he inherited different hair color genes from each parent; this would make him heterozygous for brown hair. When genes exist in a heterozygous pairing, usually one is expressed over the other. The gene which is expressed is **dominant**. The unexpressed gene is called **recessive**.

If you took the DNA from all the cells in your body and lined it up, end to end, it would form a (very thin!) strand 6000 million miles long! DNA molecules, and their important genetic material, are tightly packed around proteins called **histones** to make structures called **chromosomes**. Human beings have 23 pairs of chromosomes in every cell, for 46 chromosomes in total. The sex chromosomes determine whether you are a boy (XY) or a girl (XX). The other chromosomes are called autosomes.

Patterns of Inheritance

Biologists refer to the genetic makeup of an organism as its **genotype**. However, the collection of physical characteristics that result from the action of genes is called an organism's **phenotype.** You can remember this differentiation by looking at the beginning of each word: *geno*type is *gen*etic, and *pheno*type is *phy*sical. Patterns of inheritance can produce surprising results, because the genotype determines the phenotype.

Test Your Knowledge: Heredity

1. On paired chromosomes, two identical alleles are called:
    a) Heterozygous.
    b) Homozygous.
    c) Tetrad.
    d) Binomial.

2. The physical characteristics of an organism are known as its:
    a) Chromosomes.
    b) Genotype.
    c) DNA.
    d) Phenotype.

3. Which of the following is **NOT** a nucleotide found in DNA?
    a) Uracil.
    b) Guanine.
    c) Cytosine.
    d) Thymine.

4. The genotype describes an organism's:
    a) Appearance.
    b) Genetic code.
    c) Type of DNA.
    d) Eye color only.

5. The shape of the DNA molecule is a:
    a) Single spiral.
    b) Double spiral.
    c) Straight chain.
    d) Bent chain.

Test Your Knowledge: Heredity – Answers

1. **b)**
2. **d)**
3. **a)**
4. **b)**
5. **b)**

NUCLEIC ACIDS & DNA STRUCTURE

Nucleic acids are long chain, polymeric molecules that are known to be essential to life on Earth. They are responsible for encoding protein sequences which are necessary for life to function. there are two main types of nucleic acid: DNA – deoxyribonucleic acid, and RNA – ribonucleic acid. The primary difference between these two are the structure of their sugar backbone, and the types of nucleotide bases that are present.

DNA – DNA is the primary code of life. It is a double stranded helix. Each strand consists of a sugar backbone of deoxyribose, and associated nucleotide bases. The bases that are seen in DNA are guanine, adenine, thymine, and cytosine. They are represented respectively by the single letter codes G, A, T, and C. The nucleotide bases are complementary to one another. A & T will form a hydrogen bond between one another, and G and C will form a bond. The basic structure of these four compounds is seen below:

| Guanine | Adenine | Thymine | Cytosine |

Guanine and adenine are pyrimidine compounds, which have two rings, and thymine and cytosine are purine compounds, which have just a single ring. These nucleic acids form long sequences which are called genes. Genes are sequences of DNA that can be read by an enzyme and ribosome complex in order to produce proteins.

RNA – RNA is a single stranded nucleic acid strand that can codes for an amino acid sequence. In some species, such as viruses, RNA is the only form of genetic material that exists. In most species, both DNA and RNA are used. The sugar backbone of RNA is ribose, which is 5 carbon sugar. The nucleotides that are present in RNA are similar to DNA, with one exception. Instead of thymine, the RNA structure contains uracil, seen below:

RNA can be produced from DNA using the enzyme RNA polymerase, which binds to a DNA strand to produce a complementary copy.

236

Test Your Knowledge: Nucleic Acids & DNA Structure

1. Which of the following is true about DNA?
   a) All living species have DNA
   b) DNA and RNA have the same sugar backbone
   c) DNA is only contained in your sex cells
   d) Humans have more DNA and chromosomes than any other species

2. Which of the following molecules is a pyrimidine?
   a) Uracil
   b) Thymine
   c) Cytosine
   d) Guanine

3. A scientist extracts some DNA from a plant and finds that the nucleic acid composition is as follows: 21% A, 29% G, 29% C, and 21% T. This is:
   a) A strand of RNA
   b) A single stranded DNA fragment
   c) A double stranded DNA fragment
   d) None of the above

4. Given the sequence ATGAACT, what is the correct complementary DNA sequence?
   a) GTACCGT
   b) TACTTGA
   c) TTACCGA
   d) ATGAATC

5. Given the sequence GCCATATG, what is the correct complementary RNA sequence?
   a) CGGUAUAC
   b) CGUTAUTC
   c) AGTCCATC
   d) CGGTATAC

6. What is the backbone of a DNA molecule made of?
   a) Protein
   b) Lipid
   c) Sugar
   d) Phenol

7. In eukaryotes, DNA is typically found in the:
   a) Cytoplasm
   b) Nucleus
   c) Endoplasmic reticulum
   d) Cell membrane

8. In humans, DNA is compressed into larger bodies called:
   a) Chromosomes
   b) Histones
   c) Barr Bodies
   d) None of the above

9. Which of the following statements is *not* true regarding RNA?
   a) RNA is produced from a transcript of DNA
   b) RNA is read by a ribosome to produce proteins
   c) RNA is non-degradable and exists permanently in the cell
   d) RNA uses uracil rather than thymine as a nucleotide

10. In DNA replication, what enzyme is responsible for copying the DNA?
    a) DNA helicase
    b) DNA polymerase
    c) DNA transcriptase
    d) DNA replicase

Test Your Knowledge: Nucleic Acids & DNA Structure—Answers

1. a)
2. d)
3. c)
4. b)
5. a)
6. c)
7. b)
8. a)
9. c)
10. b)

NATURAL SELECTION & EVOLUTION

Natural selection is a biological process in which members of a species are exposed to a set of environmental conditions which causes certain traits to be "selected" for. The best way to explain natural selection is through an story/example:

Let's say there is a population of field mice. They range in size from about 50 grams to 100 grams, and they have a wide range of coat colors, including white, gray, and brown. The environment in which they live is prairie. Typically, prairie land is mostly grasses and shrubs, with few trees. The field mice have several major predators, the most important of which is the prairie falcon, which was recently introduced to the area. Before the introduction of the falcon, the major predator were canines, such as coyotes or wolves, and snakes.

After this initial assessment, a scientist waits for a period of 10-15 years, and then comes back to examine the field mouse population. He finds that the mice now have a weight of between 40-60 grams, with almost no mice larger than 60 grams. The mice are now almost entirely gray or brown. There are no white mice left.

Upon further thought, he comes to the conclusion that this was due to natural selection. The introduction of a new predator, the hawk, has selected against certain traits. Large mice are easier to see (and probably tastier), and have been hunted extensively by the falcon. Likewise, white mice are easier to see against a grassy background, which again lets the hawks catch them. As a result, the genes present in the population have changed. The field mouse population is now mostly gray/brown, and smaller in size. If selection continues over a longer period of time, it is possible that a new species will be formed.

In a nutshell, natural selection is a function of the environment around a species. If the environment changes, different traits will become more valuable, and cause a slow, but eventual shift in the characteristics of a species. This is how species evolve and change.

Test Your Knowledge: Natural Selection & Evolution

1. An mouse changes its habits to forage primarily at night, in order to avoid predators during the day. This is called a:
   a) Selection
   b) Adaptation
   c) Environmental Hazard
   d) Symbiosis

2. Which of the following evidences helped provide the strongest support for evolution?
   a) DNA comparisons between species
   b) Observation of current species
   c) The fossil record
   d) Studies of genetic inheritance

3. Which of the following was a major player in the development of the theory of evolution?
   a) Leuton van Leewenheuk
   b) Isaac Newton
   c) Charles Darwin
   d) Marie Curie

4. A faster, or more rapid rate, of evolution is usually seen in species which:
   a) Mature slowly and are able to reproduce after 20 years of age
   b) Mature quickly and are able to reproduce after 1 week of age
   c) Have a larger number of genes
   d) Have a smaller number of genes

5. According to Charles Darwin, what is the strongest driving force of evolution?
   a) Natural selection
   b) Temperature of environment
   c) Genetic inheritance
   d) None of the above

6. One of the best examples of species diversification that was noted by Darwin on the Galapagos islands was the:
   a) Variety of finches on the island
   b) Ability of the lizards to swim
   c) Variety of tortoises on the island
   d) The presence of many species

7. Which of the following phenomenon could result in the formation of a new species?
    a) Bottleneck event
    b) Genetic drift
    c) Adaptive traits
    d) Symbiosis

8. A cladogram is used to:
    a) Show the relationship between different organisms
    b) Show the relationship between different genes
    c) Depict the interaction in an ecological setting
    d) Depict the interactions between different levels of the food chain

9. Which of the following is not an assumption of the Hardy-Weinberg equilibrium model?
    a) Mating is random
    b) Population size is fixed
    c) Only sexual reproduction occurs
    d) No migration occurs between populations

10. Analysis of a fossil can be used to provide evolutionary evidence of the:
    a) Relative age of a species
    b) Life span of a species
    c) DNA of a species
    d) None of the above

Test Your Knowledge: Natural Selection & Evolution—Answers

1. b)
2. c)
3. c)
4. b)
5. a)
6. a)
7. b)
8. a)
9. b)
10. a)

MITOSIS & MEOSIS

Mitosis and Meiosis are two forms of cell division in life. Mitosis is the process of a single cell splitting to form two new somatic cells. Somatic cells are any cell that is not a reproductive sex cell. Meiosis is a form of cell division in which half the DNA from a sex cell is enclosed into a gamete, such as sperm or an egg in humans. The cell product of Meiosis has half the DNA from before, and the two sex cells can be merged to form an embryo.

Mitosis

In mitosis, there are 5 major phases: Interphase, prophase, metaphase, anaphase, and telophase. These are the 5 phases the cell will go through to produce DNA and then split. The diagram below shows the basic process.

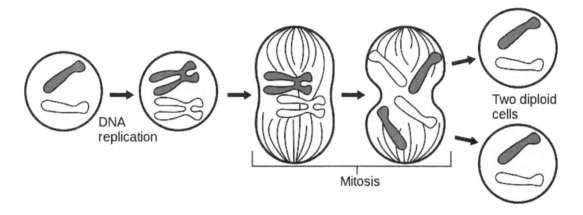

Interphase: In interphase, which is the growth phase, the cell has recently divided and is growing again. During this period of time, new proteins are being made as well as additional organelles. Additional DNA is also made during this phase.

Prophase: In this stage, the cell is preparing to divide. The DNA condenses into chromatin and forms into chromosomes. The centrioles within the cell migrate to opposite ends of the cell.

Metaphase: In metaphase, the centrioles have attached actin filaments to the individual chromosomes, and have started pulling them to opposite ends of the cell. The cell itself begins to elongate and stretch.

Anaphase: In anaphase, the chromosomes cleave, and there are now two sets of diploid chromosomes (represented in the figure as the 4th stage).

Telophase & Cytokinesis: The chromosomes are now on separate ends of the cell, and the cell membrane splits. Two new cells are now formed which are now both in interphase again.

The process of mitosis is important for growth in organisms, and is also how single celled organisms, such as bacteria and yeast, reproduce.

244

Meiosis

Meiosis only occurs in eukaryotes, and is a process necessary to produce sex cells for sexual reproduction. In short, meiosis takes random parts of chromosomes from the diploid (2n) set of chromosomes a parent has, and forms a haploid (1n) sex cell. As seen in the figure below, in the process of meiosis, homologous chromosomes are split into a total of 4 daughter nuclei.

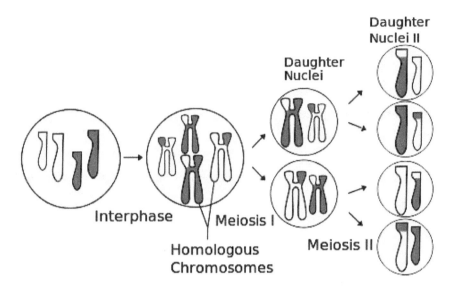

There are two major phases in meiosis: Meiosis I & Meisosi II.

Meiosis I – In the first stage of meiosis, the cell (in humans at least) starts with 23 pairs of chromosomes, or 46 total chromosomes. During Meiosis I, crossing over occurs. Crossing over is a process in which homologous (homologous means "same") chromosomes exchange parts with one another. The crossing over phenomenon is the primary generator of variation in species which use sexual reproduction.

After crossing over occurs, the cell splits into 2 daughter cells, each with a set of 23 chromosomes, but are now haploid. Each chromosome consists of a pair of sister chromatids.

Meiosis II – In Meiosis II, the process is essentially the same as mitosis, with sister chromatids being separated into a total of four cells. Each of these cells will contain one pair of sister chromatids. The sister chromatids in these now gametes will be able to fuse with another pair of sister chromatids from another sex cell to create an embryo.

Test Your Knowledge: Mitosis & Meiosis

1. During which stage of mitosis is DNA created?
   a) Interphase
   b) Metaphase
   c) Telophase
   d) Anaphase

2. The centrioles are responsible for:
   a) Organizing the mitochondria in the cell
   b) Starting cell division
   c) Organizing the mitotic spindle
   d) Pulling apart the nuclear membrane

3. If a human cell undergoes mitosis, how many copies of each chromosome will be present in the each daughter cell?
   a) 1
   b) 2
   c) 3
   d) 4

4. A single cell undergoes mitosis every 20 minutes. How many cells will be present after 2 hours?
   a) 8
   b) 16
   c) 32
   d) 64

5. Which of the following is not true of *both* mitosis and meiosis?
   a) All daughter cells end up as diploid cells in both processes
   b) In both processes, 2 or more daughter cells are produced
   c) Both processes make use of centrioles
   d) Both processes can occur in eukaryotic cells

6. Which phase of the cell cycle requires the most time?
   a) Metaphase
   b) Interphase
   c) Telokinesis
   d) Longisphase

7. A haploid cell that is used to reproduce in a sexually reproductive organism is called a:
   a) Blastocoel
   b) Gamete
   c) Zygote
   d) Barr body

8. Which of the following species would not use meiosis as a cell process?
   a) Elephant
   b) Oak tree
   c) Salmon
   d) E. coli

9. After two haploid cells a result of meiosis combine, they become a:
   a) Diploid zygote
   b) Haploid gamete
   c) Diploid morula
   d) Haploid blastosphere

10. In meiosis,
   a) The amount of DNA stays the same in all stages
   b) The end product has genes evenly split between mother and father
   c) The process results in 4 cells instead of two
   d) The period of metaphase is shorter than in that of mitosis

Test Your Knowledge: Mitosis and Meiosis—Answers

1. a)
2. c)
3. b)
4. d)
5. a)
6. b)
7. b)
8. d)
9. a)
10. c)

MENDELIAN INHERITANCE & GENETICS

Genetics is broadly defined as the study of genes and gene function in species, and also how genes are passed on from one generation to another. Is a study of how DNA (genes) affect phenotypic traits that we can see, and also how these genes are passed from parent to offspring.

Gregor Mendel was a 19th century monk who did some of the first quantitative experiments on genetics. From his work, the modern study of genetics was founded on the three laws of genetics that were developed.

First Law – The first law is the law of segregation. This law states that all traits are governed by gene alleles, which come in pairs. In sexual reproduction, each parent gives one allele to the offspring.

Second Law – The second law is the law of independent assortment. This law states that genes for separate traits are passed to the offspring independently. For example, the gene for black hair is independent from the gene for height. Having one gene does not guarantee having the other.

Third Law – The third law is the law of dominance. This states that dominant alleles will mask the effect of recessive alleles. For example, black hair is a dominant allele. If one parent has black hair and the other has red hair (which is a recessive allele), and the child receives one black hair and red hair allele, the black haired dominant allele will mask the effect of the red haired allele, resulting in a child which has black hair.

From Mendel's work, a basic tool for examining gene alleles was developed, called the Punnett Square. Below is an example of a Punnett Square.

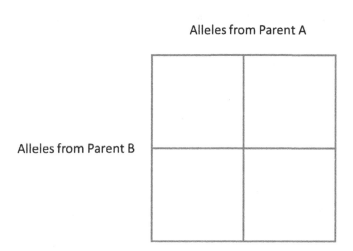

In the Punnett Square, the individual alleles are separated and placed on the X and Y-axis of the box. Then, the alleles are recombined in the box in order to predict the genes of the offspring. An example would be:

A sunflower plant has an allele which determines roundness of the flower. "R" is dominant for roundness, and "r" is recessive. A double recessive gene "rr" will cause the flower to be oval.

Two plants are mated together: One is RR and one is Rr. What is the result? See below:

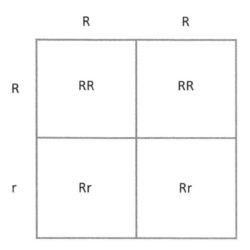

We see that the result is half the offspring have the genotype RR, and the other half have the genotype Rr. Because the R allele is dominant, all of the offspring flowers will be round, and none of them should be oval.

There are some additional terms that are important for the study of genetics. They are:
- Co-dominance: Gene alleles which can both be expressed without one being dominant over the other are termed co-dominant. An example are individuals which have an AB blood type.
- Parent generation: This is the generation which is initially studied.
- F1 generation: The F1 generation represents the 1st filial (child) generation. They are the offspring of the parent generation.
- F2 generation: The F2 generation represents the 2nd filial (child) generation. They are the offspring of the F1 generation.
- Gene pool: The gene pool is the collection of all genes in a species population.
- Homozygous: Homozygous means "same". A homozygous gene is one that has two of the same allele.
- Heterozygous: Heterozygous means "different". A heterozygous gene is one that one of each allele, for example Rr in the problem above.
- Mutation: A mutation is a change in the DNA sequence of the gene. A mutation can be caused by an error in DNA replication, exposure to chemicals, or radiation.

Test Your Knowlege: Mendelian Inheritance & Genetics

1. In roses, R is dominant for red and r is recessive for white. A gardener takes a red rose and crosses it with another red rose. Interestingly, ¼ of the offspring are white. This is because:
    a) Both red roses were homozygous dominant
    b) Both red roses were heterozygous
    c) The red roses had a hidden recessive white gene
    d) None of the above are correct

2. Gregor Mendel made many of his discoveries while working with:
    a) Roses
    b) Onions
    c) Pea plants
    d) Sunflowers

3. If a gene is sex-linked, and the recessive trait is mostly seen in males, but occasionally seen in females, then the trait is passed on through:
    a) The 22nd chromosome
    b) The X chromosome
    c) The Y chromosome
    d) The somatic cell DNA

4. Any given gene of an individual will:
    a) Always influence the phenotype of the individual
    b) Sometimes influence the phenotype of the individual
    c) Always be passed onto their offspring
    d) Never be passed onto their offspring

5. Brown eyes are dominant in humans (B), and blue eyes are recessive (b). A family has 3 children, one of which has blue eyes. Which of the following must be true?
    a) One of the parents must have blue eyes.
    b) Both of the parents must have blue eyes.
    c) One of the parents must be heterozygous Bb.
    d) Both of the parents must be heterozygous Bb.

6. In a gene with one dominant allele and one recessive allele,
    a) We will only see the influence of the dominant allele expressed in the phenotype
    b) We will see the influence of both alleles expressed in the phenotype
    c) We will only see the influence of the recessive allele expressed in the phenotype
    d) During meiosis, the dominant allele will be given to the gamete

7. Hemophilia is an X-linked recessive genetic disease that is commonly seen in males. If a female has hemophilia, then:
    a) All of her female children will have hemophilia
    b) All of her male children will have hemophilia
    c) All of her children will have hemophilia
    d) All of her children will have a 50% chance of having hemophilia

8. The F2 generation of a breed of roses were found to be all red in color. Red is dominant (R), whereas white is recessive (r). This means that:
    a) The parent generation was homozygous recessive
    b) The F1 generation was heterozygous
    c) The F1 generation was half homozygous dominant and half heterozygous
    d) The parent generation was homozygous dominant

9. A phenotype trait is a result of:
    a) Expression of a gene
    b) Expression of a gene and the environment
    c) The environment only
    d) The products of DNA replication

10. The passing on, or transmission of genes, from one generation to the next is known as:
    a) Filia
    b) Heredity
    c) Hybridization
    d) Geneticism

Test Your Knowledge: Mendelian Inheritance & Genetics—Answers

1. b)
2. c)
3. b)
4. b)
5. c)
6. a)
7. b)
8. d)
9. b)
10. b)

DNA TRANSCRIPTION & TRANSLATION

DNA transcription and translation is the process through which the DNA code is "read" and forms a product protein. The protein then functions for a variety of different operations, including catalyzing reactions, acting as a channel in the cell membrane, or breaking down substances that are no longer useful in the cell. The transcription and translation pathway follows the basic steps seen in the figure below:

DNA → RNA → Ribosome + Nucleotides → Protein

Step 1: DNA transcription: In the first step, called DNA transcription, a strand of DNA is copied by RNA polymerase into a strand of messenger RNA (mRNA). First, RNA polymerase, along with some promoter proteins, binds to DNA, unwinding it slightly. Then, RNA makes a copy of the DNA sequence using nucleotides, forming a strand of messenger RNA. The RNA is produced from the 3' end to the 5' end.

After the mRNA strand has been produced, the intron regions need to be removed. The intron regions are non-coding portions of DNA that don't "mean" anything. The introns are removed by a complex called the spliceosome, and the remaining exons (the coding regions), are spliced back together to get the final mRNA product.

Step 2: RNA translation: In the 2nd major step, the mRNA strand is carried to a ribosome. The majority of ribosomes are located on the endoplasmic reticulum in eukaryotic cells, although some ribosomes are free floating in the cytoplasm as well. The ribosome is a large complex of enzymes whose purpose is to read the mRNA and assemble a string of amino acids, which will later be folded into a protein.

The mRNA strand is read in sets of 3. Each set of 3 nucleotides, called a codon, in the mRNA strand represents an amino acid. A codon table and the represented amino acid is seen in the table below:

1st base	2nd base								3rd base
	U		C		A		G		
U	UUU	(Phe/F) Phenylalanine	UCU	(Ser/S) Serine	UAU	(Tyr/Y) Tyrosine	UGU	(Cys/C) Cysteine	U
	UUC		UCC		UAC		UGC		C
	UUA	(Leu/L) Leucine	UCA		UAA	Stop (Ochre)	UGA	Stop (Opal)	A
	UUG		UCG		UAG	Stop (Amber)	UGG	(Trp/W) Tryptophan	G
C	CUU	(Leu/L) Leucine	CCU	(Pro/P) Proline	CAU	(His/H) Histidine	CGU	(Arg/R) Arginine	U
	CUC		CCC		CAC		CGC		C
	CUA		CCA		CAA	(Gln/Q) Glutamine	CGA		A
	CUG		CCG		CAG		CGG		G
A	AUU	(Ile/I) Isoleucine	ACU	(Thr/T) Threonine	AAU	(Asn/N) Asparagine	AGU	(Ser/S) Serine	U
	AUC		ACC		AAC		AGC		C
	AUA		ACA		AAA	(Lys/K) Lysine	AGA	(Arg/R) Arginine	A
	AUG[A]	(Met/M) Methionine	ACG		AAG		AGG		G
G	GUU	(Val/V) Valine	GCU	(Ala/A) Alanine	GAU	(Asp/D) Aspartic acid	GGU	(Gly/G) Glycine	U
	GUC		GCC		GAC		GGC		C
	GUA		GCA		GAA	(Glu/E) Glutamic acid	GGA		A
	GUG		GCG		GAG		GGG		G

Note that each amino acid is represented by three or more different codons. As a result, even if there is a small mutation in the DNA strand, often there will be no result, because it may end up coding for the same amino acid anyway.

The mRNA is thus read by the ribosome, which receives amino acids carried by t-RNA molecules (transport-RNA). The amino acids are formed into a long polypeptide chain, which after completion, will be folded into a protein.

Step 3: Protein Folding: In the final step, the completed amino acid chain is folded into its correct 3D structure. A protein has 4 types of structure:

- Primary: The primary structure of a protein is the amino acid sequence.
- Secondary: The secondary structure of a protein are the substructures that are formed when protein folding begins. Certain sequences of amino acids are able to form into structures that resemble a sheet, called a beta-sheet, or a helix, called an alpha helix.
- Tertiary: The majority of proteins have a 3D structure called a tertiary structure. This structure is formed from the interaction of all the secondary structures in a protein. Some proteins may be globular, or round in nature, whereas others might be cylindrical or flat.
- Quaternary: Some proteins, but not all, have a quaternary structure. A quaternary structure is one that is an interaction between multiple proteins. For example, the hemoglobin protein, which carries oxygen in blood, will interact as a set of 4 hemoglobin proteins surround iron heme groups.

The proteins which are produced from the DNA transcription and translation process are then exported from the endoplasmic reticulum or freely released into the cytosol, where they can perform their work.

Test Your Knowledge: DNA Transcription & Translation

1. Which of the following enzymes is responsible for making a copy of DNA to RNA?
    a) RNA polymerase
    b) DNA polymerase
    c) RNA ligase
    d) DNA helicase

2. If mRNA produced by transcription is used immediately, with no further processing, which of the following would occur?
    a) The protein coded by the mRNA would be functional
    b) The protein coded by the mRNA will not be exported from the cell
    c) The protein coded by the mRNA will not be functional
    d) No polypeptide chain will be produced

3. During transcription, the mRNA is written in which direction?
    a) 5' → 3'
    b) 3' → 5'
    c) 2' → 7'
    d) 7' → 2'

4. When a ribosome reads an mRNA strand, how many base pairs are read at a time?
    a) 1
    b) 2
    c) 3
    d) 4

5. If a single mutation occurs in the third base pair of the codon for histidine, what is the percent chance that the amino acid will be changed?
    a) 0%
    b) 25%
    c) 50%
    d) 66%

6. Which of the following species is not important in DNA transcription and translation?
    a) mRNA
    b) tRNA
    c) Ribosome
    d) All of the above are important

7. A researcher is trying to create some protein, and is trying to get a ribosome to read the DNA he has prepared. This will not work, because:
    a) Ribosomes can only read DNA if tRNA is present.
    b) Ribosomes can only read RNA, not DNA.
    c) The DNA is double stranded and not single stranded, which is required for a ribosome to use.
    d) This should work, and nothing is wrong.

8. The RNA strand AUGCACAGG codes for which sequence of amino acids?
    a) M-H-V
    b) V-H-R
    c) M-H-R
    d) R-A-V

9. An exon coding for a protein was found to be 63 base pairs in length. This protein would contain:
    a) 12 amino acids
    b) 21 amino acids
    c) 27 amino acids
    d) 60 amino acids

10. Which of the following is a difference between eukaryotic and prokaryotic DNA transcription?
    a) DNA transcription only occurs in eukaryotic cells.
    b) In prokaryotic cells, the mRNA is read by a complex called a spliceosome, not a ribosome.
    c) In eukaryotic cells, DNA is transcribed by DNA polymerase, not RNA polymerase.
    d) None of the above is a difference.

Test Your Knowledge: DNA Transcription & Translation—Answers

1. a)
2. c)
3. b)
4. c)
5. d)
6. d)
7. b)
8. c)
9. b)
10. d)

Practice Test #1

Mathematics

1. $(4^3 + 2 - 1) =$ _____

2. $(7^2 - 2^3 - 6) =$ _____

3. The sales price of a car is \$12,590, which is 20% off the original price. What is the original price?
    a) \$14,310.40.
    b) \$14,990.90.
    c) \$15,290.70.
    d) \$15,737.50.
    e) \$16,935.80.

4. Which of the following is not a rational number?
    a) -4.
    b) 1/5.
    c) 0.8333333...
    d) 0.45.
    e) $\sqrt{2}$.

5. What is 1230.932567 rounded to the nearest hundredths place?
    a) 1200.
    b) 1230.9326.
    c) 1230.93.
    d) 1230.
    e) 1230.933.

6. What is the absolute value of –9?
    a) –9.
    b) 9.
    c) 0.
    d) –1.
    e) 1.

7. Add 0.98 + 45.102 + 32.3333 + 31 + 0.00009.
  a) 368.573.
  b) 210.536299.
  c) 109.41539.
  d) 99.9975.
  e) 80.8769543.

8. (9 ÷ 3) * (8 ÷ 4) equals:
  a) 1.
  b) 6.
  c) 72.
  d) 576.
  e) 752.

9. 7.95 ÷ 1.5 equals:
  a) 2.4.
  b) 5.3.
  c) 6.2.
  d) 7.3.
  e) 7.5.

10. What is the volume of a cube whose width is 5 inches?

  a) 15 cubic inches.
  b) 25 cubic inches.
  c) 64 cubic inches.
  d) 100 cubic inches.
  e) 125 cubic inches.

11. If a discount of 25% off the retail price of a desk saves Mark $45, what was desk's original price?
  a) $135.
  b) $160.
  c) $180.
  d) $210.
  e) $215.

12. **What number is 5% of 2000?**
    a) 50.
    b) 100.
    c) 150.
    d) 200.
    e) 250.

13. **You need to purchase a textbook for nursing school. The book costs $80.00, and the sales tax is 8.25%. You have $100. How much change will you receive back?**
    a) $5.20.
    b) $7.35.
    c) $13.40.
    d) $19.95.
    e) $21.25.

14. **Jim's belt broke, and his pants are falling down. He has 5 pieces of string. He needs to choose the piece that will be able to go around his 36-inch waist. The piece must be at least 4 inches longer than his waist so that he can tie a knot in it, but it cannot be more that 6 inches longer so that the ends will not show from under his shirt. Which of the following pieces of string will work the best?**
    a) 3 feet.
    b) 3 ¾ feet.
    c) 3 5/8 feet.
    d) 3 1/3 feet.
    e) 2 ½ feet.

15. **What will it cost to carpet a room with indoor/outdoor carpet if the room is 10 feet wide and 12 feet long? The carpet costs $12.51 per square yard.**
    a) $166.80.
    b) $175.90.
    c) $184.30.
    d) $189.90.
    e) $192.20.

16. **You have orders to give a patient 20 mg of a certain medication. The medication is stored as 4 mg per 5-mL dose. How many milliliters will need to be given?**
    a) 15 mL.
    b) 20 mL.
    c) 25 mL.
    d) 30 mL.
    e) 35 mL.

17. Sarah needs to make a cake and some cookies. The cake requires 3/8 cup of sugar, and the cookies require 3/5 cup of sugar. Sarah has 15/16 cups of sugar. Does she have enough sugar, or how much more does she need?
   a) She has enough sugar.
   b) She needs 1/8 of a cup of sugar.
   c) She needs 3/80 of a cup of sugar.
   d) She needs 4/19 of a cup of sugar.
   e) She needs 1/9 of a cup of sugar.

18. If $|3x + 2| = 5$, which of the following options give us the correct values of 'x'?
   a) $(1, -\frac{7}{3})$
   b) $(-1, \frac{7}{3})$
   c) $(3, 7)$
   d) $(\frac{7}{3}, \frac{3}{7})$

19. $\frac{|2k+4|}{8} = 2$ Which of the following values of 'k' satisfies this equation?
   a) $(12, 2)$
   b) $(4, 5)$
   c) $(3, 6)$
   d) $(-10, 6)$

20. If $\frac{2x+7}{9} < 2$, which of the following options is correct?
   a) $3x < \frac{21}{3}$
   b) $x > -3$
   c) $x < \frac{11}{2}$
   d) $2x > 1$

21. What is the result when we multiply these given fractions?
$$\frac{4}{5} * \frac{14}{25} * \frac{125}{7} * \frac{4}{2}$$

22. What is the result when we multiply these given fractions?
$$\frac{2}{9} * \frac{3}{25} * \frac{125}{6} * \frac{3}{10}$$

23. $\frac{1}{5} + \frac{4}{25} =$ _____

24. Alan bought a pizza which had 8 slices. Alan ate 3 slices of pizza in lunch, and left the remaining pizza for Alana. What fraction of pizza did he leave for Alana?

    a) $\frac{3}{8}$

    b) $\frac{1}{2}$

    c) $\frac{4}{5}$

    d) $\frac{5}{8}$

25. $\left(\frac{3}{4} + \frac{1}{5}\right) - \left(\frac{2}{3} + \frac{3}{2}\right) =$ _____

26. What is the result of following expression?

    $\frac{2}{9} + \left(\frac{5}{6} - \frac{1}{2}\right) =$ _____

27. If $3x + 2 > 5$, which of the following options is correct?

    a) $x < 1$

    b) $x > -1$

    c) $x > 1$

    d) $x > 3$

28. Which of the following is the Roman numeral CLVII equal?

    a) 202

    b) 157

    c) 752

    d) 257

    e) None of the above

29. Simply the following expression: $5\frac{1}{3} - 2\frac{1}{3}$

    a) $5\frac{1}{3}$

    b) $5\frac{2}{3}$

    c) 5

    d) 3

    e) $3\frac{2}{3}$

30. Convert the following into a fraction: $5.25 + 1.5$

    a) $5\frac{3}{4}$

    b) $7\frac{3}{4}$

    c) $6\frac{3}{4}$

    d) $7\frac{1}{4}$

    e) None of the Above

31. Convert 0.28 into a fraction.

    a) 9/25

    b) 7/45

    c) 7/25

    d) 8/15

    e) 7/15

32. Convert $\frac{5}{20}$ **into decimal form.**

    a) 0.55

    b) 0.35

    c) 0.15

    d) 0.25

    e) 0.20

Use the below chart to answer questions #33 and #34

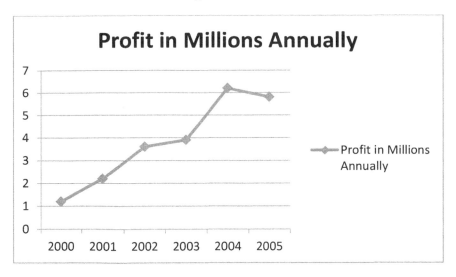

33. Referencing the above line graph, approximately how much did profit increase from 2003 to 2004 in dollars?
   a) 2.3 Million
   b) 6.2 Million
   c) 3.9 Million
   d) 3.2 Million
   e) None of the Above

34. Approximately how much more profit was earned in 2001 than 2000?
   a) 2.2 million
   b) 1 million
   c) 3.5 million
   d) 6.1 million
   e) None of the above

Mathematics – ANSWER KEY

1. Answer: 65

Explanation: We need to remember the order of operations (PEMDAS) to solve this question. First of all, we solve the parenthesis, and then the exponents. In this particular question, 4^3 is within the parenthesis so we solve it first. $4^3 = 64$. Now, the expression becomes (64+2-1). So, we add 2 in 64 first, and then subtract 1 from the answer. This gives us 66-1 = 5.

2. Answer: 35

Explanation: We need to remember the order of operations (PEMDAS) to solve this question. First of all, we solve the parenthesis, and then the exponents. However, in order to solve the parenthesis, we need to know the values of 7^2 and 2^3. Therefore, we find these exponents first and then proceed with PEMDAS. Since $7^2 = 49$ and $2^3 = 8$, the expression becomes (49-8-6) i.e. we simply subtract 6 and 8 from 49 to get our final answer which is equal to 35.

3. Answer: Option (d)

Explanation: The sales price of the car is 20% off the original price (20% discount) which means that the given price of $12590 is 80% of the original price. Let's say that 'x' is the original price of the car, then

(80/100)*x = 12590 (i.e. 80% of 'x' equals $12590)
Solving the above equation, x = 12590*(100/80) ➜ $15,737 Option (d)

4. Answer: Option (e)

Explanation: A rational number is the one which can be written in form of a simple fraction. If we observe closely, only option (e) gives us a number which cannot be written in form of a fraction.

5. Answer: Option (c)

Explanation: We are asked to round off this given number to the nearest hundredth place. Considering the numbers on the right of the decimal, our answer comes out to be 1230.93

6. Answer: Option (b)

Explanation: We know that the absolute value of any negative number gives the positive of that same number i.e. Absolute value of -9 is +9.

7. Answer: Option (c)

Explanation: There are two ways to solve this question. Either you can add all the given numbers and find the exact answer. This method is time consuming and is less efficient.
The second method to solve this question is by adding only the numbers on the left of the decimal and then comparing your answer with the answer choices that you are given. We add 45, 32 and 31 to get 45+32+31 = 108. Now, we can easily interpret that our answer must be very close to 108 when we add the decimal points as well for each given number. In the answer choices, Only option (c) gives us a number which is closest to 108. (Note that this method of

approximation saves time but it is not very accurate if all the answer choices are very close to each other.)

8. Answer: Option (b)
Explanation: This is a very simple question. All you need to know is PEMDAS rule. First of all, we solve what is within the parenthesis, and then we multiply the answers of each parenthesis.
9 divided by 3 equals 3.
8 divided by 4 equals 2.
We multiply 3 and 2 to get our final answer: $3*2 = 6$

9. Answer: Option (b)
Explanation: It is a simple division question. When we divide 7.95 by 1.5, we get 5.3 as answer. In order to re-confirm your answer, you can cross check by multiplying 5.3 by 1.5, and it would give 7.95.

10. Answer: Option (e)
Explanation: We are given with the width of the cube. As we know that all sides of the cube are equal to each other, we say that the length and height of this cube is also 5. So, the volume of this cube becomes;
Volume = Length * Width * Height = $5 * 5 * 5 = 125$

11. Answer: Option (c)
Explanation: From the given information in the question, we know that 25% of the actual price of desk is $45. If we write this in form of an equation, it becomes;
$(25/100) * x = \$45$ (25% of 'x' equals $45)
$x = 45/0.25 \rightarrow \$180$
Therefore, the actual price of the desk equals to $180.

12. Answer: Option (b)
Explanation: In order to find 5% of 2000, we need to multiply 2000 by (5/100) i.e.
$2000*0.05 = 100$

13. Answer: Option (c)
Explanation: This is a tricky question. We are given with the sales tax percentage and the actual amount of the book. First of all, we need to find out the amount we would be charged for this including sales tax, and then we need to subtract it from 100, to find out the change we will receive from them.

8.5% tax on $80 becomes $0.085*80 = \$6.8$
So, the total amount that we will be charged becomes $80+ 6.8 = \$86.8$
Subtracting it from $100 to find the change, we get $100 - 86.8 = \$13.40$

14. Answer: Option (d)
Explanation: From the statement of the question, it is clear that we need string that is at least 40 inches long (i.e. 36 inch waist and 4 inches for knot) but not longer than 42 inches.
Let's examine the length of strings available in answer options.

Option (a) = 3 feet = 36 inches Incorrect
Option (b) = 3(3/4) feet = 45 inches Incorrect
Option (c) = 3(5/8) feet = 43.5 inches Incorrect
Option (d) = 3 (1/3) feet = 40 inches **Correct**
Option (e) = 2(1/2) feet = 30 inches Incorrect

15. **Answer: Option (a)**

Explanation: It is important to note that the rate of the carpet is given is per sq. yard and the dimensions of the room are given in feet. So, we need to convert the width and length of the room in yards, and then calculate the total area of the room. We know that 1 foot = 0.33 yards
10 feet = 3.33 yards
12 feet = 4 yards
Area of the room = 4*3.33 = 13.32 sq yards
So, the total cost to carpet this room equals 13.32 * 12.51 → $166.6

16. **Answer: Option (c)**

Explanation: There are 4mg of medication in 5 mL dose. We need to give 20 mg to the patient and $\frac{20}{4}$ = 5 so we multiply the dose by 5 to give our desired amount of medication to the patient. Therefore, 5* 5mL = 25 mL

17. **Answer: Option (c)**

Explanation: Cake requires $\frac{3}{8}$ = 0.375 cup of sugar, whereas, cookies require $\frac{3}{5}$ = 0.6 cup of sugar. This makes a total of 0.375+0.6 = 0.975 cup of sugar.
Sarah has got $\frac{15}{16}$ = 0.9375 cup of sugar.
Therefore, it is clear that Sarah needs more sugar than she already has got. The exact amount of sugar required can be calculated by subtracting total sugar from required sugar.
i.e. 0.975-0.9375 = 0.0375
Therefore, Option (c) is correct. [$\frac{3}{80}$ = 0.0375]

18. **Answer: Option (a)**

Explanation: We re-write the given equation as:

$|3x+2| = 5$

$+ (3x+2) = 5$ or $-(3x+2)= 5$

$3x= 5-2$ or $-3x-2=5$

$x = 1$ or $x= -\frac{7}{3}$

Therefore, $(1, -\frac{7}{3})$.

19. **Answer: Option (d)**

Explanation: The given equation can be re-written as:

273

$\frac{|2k+4|}{8} = 2$ ➜ |2k+4| = 16

$+(2k + 4) = 16$ ➜ 2k = 12 ➜ k= 6

$Or, -(2k + 4) = 16$ ➜ -2k-4 = 16 ➜ -2k = 20 ➜k = -10

$Therefore, k = -10, 6$

20. Answer: Option (c)

Explanation: Considering the given inequality;

$\frac{2x+7}{9} < 2$

Multiplying by '9' on both sides, we get;

2x+7 < 18

Subtracting 7 on both sides, we get;

2x < 18-7

2x < 11

Dividing by '2' on both sides, we get;

$x < \frac{11}{2}$

21. Answer: 16

Explanation: This question looks like a lengthy multiplication question but actually its not. We know that 25*5 = 125. Similarly, 7*2 = 14. This means that the denominators of all the fractions are cancelled out by numerators of second and third fraction, and we are left with only 4*4 = 16.

22. Answer: $\frac{5}{30}$ or $\frac{1}{6}$

Explanation: A simple trick in solving these complex fraction-multiplication questions is to look for the numbers which can cancel each other. For example, in this given question, we see that 3*3 = 9 which cancels the 9 of denominator. Similarly, $\frac{125}{25} = \frac{5}{1} = 5$.

The net result of this multiplication after cancellation of numerators and denominators becomes;

$\frac{2}{6} * 5 * \frac{1}{10} = \frac{1}{6}$ or $\frac{5}{30}$

23. Answer: $\frac{9}{25}$

Explanation: Adding the given fractions, we get;

$\frac{1(5)+4}{25}$ ➜ $\frac{5+4}{25}$ ➜ $\frac{9}{25}$

24. Answer: Option (d)

Explanation: As we know that there were a total of 8 slices of pizza, this means that each slice was $\frac{1}{8}th$ of the total pizza. Alan ate 3 slices i.e. $\frac{1}{8}+\frac{1}{8}+\frac{1}{8}=\frac{3}{8}$.

Remaining pizza = $1-\frac{3}{8}$ ➔ $\frac{8-3}{8}$ ➔ $\frac{5}{8}$

25. **Answer:** $\frac{-73}{60}$

   Explanation: Finding the sum of the expressions in parenthesis first, we get;

   $(\frac{3}{4}+\frac{1}{5})$ ➔ $\frac{15+4}{20}=\frac{19}{20}$

   $(\frac{2}{3}+\frac{3}{2})$ ➔ $\frac{4+9}{6}$ ➔ $\frac{13}{6}$

   Now, $\frac{19}{20}-\frac{13}{6}=\frac{19(6)-13(20)}{120}$ ➔ $\frac{-146}{120}$ ➔ $\frac{73}{60}$

26. **Answer:** $\frac{5}{9}$

   Explanation: Finding the difference of fractions given in the parenthesis first, we get;

   $\frac{5}{6}-\frac{1}{2}=\frac{5-(3)}{6}=\frac{2}{6}=\frac{1}{3}$

   Now, $\frac{2}{9}+\frac{1}{3}$ ➔ $\frac{2+3}{9}$ ➔ $\frac{5}{9}$

27. **Answer: Option (c)**

   Explanation: Considering the given inequality;

   $3x > 5-2$

   $3x > 3$

   $x > 1$

28. **Answer: Option (b)**

   Explanation: 157 (correct: C = 100, L = 50, V = 5, I = 1)

29. **Answer: Option (d)**

   Explanation: Simply the following expression: $5\frac{1}{3}-2\frac{1}{3}$

   $5.33 - 2.33 = 3$

30. **Answer: Option (c)**

   Explanation: Answer is $6\frac{3}{4}$

   5 ¼ + 1 ½ = 6 + ¼ + 2/4 = 6 ¾

31. Answer: Option (c)
Explanation: 0.28 = 28/100.

The lowest common denominator is 4.

28/4 = 7

100/4=25

= 7/25

32. Answer: Option d)
Explanation:

$$
\begin{array}{r}
.25 \quad R \ 0 \\
20\overline{)5.0} \\
-40 \\
\hline
100 \\
-100 \\
\hline
0
\end{array}
$$

33. Answer: Option (a)
The question is straight forward, but the exact dollar amounts are a little more difficult to interpret. Since the question asks for "approximately" how much, we know we have a little wiggle room and the answer choices will not be very similar, so if we see one that is possibly right, we know we have our answer. In 2003, the profit was just a little bit under the 4MM line, so we know it is about 3.8 or 3.9. In 2004, the profit jumps to just over the 6MM line, so we know it is probably about 6.1 or 6.2. In either case, 6.1 – 3.8 = 2.3 as does 6.2 – 3.9 = 2.3 so we know answer choice (a) is correct. Even if you arrived at an estimate of 6.2 – 3.8 = 2.4, that is certainly "approximate" for this exam.

34. Answer: Option b)
Explanation: The question asks for the difference in profit between 2001 and 2000. In 2001 approximately 2.2 Million was earned and in 2000, approximately 1.2 Million was earned. 2.2 – 1.2 = 1Million

Science

1. Blood is prevented from changing direction in the veins by:
   a. Pressure from the heart
   b. Valves
   c. Suction from the heart
   d. None of the above

2. The liquid part of the blood is called:
   a. Plasma
   b. Blood fluid
   c. Serous fluid
   d. None of the above

3. Which of the following is a true statement about the periodic table?
   a. The size of elements increases from right to left
   b. The electron shell size increases from top to bottom
   c. The electronegativity increases from top to bottom
   d. The radioactivity of elements decreases from left to right

4. Blood cells that are responsible for transportation of oxygen are called:
   a. Leukocytes
   b. Thrombocytes
   c. Erythrocytes
   d. None of the above

5. What is the thyroid cartilage commonly known as?
   a. Vocal box
   b. Adams apple
   c. Vocal cords
   d. None of the Above

6. When breathing out, the diaphragm:
    a. Relaxes
    b. Contracts
    c. Does nothing
    d. None of the Above

7. A double bond between two atoms, for example the double bond between oxygen in O_2, has how many electrons?
    a. 2
    b. 4
    c. 6
    d. 8

8. Which bone forms the rib cage of the thoracic region with the ribs?
    a. Sternum
    b. Fibula
    c. Occipital bone
    d. None of the Above

9. A 50 liter volume of water vapor is condensed into liquid. Approximately how much volume will the liquid be?
    a. Less than 50 mL
    b. Between 50 mL and 200 mL
    c. About 1 liter
    d. More than 1 liter

10. The humerus and ulna form the:
    a. Shoulder joint
    b. Elbow joint
    c. Writs joint
    d. None of the Above

11. Patella is also called:
    a. Breastbone
    b. Kneecap
    c. Finger bone
    d. None of the Above

12. The bone that is stationary during the movement is called the:
    a. Insertion
    b. Agonist
    c. Origin
    d. None of the Above

13. Which of the following is the process that produces a liquid from a gas?
    a. Vaporization
    b. Condensation
    c. Sublimation
    d. Denitrification

14. How many origins does a quadriceps have?
    a. 4
    b. 5
    c. 3
    d. None of the Above

15. Which part of the brain is responsible for higher brain functions?
    a. The pons
    b. The cerebral cortex
    c. The cerebellar cortex
    d. None of the Above

16. How many thoracic spinal nerves are there in the human body?
    a. 8
    b. 9
    c. 12
    d. None of the Above

17. Which of the following is **not** a specialized sense?
    a. Touch
    b. Balance
    c. Sight
    d. None of the Above

18. In which region of the small intestine are most of the nutrients absorbed?
    a. The jejunum
    b. The ileum
    c. The duodenum
    d. None of the Above

19. Which type of nutrients is broken down by trypsin?
    a. Proteins
    b. Fats
    c. Sugars
    d. None of the Above

20. Chemical bonding:
    a. Uses electrons that are closest to the nucleus of the atoms bonding.
    b. Always uses electrons from only one of the atoms involved.
    c. Uses all the electrons in all atoms involved.
    d. Uses the valence electrons of all the atoms involved.

21. Which of the following would have the most dramatic effect in changing the reaction rate?
    a. Increasing the temperature by 2 fold
    b. Increasing the pressure by 2 fold
    c. Decreasing the activation energy by 3 fold
    d. Decreasing the concentration of reactants by 2 fold

22. A student notices that a reaction has a reaction rate of 0. In order for this to be true, which of the following must be true?
    a. The activation energy must be lower than 0.
    b. The temperature is 0 Kelvin.
    c. The Arrhenius constant is 0.
    d. The reactants must be lower than 1 M in concentration.

23. Enzymes are created from amino acid chains. As such, what might prevent the action of an enzyme?
    a. A pH close to 7
    b. A high temperature
    c. The lack of hydrogen ions in solution
    d. A lack of ATP in the cell

24. If a scientist wants to determine the rate at which an enzyme works, what could he or she measure?
    a. The rate at which the enzyme is degraded
    b. The rate at which the product disappears
    c. The rate at which the reactants disappear
    d. The rate at which the products appear

25. In the graph shown below, showing reaction rate of the enzyme over time, what is the rate at 2 hours?

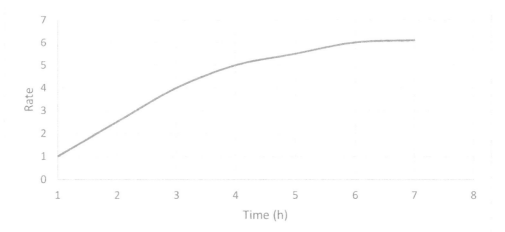

a. 1
b. 2.5
c. 3
d. 4.5

26. What is true of elements found in the same group (column) in the periodic table?
    a. They have the same atomic mass
    b. They have the same level of reactivity
    c. They have the same number of protons
    d. The have the same number of valence electrons

27. Compounds that are acidic will be able to lower the pH of a solution, by doing which of the following?
    a. Accepting H+ ions
    b. Releasing H+ ions
    c. Binding with acidic species in solution
    d. Reducing oxidative species in solution

28. Which of the following elements is the most electronegative?
    a. Chlorine
    b. Iron
    c. Magnesium
    d. Silicon

29. According to Newton's first law, F = M x A, how fast will a 10 kilogram object accelerate when pushed with 50 Newtons of force?
    a. 2.5 m/s^2
    b. 5.0 m/s^2
    c. 8.0 m/s^2
    d. 15.0 m/s^2

30. Upon touching a chair cushion and then a metal plate, John notices that the metal plate feels much colder than the cushion, although the surrounding air temperature is the same. What is an explanation for this?
    a. The chair cushion has a higher heat capacity than the metal plate.
    b. The metal plate has a higher heat transfer rate than the chair cushion.
    c. The metal plate is able to absorb more heat from the air than the cushion.
    d. The chair cushion produces some internal heat.

31. If a pitcher throws a baseball into the air, and notices that it takes 5 seconds to reach its peak, how long will the baseball need to fall back to the ground? Neglect air resistance.
    a. 2.5 seconds
    b. 9.8 seconds
    c. 5.0 seconds
    d. 10.0 seconds

32. Which of the following is true regarding deoxyribonucleic acid (DNA) in the human body?
    a. DNA is used as an energy source.
    b. DNA is used as a template for creation of proteins.
    c. DNA is only found in the brain.
    d. DNA is made of sugar.

33. Testes are an organ found in:
    a. Females
    b. Plants
    c. Males
    d. Amoebas

34. How many kingdoms of life are there?
    a. 3
    b. 6
    c. 7
    d. 9

35. Plants absorb carbon dioxide (CO_2) to create sugar for energy. What is the primary byproduct of this process?
    a. Oxygen
    b. Nitrogen
    c. Carbon Monoxide
    d. Carbon

36. What prevents ultraviolet radiation produced by the sun from damaging life on earth?
    a. The ozone layer
    b. Greenhouse gases
    c. The vacuum between earth and the sun
    d. The water layer

37. Which of the following is *not* present in an animal cell?
    a. Nucleus
    b. Mitochondria
    c. Cytoplasm
    d. Cell Wall

38. Mitosis is the process of cell division to create new cells. What is the process of cell division required to create new sex cells, or gametes?
    a. Telosis
    b. Meiosis
    c. Kinesis
    d. Phoresis

39. What are the two main parts of the human body's central nervous system?
    a. The heart and the spinal cord
    b. The brain and the spinal cord
    c. The peripheral nerves and the brain
    d. The spinal cord and the peripheral nerves

40. Which of the following is not an organ system in humans?
    a. The endocrine system
    b. The respiratory system
    c. The exophatic system
    d. The muscular system

41. Humans can turn glucose into ATP, the basic energy molecule in the body. What is a byproduct of this process?
    a. Carbon dioxide
    b. Oxygen
    c. Nitrogen
    d. Phosphorus

42. Which of the following is not in the Kingdom Plantae?
    a. Cactus
    b. Algae
    c. Oak Tree
    d. Sunflower

43. What is the primary difference between a cell membrane and a cell wall?
    a. A cell membrane is flexible and a cell wall is rigid.
    b. A cell membrane is not found in plants, whereas a cell wall is.
    c. A cell membrane is not found in animals, whereas a cell wall is.
    d. A cell membrane is composed of protein, whereas a cell wall is composed of sugar.

44. What skill is a scientist using he or she observes the way in which different mammals climb trees?
    a. drawing conclusions
    b. interpreting data
    c. making observations
    d. making a hypothesis

45. When conducting an experiment, the factor that is being measured is called what?
    a. independent variable
    b. dependent variable
    c. conclusion
    d. controlled variable

46. Select which of the following question is the best high level scientific question?
    a. Who is credited with inventing the electromagnet?
    b. How many penguins live in Antartica?
    c. Is the boiling or freezing point of water affected by how much salt is in it?
    d. When did dinosaurs become extinct?

47. What is the correct order of the steps in the scientific method.
    a. Ask a question, analyze results, make a hypothesis, test the hypothesis, draw conclusions, communicate results.
    b. Make a hypothesis, test the hypothesis, analyze the results, ask a question, draw conclusions, communicate results.
    c. Ask questions, make a hypothesis, test the hypothesis, analyze results, draw conclusions, communicate results.
    d. Ask a question, make a hypothesis, test hypothesis, draw conclusions, analyze results, communicate results.

48. When determining the mass of an ant, you should use
     a. Meters
     b. Grams
     c. Liters
     d. kilograms

Science – ANSWER KEY

1.	B	25.	B
2.	A	26.	D
3.	B	27.	B
4.	C	28.	A
5.	B	29.	B
6.	A	30.	B
7.	B	31.	C
8.	A	32.	B
9.	A	33.	C
10.	B	34.	B
11.	B	35.	A
12.	C	36.	A
13.	B	37.	D
14.	A	38.	B
15.	B	39.	B
16.	C	40.	C
17.	A	41.	A
18.	A	42.	B
19.	A	43.	A
20.	D	44.	C
21.	C	45.	B
22.	C	46.	C
23.	B	47.	C
24.	D	48.	B

English & Language Arts

1. Which word best completes the sentence? She told them to _____ their room before they left for the party.
    - a. Cleaned
    - b. Tidy
    - c. Clears
    - d. Neat

2. Which pronoun best completes the sentence? They left for the party, but had to return home because _____ forgot her purse.
    - a. He
    - b. They
    - c. We
    - d. She

3. Which is correctly punctuated?
    - a. Lets eat Grandma.
    - b. Let's eat Grandma.
    - c. Let's eat, Grandma.
    - d. Let us eat Grandma.

4. Which has a correct subject-verb agreement?
    - a. We has gone to school.
    - b. We goes to school.
    - c. He went to school.
    - d. He go to school.

5. Which has the best sentence fluency?
    - a. To the Laundromat, take the laundry please.
    - b. Please take the laundry to the Laundromat.
    - c. Take the laundry please to the Laundromat.
    - d. The laundry please take to the Laundromat.

6. Which is a simple sentence?
    - a. He threw the ball.
    - b. He threw the ball to the dog, and the dog ran after it and caught it in his mouth.
    - c. He threw the ball all the way across the field so he scored the winning goal.
    - d. He threw the ball at the game last week, but did not do well.

7. Which underlined word is spelled correctly?
   a. The threat from the storm was <u>immenent,</u> and an evacuation order was issued.
   b. The hurricane made landfall in the wee hours of the morning, but damage was <u>minimal.</u>
   c. The storm shelter was <u>constructd</u> of heavy concrete for safety.
   d. The tornado sirens were <u>desined</u> to be heard for miles.

8. Which best defines irate?
   a. Sad
   b. Happy
   c. Angry
   d. Frightened

9. Which conjunction best completes the sentence? I had worked a very long shift, _____ still had to run errands after work.
   a. And
   b. Or
   c. But
   d. So

10. Which is the correct part of speech of the underlined word? He ran <u>quickly,</u> training hard for the race that weekend.
    a. Verb
    b. Adjective
    c. Noun
    d. Adverb

11. Which has a correct subject-verb agreement?
    a. The dogs ran from one end of the fence to the other, barking loudly.
    b. The dogs was running from one end of the fence to the other, barking loudly.
    c. The dogs barks loudly, runs from one end of the fence to the other.
    d. The dog runs from one end of the fence to the other and bark loudly.

12. Which is correctly capitalized?
    a. We went to Paris, Rome, and London on our vacation in june.
    b. We went to paris, rome and London on our vacation in June.
    c. We went to Paris, Rome and London on our Vacation in June.
    d. We went to Paris, Rome and London on our vacation in June.

13. Which best defines conscientious?
    a. Thoughtful
    b. Considerate
    c. Careful
    d. Cruel

14. Which is a simple sentence?
    a. I forgot my homework.
    b. I forgot my homework because I was late for school
    c. Because I was sick yesterday, I forgot my homework.
    d. I forgot my homework, leaving it on the table at home.

15. Which uses a third-person point of view?
    a. You need to check on the patient in room 302.
    b. Check on the patient in room 302.
    c. He checked on the patient in room 302.
    d. I will check on the patient in room 302.

16. Which is correctly punctuated?
    a. Which school will you be attending in the fall, Harvard or Yale?
    b. Which school will you be attending in the fall, Harvard or Yale.
    c. Which school will you be attending in the fall Harvard or Yale?
    d. Which school will you be attending in the fall; Harvard or Yale?

17. Which is correctly punctuated?
    a. You need to call the lab, check the test results and contact the patient's doctors.
    b. You need to call the lab check the test results, and contact the patients doctors.
    c. You need to: call the lab, check the test results and contact the patient's doctors.
    d. You need to call the lab, check the test results and contact the patients doctors.

18. Which word best completes the sentence? The patient came to the office complaining of _____ distress.
    a. Respiration
    b. Respiratory
    c. Perspiratory
    d. Perspiration

19. Which word best completes the sentence? Chest pain can be a sign of _____ troubles.
    a. Cardiac
    b. Orthopedic
    c. Urinary
    d. Muscular

20. Which ending would make the sentence a simple sentence? He waited…
    a. He waited for the bus.
    b. He waited for the bus, but it was running late.
    c. He waited for the bus, so he could get to work on time.
    d. He waited for the bus because he had an appointment.

21. Which is the correct spelling of the underlined word?
    a. The heart rate <u>veries</u> for a number of reasons.
    b. The heart rate <u>varies</u> for a number of reasons.
    c. The heart rate <u>varries</u> for a number of reasons.
    d. The heart rate <u>varys</u> for a number of reasons.

22. Which is correctly capitalized?
    a. Mr. Smith is a patient in the University Hospital.
    b. Mr. Smith is a Patient in the University Hospital.
    c. Mr. Smith is a patient in the university Hospital.
    d. Mr. Smith is a patient in the University hospital.

23. Which punctuation mark correctly completes the sentence?
    a. We went to the store, where we shopped for groceries!
    b. We went to the store, where we shopped for groceries.
    c. We went to the store, where we shopped for groceries?
    d. We went to the store, where we shopped for groceries,

24. Which word best completes the sentence? Take the patient's _____ before the doctor comes into the office.
    a. Symptoms
    b. Insurance
    c. Vitals
    d. Temperatures

25. Which is correctly punctuated?
    a. He returned the books, to the library, using the drop slot by the front door.
    b. He returned the books to the library; using the drop slot by the front door.
    c. He returned the books to the library using the drop slot by the front door.
    d. He returned the books to the library. Using the drop slot by the front door.

26. Which point of view is used in the passage? I did not, when a slave, understand the deep meaning of those rude and apparently incoherent songs. I was myself within the circle; so that I neither saw nor heard as those without might see and hear. They told a tale of woe which was then altogether beyond my feeble comprehension; they were tones loud, long, and deep; they breathed the prayer and complaint of souls boiling over with the bitterest anguish.
    a. First person
    b. Second person
    c. Third person
    d. First person omniscient

27. Which is a simple sentence?
    a. After they finished their homework, they left for the zoo.
    b. They left for the zoo.
    c. They left for the zoo, because they had already finished their homework.
    d. They left for the zoo in order to complete their homework.

28. Which is the correct part of speech of the underlined word? The dress was beautiful, <u>but</u> it was too expensive for her budget.
    a. Adjective
    b. Preposition
    c. Conjunction
    d. Article

29. Which word in the sentence should be capitalized? He went to the doctor on the other side of town on the first of june.
    a. Doctor
    b. Town
    c. June
    d. First

30. Which word best completes the sentence? She hurried up that morning ____ she wouldn't be late for her first day at work.
    a. Because
    b. For
    c. But
    d. So

31. Which part of speech is the underlined word? She threw the ball <u>to the dog</u>.
    a. Subject
    b. Direct object
    c. Verb
    d. Prepositional phrase

32. Which is correctly punctuated?
    a. Today, we will learn proper hand-washing procedures for hospital employees.
    b. Today we well learn proper hand-washing procedures, for hospital employees.
    c. Today: we will learn proper hand-washing procedures for hospital employees.
    d. Today, we will learn proper hand-washing procedures for hospital employees?

33. Which uses a second-person point of view?
    a. You need to take the patient his medication.
    b. I took the patient his medication.
    c. The patient needs his medication.
    d. She already gave him his medication.

34. Which underlined word is spelled correctly?
    a. Take the <u>patience</u> blood pressure.
    b. Take the <u>patients</u> blood pressure.
    c. Take the <u>patent's</u> blood pressure.
    d. Take the <u>patient's</u> blood pressure.

35. Which has a correct subject-verb agreement?
    a. We have taken the patients to their rooms.
    b. We takes the patients to their rooms.
    c. He has took the patients to their rooms.
    d. They has taken the patients to their rooms.

English & Language Arts – ANSWER KEY

1. b.
2. d.
3. c.
4. c.
5. b. The most fluent word order is subject, an implied you, verb, direct object, prepositional phrase.
6. a. The other sentences include dependent or independent clauses.
7. b.
8. c.
9. c.
10. d.
11. a.
12. d.
13. c.
14. a.
15. c.
16. a.
17. a.
18. b.
19. a.
20. a.
21. b.
22. a.
23. b.
24. c.
25. c.
26. a. First person uses I or we.
27. b. Other options have additional dependent or independent clauses.
28. c.
29. c.
30. d.
31. d.
32. a.
33. a.
34. d.
35. a.

Reading

Many persons plead a love of truth as an apology for rough manners, as if truth was never gentle and kind, but always harsh, morose, and forbidding. Surely good manners and a good conscience are no more inconsistent with each other than beauty and innocence, which are strikingly akin, and always look the better for companionship. Roughness and honesty are indeed sometimes found together in the same person, but he is a poor judge of human nature who takes ill-manners to be a guarantee of probity of character. Some persons object to politeness, that its language is unmeaning and false. But this is easily answered. A lie is not locked up in a phrase, but must exist, if at all, in the mind of the speaker. In the ordinary compliments of civilized life, there is no intention to deceive, and consequently no falsehood. Polite language is pleasant to the ear, and soothing to the heart, while rough words are just the reverse; and if not the product of ill temper, are very apt to produce it. The plainest of truths, let it be remembered, can be conveyed in civil speech, while the most malignant lies may find utterance, and often do, in the language of the fish market.

1. What is the first sentence in the passage?
   a. Main idea
   b. Topic
   c. Theme
   d. Supporting detail

2. Which is a logical prediction?
   a. The next paragraph will discuss manners at the fish market.
   b. The next paragraph will discuss ways to speak politely.
   c. The next paragraph will discuss table manners.
   d. The next paragraph will discuss how to respond to an invitation.

3. What is the intent?
   a. Persuade
   b. Inform
   c. Entertain
   d. Express feeling

4. Which is an opinion?
   a. Polite language is pleasant to the ear.
   b. Many persons plead a love of truth.
   c. Roughness and honesty are indeed sometimes found together
   d. Some persons object to politeness

I do not mean to prescribe rules to strong and valiant natures, who will mind their own affairs whether in heaven or hell, and perchance build more magnificently and spend more lavishly than the richest, without ever impoverishing themselves, not knowing how they live—if, indeed, there are any such, as has been dreamed; nor to those who find their encouragement and inspiration in precisely the present condition of things, and cherish it with the fondness and enthusiasm of lovers—and, to some extent, I reckon myself in this number; I do not speak to those who are well employed, in whatever circumstances, and they know whether they are well employed or not;—but mainly to the mass of men who are discontented, and idly complaining of the hardness of their lot or of the times, when they might improve them. There are some who complain most energetically and inconsolably of any, because they are, as they say, doing their duty. I also have in my mind that seemingly wealthy, but most terribly impoverished class of all, who have accumulated dross, but know not how to use it, or get rid of it, and thus have forged their own golden or silver fetters.

5. Which is a topic sentence?
   a. There are some who complain most energetically and inconsolably of any, because they are, as they say, doing their duty.
   b. I do not speak to those who are well employed, in whatever circumstances.
   c. I also have in my mind that seemingly wealthy, but most terribly impoverished class of all, who have accumulated dross, but know not how to use it, or get rid of it, and thus have forged their own golden or silver fetters.
   d. I do not mean to prescribe rules to strong and valiant natures, who will mind their own affairs whether in heaven or hell, and perchance build more magnificently and spend more lavishly than the richest, without ever impoverishing themselves, not knowing how they live—if, indeed, there are any such, as has been dreamed; nor to those who find their encouragement and inspiration in precisely the present condition of things, and cherish it with the fondness and enthusiasm of lovers—and, to some extent, I reckon myself in this number; I do not speak to those who are well employed, in whatever circumstances, and they know whether they are well employed or not;—but mainly to the mass of men who are discontented, and idly complaining of the hardness of their lot or of the times, when they might improve them.

6. What is the third sentence in the passage?
   a. Main idea
   b. Topic
   c. Theme
   d. Supporting detail

7. What can be inferred?
   a. The author believes that money is essential for happiness.
   b. The author wants people to find contentment.
   c. The author dislikes wealth.
   d. The author does not believe happiness is possible.

8. Which is a logical conclusion?
    a. The author is going to offer help finding new, meaningful employment.
    b. The author is going to recommend saving money, rather than spending.
    c. The author is going to suggest a path to contentment.
    d. The author is going to suggest that people give away their money.

9. What is the main purpose?
    a. To explain why wealth causes unhappiness
    b. To explain why wealth causes happiness
    c. To differentiate to whom the author is speaking
    d. To tell the reader the topic of the essay

10. Which type of passage is this?
    a. Narrative
    b. Expository
    c. Technical
    d. Persuasive

11. Which is a summary sentence?
    a. The wealthy spend lavishly.
    b. New money causes unhappiness.
    c. Hard work will bring happiness.
    d. Happiness and contentment is largely a matter of attitude and personality, rather than wealth.

I did not, when a slave, understand the deep meaning of those rude and apparently incoherent songs. I was myself within the circle; so that I neither saw nor heard as those without might see and hear. They told a tale of woe which was then altogether beyond my feeble comprehension; they were tones loud, long, and deep; they breathed the prayer and complaint of souls boiling over with the bitterest anguish. Every tone was a testimony against slavery, and a prayer to God for deliverance from chains. The hearing of those wild notes always depressed my spirit, and filled me with ineffable sadness. I have frequently found myself in tears while hearing them. The mere recurrence to those songs, even now, afflicts me; and while I am writing these lines, an expression of feeling has already found its way down my cheek. To those songs I trace my first glimmering conception of the dehumanizing character of slavery. I can never get rid of that conception. Those songs still follow me, to deepen my hatred of slavery, and quicken my sympathies for my brethren in bonds. If any one wishes to be impressed with the soul-killing effects of slavery, let him go to Colonel Lloyd's plantation, and, on allowance-day, place himself in the deep pine woods, and there let him, in silence, analyze the sounds that shall pass through the chambers of his soul,—and if he is not thus impressed, it will only be because "there is no flesh in his obdurate heart."

12. Which is a logical conclusion?
    a. The narrator was once a slave.
    b. The narrator is still a slave.
    c. This is a work of fiction.
    d. Colonel Lloyd is the narrator.

13. Which type of passage is this?
    a. Narrative
    b. Expository
    c. Technical
    d. Persuasive writing

14. What is the main purpose?
    a. To explain the history of slave music
    b. To convince the reader to abolish slavery
    c. To share a personal story
    d. To explain why Colonel Lloyd was unkind

The following questions will test informational source comprehension.

15. You start with one red marble and two green marbles in a pouch. After following the directions below, how many marbles are in the pouch?
    1) Remove one red marble
    2) Add one green marble
    3) Add one red marble
    4) Add one green marble
    5) Remove one red marble
    6) Remove one green marble
    7) Add three red marbles
    8) Add two green marbles

16. According to the index below, where might the reader find information about truthfulness?

> Ethics, 225-275
>   self-determination, 227-231
>   veracity, 232-235
>   justice, 236-241
>   beneficence, 242-249

17. According to the index above, where might the reader find information about autonomy?

18. If the thermometer below indicated a temperature of -30° C, what would the temperature be in degrees Fahrenheit?

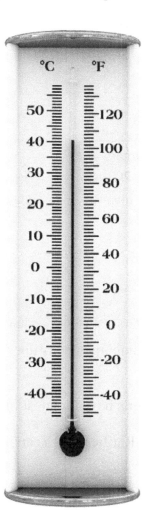

19. If the thermometer above dropped 10° F, what would the temperature be in degrees Centigrade?

20. According to the graph below, which food does Gigi's have the least of?

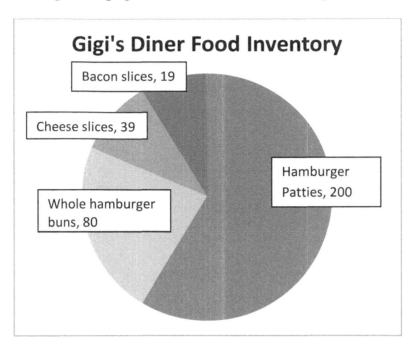

21. According to the graph above, how many more hamburger buns does Gigi's need in order to make 200 hamburgers?

22. According to the graph above, which food does Gigi's have the most of?

23. According to the table of contents below, is The Ratification Years a heading or subheading?

Early American History

Early Settlement
      Plymouth
      Jamestown
The American Revolution
      American Victories
      British Victories
A New Century
      The Constitutional Convention
      The Ratification Years

24. According to the table of contents above, what are the three headings?

25. According to the map below, in relation to Emerald Lake, which direction is Hildred Forest?

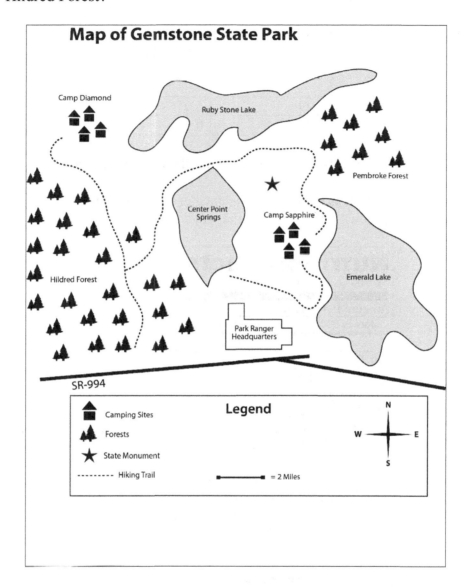

26. According to the map above, how many miles is it from Camp Diamond to Camp Sapphire?

27. According to the map above, which geographical location is directly south of Pembroke Forest?

28. Dennis wants to buy shoes and has $100 to spend, but wants to get the best deal. According to the table below, from which retailer should he buy?

Retailer	Base Price	Shipping & Handling	Taxes
Wholesale Footwear	59.99	10.95	7.68
Bargain Sales	65.99	5.95	5.38
Famous Shoes	79.99	0.00	4.89

29. According to the table above, which retailer has the lowest total price?

30. Sonia is trying to limit her carbohydrate intake. According to the nutrition label below would the product help or hinder that goal?

Nutrition Facts
Serving Size 172 g

Amount Per Serving

Calories 200   Calories from Fat 8

% Daily Value*

Total Fat 1g	1%
Saturated Fat 0g	1%
Trans Fat	
Cholesterol 0mg	0%
Sodium 7mg	0%
Total Carbohydrate 36g	12%
Dietary Fiber 11g	45%
Sugars 6g	
Protein 13g	

Vitamin A   1%   •   Vitamin C   1%
Calcium   4%   •   Iron   24%

*Percent Daily Values are based on a 2,000 calorie diet. Your daily values may be higher or lower depending on your calorie needs.

NutritionData.com

31. Mark is starting a Paleo diet in which he cannot eat carbohydrates. According to the nutrition label above, is this food permitted in the diet?

32. You start with $20 in your wallet. After following the directions below, how much money do you have?
    1) You spend $5 on lunch.
    2) You receive $20 from mowing your neighbor's yard.
    3) You spend $10 on a new shirt.
    4) You receive $10 for driving a friend to work.
    5) You spend $30 on fuel for your vehicle.

33. In the dialogue below, why is the text laid out the way it is?

> Craig: Today is my 40th birthday. *I'm an old man.*
>
> Jennifer: Happy birthday!

34. In the dialogue above, which sentence is thought instead of spoken?

35. If the thermometer below indicated a temperature of -40° C, what would the temperature be in degrees Fahrenheit?

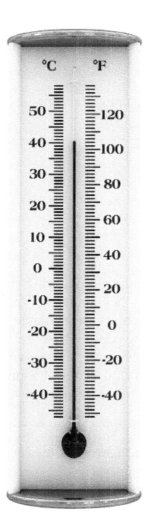

36. If the thermometer above rose 10° C, what would the temperature be in degrees Fahrenheit?

37. An ecological protection group wants to buy XL green t-shirts for their demonstration on campus. According to the table below, which company can accommodate them?

Company	Price	Color	Size
Maximum Tees	15.99/dozen	Red	M
Wholesale Tees	12.99/dozen	Blue	L
Total Tees	19.99/dozen	Green	XL

38. Ed wants to buy t-shirts for his youth hockey team. Some of his players wear M, and some of them wear L. According to the table above, which companies must he buy from?

39. According to the memo below, personal use of computers should be limited to how many minutes per day?

40. According to the memo below, what are employee computers supposed to be used for?

MEMO

To: Human Resources Department
From: Corporate Management
Date: December 6, 2013
Subject: Personal Use of Computers

The corporate office has been conducting standard monitoring of computer usage, and we have been quite dismayed at the amount of personal use occurring during business hours. Employee computers are available for the sole purpose completing company business, nothing else. These rules must be respected. If not, steps will be taken to ensure maximum productivity. Personal use should occur only in emergency situations and should be limited to 30 minutes per day. Please communicate these requirements to lower management and personnel.

41. According to the memo above, would you say the corporate office is pleased or disappointed by the amount of personal use of computers?

42. You have 3 gallons of water. After following the directions below, how much water is left?
   1) You use half a gallon to water your lawn.
   2) You use one gallon to refill your dog's water bowl.
   3) You put half a gallon in an ice tray to make ice cubes.

Reading – ANSWER KEY

1. a.
2. b.
3. a.
4. a.
5. d.
6. d.
7. b.
8. c.
9. c.
10. d.
11. d.
12. a.
13. a.
14. c.
15. After following these directions, you have three red marbles and five green marbles in the pouch.
16. Veracity is truthfulness, so pages 232-235.
17. Autonomy is self-determination, so pages 227-231.
18. -30° C is approximately -20° F.
19. Approximately 30° C.
20. Bacon slices, at 19.
21. 120 since Gigi's already has 80.
22. Hamburger patties, at 200.
23. The subject is Early American History. A New Century is a heading. Since a subheading is a subcategory of a heading, The Ratification Years is classified as a subheading.
24. The subject is Early American History. Since a heading is a subcategory of a subject, the three headings are Early Settlement, The American Revolution, and A New Century.
25. West.
26. About 11 miles.
27. Emerald Lake.
28. When you add the base price, shipping & handling fee, and taxes, Bargain Sales is the least expensive option, with a total cost of $77.32.
29. Bargain Sales. Its total price of $77.32 is lower than Wholesale Footwear's $78.62 and Famous Shoes' $84.88.
30. Since the food contains36 grams of carbohydrates per serving, it would more than likely hinder Sonia's goal.
31. No, since the food contains 36 grams of carbohydrates.
32. After following these directions, you have $5 in your wallet.
33. When writing dialogue, skip lines to indicate a verbal conversation between two or more people.

34. *I'm an old man* is thought, not spoken. Italicized text within dialogue is a text feature that indicates a thought.
35. -40° C is approximately -40° F.
36. Approximately 123° F.
37. Total Tees because they sell XL green shirts.
38. Ed must buy from Maximum Tees and Wholesale Tees because they sell M and L shirts, respectively.
39. 30 minutes per day.
40. Employee computers are supposed to be used for completing company business and nothing else.
41. The tone and context clues suggest that the corporate office is disappointed by the amount of personal use of computers.
42. After following these directions, there is 1 gallon of water left.

Practice Test #2

Mathematics

1. $3 * (2 * 4^3) \div 4 =$ _____

2. $(5 * 3) * 1 + 5 =$ _____

3. $(5^3 + 7) * 2 =$ _____

4. If $y = 3$, then what is $y^3(y^3 - y)$?

      a) 300.
      b) 459.
      c) 648.
      d) 999.
      e) 1099.

5. Round 907.457 to the nearest tens place.

      a) 908.0.
      b) 910.
      c) 907.5.
      d) 900.
      e) 907.46.

6. Subtract the following numbers and round to the nearest tenths place:

    134.679
    − 45.548
    − 67.8807

      a) 21.3.
      b) 21.25.
      c) -58.97.
      d) -59.0.
      e) 1.

7. What is the median of the following list of numbers: 4, 5, 7, 9, 10, and 12?

    a) 6.
    b) 7.5.
    c) 7.8.
    d) 8.
    e) 9.

8. Find $0.12 \div 1$.

    a) 12.
    b) 1.2.
    c) .12.
    d) .012.
    e) .0012.

9. 6 * 0 * 5 equals:

    a) 30.
    b) 11.
    c) 25.
    d) 0.
    e) 27.

10. If a rectangular house has a perimeter of 44 yards, and a length of 36 feet, what is the house's width?

    a) 30 feet.
    b) 18 yards.
    c) 28 feet.
    d) 32 feet.
    e) 36 yards.

11. If the area of a square flowerbed is 16 square feet, then how many feet is the flowerbed's perimeter?

    a) 4.
    b) 12.
    c) 16.
    d) 20.
    e) 24.

12. 35% of what number is 70?

   a) 100.
   b) 110.
   c) 150.
   d) 175.
   e) 200.

13. A car dealer sells an SUV for $39,000, which represents a 25% profit over the cost. What was the actual cost of the SUV to the dealer?

   a) $29,250.
   b) $31,200.
   c) $32,500.
   d) $33,800.
   e) $33,999.

14. Your supervisor instructs you to purchase 240 pens and 6 staplers for the nurse's station. Pens are purchased in sets of 6 for $2.35 per pack. Staplers are sold in sets of 2 for $12.95. How much will purchasing these products cost?

   a) $132.85.
   b) $145.75.
   c) $162.90.
   d) $225.25.
   e) $226.75.

15. During a 5-day festival, the number of visitors tripled each day. If the festival opened on a Thursday with 345 visitors, what was the attendance on that Sunday?

   a) 345.
   b) 1,035.
   c) 1,725.
   d) 3,105.
   e) 9,315.

16. A vitamin's expiration date has passed. It was supposed to contain 500 mg of Calcium, but it has lost 325 mg of Calcium. How many mg of Calcium are left?

    a) 135 mg.
    b) 175 mg.
    c) 185 mg.
    d) 200 mg.
    e) 220 mg.

17. Jim works for $15.50 per hour at a health care facility. He is supposed to get a $0.75 per hour raise after one year of service. What will be his percent increase in hourly pay?

    a) 2.7%.
    b) 3.3%.
    c) 133%.
    d) 4.8%.
    e) 105%.

18. What is the least common multiple of 2, 3, 4, and 5?

    a) 30
    b) 60
    c) 120
    d) 40
    e) 50

19. $2 - 3|4n| = 26$ Which of the following correctly gives us the value of 'n'?

    a) (1, 2)
    b) (-2, 2)
    c) (3, 4)
    d) (-1, -4)

20. $|2r+1|-10 = 13$ which of the following values of 'r' satisfies the given equation?

    a) (12, -2)
    b) (11, −11)
    c) (12, -11)
    d) (-12, 11)

323

21. $\dfrac{3}{4} * \dfrac{4}{5} * \dfrac{5}{3} =$ _____

22. If 3x+33 > -6x+3, which of the following options is correct?

        a) 2x < 10
        b) 3x > -10
        c) x > 11
        d) 4x > 31

23. What is the result of multiplication of $\dfrac{100}{30} * \dfrac{3}{6} * \dfrac{300}{50}$

24. $\dfrac{2}{3} + \dfrac{4}{5} - \dfrac{5}{6} =$ _____

25. $\dfrac{11}{22} + \dfrac{22}{44} + \dfrac{1}{2} =$ _____

26. $\dfrac{13}{4} + \dfrac{5}{8} =$ _____

27. David had 12 chocolates which he decided to distribute among his friends. Alex got $\dfrac{2}{3}$ of the total chocolates. How many chocolates did he get?

        a) 2
        b) 4
        c) 8
        d) 9

28. If 4x-12 < 12, which of the following options is correct?

        a) 2x <12
        b) x >12
        c) x >11
        d) x >21

29. Convert the following to Roman numerals: 240

    a) CCL

    b) DXL

    c) CCXXX

    d) CCXL

    e) None of the above

30. Convert the following into decimal form: $2\frac{1}{2} - 1\frac{1}{4}$

    a) 1.5

    b) 2.25

    c) 1.25

    d) 0.25

    e) 0.75

31. Convert 0.55 into a fraction.

    a) 11/20

    b) 5/9

    c) 5/10

    d) 11/50

    e) 10/20

32. Convert $\frac{7}{20}$ into a decimal form.

    a) 0.45

    b) 0.35

    c) 0.28

    d) 0.65

    e) 0.12

Use the below chart to answer the next two questions:

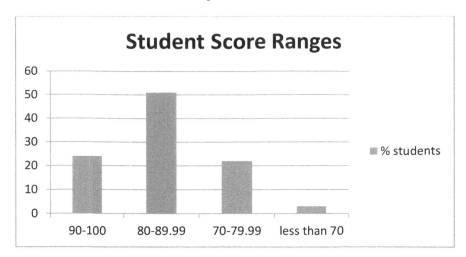

33. Referencing the chart above, if only scores below 85 are considered average, scores above 90 are considered exceptional, and scores below 70.0 are considered failing, what percentage of students pass this exam?
    a) 51%
    b) 22%
    c) 3%
    d) 97%
    e) None of the Above

34. A score of 70 or higher is considered passing. A score of 70 to 79.99 is considered a C. A score of 80-89.99 is considered a B. A score of 90-100 is considered an A. Based on the above chart, which of the following must NOT be true?
    a) Over half the class passed
    b) Less than 30% made an A
    c) The highest occurrence of scores earned by the class was a B
    d) Only 75% of the class passed
    e) None of the above

Mathematics – ANSWER KEY

1. Answer: 96

> **Explanation:** We need to remember the order of operations (PEMDAS) to solve this question. First of all, we solve the parenthesis, and then the exponents. In this particular question, 4^3 is within the parenthesis so we solve it first. $4^3 = 64$. Now, multiplying it with 2 to solve the parenthesis, it becomes 64*2 = 128. So, the expression becomes 3*128÷4. Following PEMDAS, we multiply 128 by 3, and then divide the answer by 4. This gives us 384÷4 = 96

2. Answer: 20

> **Explanation:** This question also involves the order of operations (PEMDAS). To solve this question, we solve the parenthesis first, and then multiply the answer by 1. After that, we add 5 to get our final answer. (5*3) = 15, so the expression becomes 15*1+5 = 15 + 5 = 20

3. Answer: 264

> **Explanation:** First of all, we find the value of 5^3 to solve the parenthesis (remember the order of operations PEMDAS). As we know that $5^3 = 5*5*5 = 125$, the expression becomes (125+7)*2.
>
> We solve the parenthesis first because it is given more preference in PEMDAS, it becomes132*2.
>
> Multiplying these two numbers, we get our final answer which is 264.

4. Answer: Option (c)

> **Explanation:** It's a relatively simple question. The value of 'y' is given as 3. We know that $3^3 = 27$. So, the expression becomes 27 * (27-3) = 27*24 ➜ **648** Option (c)

5. Answer: Option (b)

> **Explanation:** We are asked to round off 907.457 to the nearest tens place. As the units place in 907.457 is '7' which is greater than 5, we make is 910.

6. Answer: Option (a)

> **Explanation:** When we subtract 45.548 and 67.8807 from 134.679, we get 21.2503. Now, applying the rounding off rules, 21.3(Note that we were asked to round off up to the nearest tenth place only).

7. Answer: Option (d)

> **Explanation:** In order to find the median of any given list, first of all, we need to check if the numbers are arranged in an ascending order or not. In this case, these given numbers are already arranged in order. Secondly, we need to check if the total number of entries in the list is even or odd. Since the total number of entries in this list is 6, and 6 is an even number, the median of this list equals the average of two entries which are at the middle of this list. i.e. Median $=\frac{7+9}{2} = 8$.

8. Answer: Option (c)

Explanation: Any number divided by '1' gives the same number as a result. Therefore, 0.12/1 = 0.12

9. Answer: Option (d)

Explanation: Anything multiplied by zero gives zero as answer. We are multiplying 0 by 5 and 6, so the answer is still 0.

10. Answer: Option (a)

Explanation: Please note that it's a tricky question. The perimeter of the rectangular house is given as 44 yards, and the length of the house is given as 36 feet (units are different).
1 yard = 3 feet
44 yards = 132 feet

As we know that the perimeter of the rectangular house equals,
Perimeter = 2*(length) + 2*(width)
132 = 2(36) + 2* width
Width = (132-72)/2 = 30 feet

11. Answer: Option (c)

Explanation: The area of this square flower bed is given as 16. This means that when the length and width of this square flowerbed was multiplied, we got 16. Only 4*4 gives us 16. Therefore, we are left with only one option for the length of the each side of this square i.e. 4.

Now, we know that the length of each side of the square flowerbed is 16, Therefore, the perimeter becomes 4+4+4+4 = 16.
Important thing to note in this question is that the flowerbed is a 'square'. If it were a rectangular flowerbed, it could have a perimeter of 16 or 20.

12. Answer: Option (e)

Explanation: Let's suppose that the unknown number is 'x'. So, 35% of 'x' is equal to 70. Writing this in form of an equation,
(35/100)* x = 70
x = 70/0.35
x= 200

13. Answer: Option (b)

Explanation: First of all, you should know that 25% profit on the actual price means that we have multiplied the original price by 1.25 i.e. (1+ 0.25). So, in order to find the actual price of SUV, we divide it by 1.25. This gives us $39000/1.25 ➔ $31200 which is the original price of the SUV.

14. Answer: Option (a)

Explanation: From the given information in the question, we get to know that the pens are sold in packs of 6 at \$2.35 per pack, and we need to buy $\frac{240}{6}$ = 40 packs. Therefore, the total amount required for 240 pens is 40*2.35 = \$94.

Also, the staplers are sold in sets of 2 at \$12.95 per set, and we need to buy $\frac{6}{2}$ = 3 sets of staplers. Therefore, the total amount for staplers equals 3*12.95 = \$38.85

Total cost = \$94 + \$38.85 ➔\$132.85

15. Answer: Option (e)

Explanation: The number of people on Thursday is 345. Every next day the number of people triples. On Friday, it becomes 3*345 = 1035

On Saturday, the number of people who came to this festival became 3 * 1035 =3105

On Sunday, the number of people who came to this festival became 3 * 3105 = 9315

16. Answer: Option (b)

Explanation: The amount of calcium actually required was 500 mg in that vitamin, but it has lost 325mg of calcium in it. Therefore, it has got 500-325 = 175 mg calcium left in it after expiration.

17. Answer: Option (d)

Explanation: His new hourly salary would become \$15.50+\$0.75 = \$16.25

Percentage change = $\frac{Final\ value\ -\ Original\ Value}{Original\ Value}$*100

$\frac{16.25-15.50}{15.50}$ *100

$\frac{0.75}{15.50}$ * 100 = 4.8%

18. Answer: Option (b)

Find all the prime numbers that multiply to give the numbers.

For 2, prime factor is 2; for 3, prime factor is 3; for 4, prime factors are 2, 2; for 5, prime factor is 5. Note the maximum times of occurrence of each prime and multiply these to find the least common multiple. The LCM is 2 * 2 * 3 * 5 = 60.

19. Answer: Option (b)

Explanation: Re-arranging the given equation, we get:

$-3|4n| = 26 - 2$

$-3|4n| = 24$

$|4n| = -8$

$+4n = -8$ or $-4n = -8$

Therefore, n = -2, or n = +2 (Option B)

20. Answer: Option (d)

Explanation: The given equation can be re-written as:

|2r+1|-10 = 13 ➔ |2r+1| = 23

+(2r+1) = 23 ➔ r= 11

$-(2r+1) = 23$ ➜ $-2r-1 = 23$ ➜ $-2r = 24$ ➜ $r = -12$

Therefore, r = 11, -12

21. Correct Answer: 1

Explanation: If we observe closely, we note that for every number in the numerator, there is an equivalent denominator which cancels the numerator. Therefore the net result of this multiplication comes out to be 1.

22. Answer: Option B

Explanation: Considering the given inequality;

$3x+33 > -6x+3$

Adding 6x on both sides, we get

$3x+33+6x > -6x+6x+3$

$9x +33 > 3$

Subtracting 33 on both sides, we get;

$9x > 3-33$

$9x > -30$

Dividing by '3' on both sides, we get

$3x > -10$

23. Answer: 10

Explanation: As explained in the previous questions, you need to look for the numbers which can be cancelled with each other in numerator and denominator. Observing closely, we see that $\frac{300}{30} = 10$. Also, $\frac{100}{50} = 2$, and $\frac{3}{6} = \frac{1}{2}$.

So, $\frac{1}{2} * 10 * 2 = 10$

24. Answer: $\frac{19}{30}$

Explanation: In this question, we find the sum of the given fractions first, and then subtract $\frac{5}{6}$ from that sum.

$\frac{2}{3} + \frac{4}{5}$ ➜ $\frac{10+12}{15} = \frac{22}{15}$

Now, subtracting $\frac{5}{6}$ from it, we get;

$\frac{22}{15} - \frac{5}{6}$ ➜ $\frac{22(6)-5(15)}{90}$ ➜ $\frac{19}{30}$

25. Answer: $\frac{3}{2}$

Explanation: We know that $\frac{11}{22}$ can be written as $\frac{1}{2}$. Similarly, $\frac{22}{44}$ equals $\frac{1}{2}$. Therefore, the expression becomes,

$$\frac{1}{2} + \frac{1}{2} + \frac{1}{2} \rightarrow \frac{3}{2}$$

26. Answer: $\frac{31}{8}$

Explanation: This is a relatively simple question. Adding the given fractions, we get;

$$\frac{13}{4} + \frac{5}{8} \rightarrow \frac{13(2)+5}{8} \rightarrow \frac{26+5}{8} \rightarrow \frac{31}{8}$$

27. Answer: Option (c)

Explanation: $\frac{2}{3}$ of the actual number of chocolates means that Alex got;

$12 * \frac{2}{3} = 4*2 \rightarrow 8$ Chocolates.

28. Answer: Option (a)

Explanation: Considering the given inequality;

$4x - 12 < 12$

$4x < 12+12$

$4x < 24$

Dividing by '2' on both sides, we get;

$2x < 12$ (Option A)

29. Answer: Option (d)

Explanation: CCXL (correct; C = 100, X = 10, L =50. Since X is before L and X is a smaller value than L, it means that you subtract instead of add. So you could visualize it as $100 + 100 - 10 + 50 = 240$. This avoids having to write XXXX to equal 40.)

30. Answer: Option (c)

Explanation: Answer is 1.25

$2(1/2) = 2.5$

$1(1/4) = 1.25$

$2.5 - 1.25 = 1.25$

31. Answer: Option (a)

Explanation: Answer is 11/20

0.55 equals 55/100. The lowest common denominator or 55/100 is 5.

$55/5 = 11$ & $100/5 = 20.$

32. Answer: Option (b)

   Explanation:

$$.35 \ R \ 0$$
$$20\overline{)7.00}$$
$$\underline{-60}$$
$$100$$
$$\underline{-100}$$
$$0$$

33. Answer: Option (d)

   There is additional information provided in the question that is irrelevant to the answer you need to find. The question wants to know how many people passed the exam, and only scores above 70.0 are considered passing. Approximately 3% scored below 70, so that means 97% passed. 100% - 3% = 97%.

34. Answer: Option (d)

   Explanation: Choice A is true, approximately 96% of the class passed the test. Choice B is true, only about 23% of students made an A. Choice C is true, overwhelmingly a score of B was the most. Choice D is the right answer choice, because only a score of less than 69.99 or lower fails, and only about 4% of the class scored less than 70.

Science

1. When measuring blood pressure, the numbers represent:
   a) The systolic and diastolic pressures, respectively.
   b) The diastolic and systolic pressures, respectively.
   c) The pressure in the arteries and the veins, respectively.
   d) None of the Above

2. The superior vena cava:
   b) Ascends from the right atrium.
   c) Ascends from the left atrium.
   d) Descends from the right atrium.
   e) None of the Above

3. A scientist has isolated Fe (III), a variant of iron that has a charge of 3+. Which of the following compounds could be created from this element?
   a) FeO2
   b) FeCl
   c) FeCa3
   d) Fe2O3

4. What is the VSEPR structure of a PO_4 (phosphate) molecule?
   a) Tetrahedral
   b) Octahedral
   c) Linear
   d) Trigonal Bi-planar

5. Rectum is a part of:
   a) The anus
   b) The large intestine
   c) The small intestine
   d) None of the Above

6. Where does digestion start?
   a) The stomach
   b) The small intestine
   c) The mouth
   d) None of the Above

7. The large intestine:
   a) Absorbs water
   b) Digests food
   c) Moves the food from the esophagus to the small intestine
   d) None of the Above

8. What type of reaction is the following?

$$CaCl_2 + 2NaOH \rightarrow Ca(OH)_2 + 2NaCl$$

   a) Single replacement
   b) Double replacement
   c) Synthesis
   d) Acid Base

9. What are the products of the following reaction?

$$NaOH + HCl \rightarrow ?$$

   a) Dihydrogen monoxide and sodium chloride
   b) Sodium hydride and chlorohydroxide
   c) Hydrochloride and sodium monohydroxide
   d) Sodium chloride and sodium hydroxide

10. In the following chemical reaction, what is the correct stoichiometric coefficient for silicon dioxide?

$$4Si + 2O_2 \rightarrow Si + SiO_2$$

a) 1
b) 2
c) 3
d) 4

11. When you notice that a chemical reaction equation is not balanced stoichiometrically, which of the following can be performed to balance the equation?
a) Change the formula of the products
b) Change the subscripts of the molecular formulas
c) Change the coefficients of the reactants or products
d) Change the reaction type

12. A scientist places mercury oxide (HgO) into a sealed chamber and heats it to 400 °C, causing a reaction to occur. When she opens the chamber, she notices liquid mercury has formed as well as oxygen gas. This reaction is a:
a) Endothermic synthesis reaction
b) Exothermic combustion reaction
c) Endothermic decomposition reaction
d) Exothermic replacement reaction

13. What is the name of the process that happens in the red bone marrow?
a) Hematopoiesis
b) Bone fusing
c) Calcification
d) Nonc of the Above

14. The vertebral column protects the:
   b) Brain
   c) Heart
   d) Spinal column
   e) None of the Above

15. Which unit of measure is NOT used in the International System of Units
   a) Centimeters
   b) Milliliters
   c) Grams
   d) inches

16. A conclusion reached on the basis of evidence and reasoning is a/an
   a) theory
   b) conclusion
   c) inference
   d) hypothesis

17. Plants are autotrophs, meaning that they:
   a) Consume organic material produced by animals
   b) They produce their own food
   c) They are able to move by themselves
   d) They can automatically transform from a seed into a plant.

18. Which of the following is *not* true of a virus?
   a) Viruses have DNA
   b) Viruses do not have a nucleus
   c) Viruses cannot survive without water
   d) Viruses can be infectious

19. In the digestive system, the majority of nutrients are absorbed in the:
    a) Esophagus
    b) Stomach
    c) Small Intestine
    d) Large Intestine

20. How many pairs of human chromosomes exist?
    a) 17
    b) 13
    c) 23
    d) 29

21. Animals engaging in a symbiotic relationship will do which of the following?
    a) Help each other survive
    b) Take one another's food
    c) Attack one another
    d) Eat each other

22. What are the motor units made of?
    a) Motor neurons
    b) Muscle cells
    c) Tendons
    d) None of the Above

23. What is the name of a state of constant muscle contraction caused by rapid successive nerve signals?
    a) Tetanus
    b) Muscle tone
    c) Temporal summation
    d) None of the Above

24. Which of the following can be found in abundance in a fatigues muscle?
    b) Glucose
    c) Lactic acid
    d) ATP
    e) None of the Above

25. Which of the following produces a gas from a solid?
    a) Melting
    b) Plasmification
    c) Condensation
    d) Sublimation

26. A student isolates a substance, and succeeds in purifying it. She then puts it into the lab refrigerator, at 4 °C. When she comes back the next day, she notices that it has solidified! Which of the following statements should be true about the substance?
    a) It has a melting point below 4 °C
    b) It has a boiling point less than that of water
    c) It has a freezing point higher than that of water
    d) It has a vaporization point at around 90 °C

27. The specific heat of ethanol is about 2.3 J/g*K. If you want to heat 100g of ethanol from 25 °C until its boiling point, and have it all be vaporized, how much energy do you need?
    a) 545 kJ
    b) 977 kJ
    c) 129 kJ
    d) 822 kJ

28. In science, an educated guess is called a/an
    a) Observation
    b) Question
    c) Conclusion
    d) hypothesis

29. In an experiment, what do you call the variable that is changed?
   a) controlled variable
   b) dependent variable
   c) independent variable
   d) experimental variable

30. What organ system contains your skin?
   a) The respiratory system
   b) The epithelial system
   c) The lymphatic system
   d) The circulatory system

31. If a gene is expressed, then that means that:
   a) It is influencing a phenotype trait
   b) It is being copied into another set of DNA
   c) It will be passed on from mother to son
   d) The gene will produce some hormones

32. Which of the following structures is found in eukaryotes but not in prokaryotes?
   a) A cell wall
   b) Mitochondria
   c) A nuclear membrane
   d) Vacuoles

33. A mutation in DNA can be caused by all of the following except:
   a) Ultraviolet radiation
   b) Chemical exposure
   c) DNA replication error
   d) Exonic duplication

34. Where does integration happen?
    a) ANS
    b) CNS
    c) PNS
    d) None of the Above

35. Which part of the PNS is responsible for the fight or flight reaction?
    b) The parasympathetic
    c) The sympathetic
    d) The ENS.
    e) None of the Above

36. People who suffer from Type I diabetes are lacking function in which organ?
    a) Liver
    b) Pancreas
    c) Stomach
    d) Heart

37. One of the primary differences between fungi and plants is that:
    a) Fungi can produce their own food and plants cannot.
    b) Plants have chlorophyll and fungi do not.
    c) Fungi are able to grow without water and plants cannot.
    d) Fungi and plants have no major differences.

38. Which of the following organisms is capable of asexual reproduction?
    a) Squash plant
    b) Amoeba
    c) Salmon
    d) Koala bear

39. In our atmosphere, nitrogen is the most common element, and makes up approximately what percentage?
    a) 25%
    b) 51%
    c) 65%
    d) 78%

40. In the human body, which of the following is responsible for clotting blood?
    a) Platelets
    b) White blood cells
    c) Red blood cells
    d) Osteoplasts

41. Which of the following is correct regarding an aqueous substance?
    a) It is soluble in water
    b) It is very reactive
    c) It is soluble in hydrocarbon
    d) It is able to dissolve most other compounds

42. In order for work to be performed, a force has to be:
    a) Applied to an object
    b) Applied to a surface
    c) Applied to a moving object
    d) Applied over a distance to an object.

43. According to electron theory, what is the maximum number of bonds a carbon atom can have?
    a) 2
    b) 3
    c) 4
    d) 5

44. If a rowboat weighs 50 kilograms, how much water needs to be displaced in order for the boat to float?
   a) 25 liters
   b) 50 liters
   c) 100 liters
   d) 500 liters

45. Where are the cilia found?
   a) In the bronchi
   b) In the alveoli
   c) In the upper airways
   d) None of the Above

46. The tidal volume is the amount of air moved during:
   a) Deep breathing
   b) Shallow breathing
   c) Coughing
   d) None of the Above

47. A ball with a mass of 0.5 kg is moving at 10 m/s. How much kinetic energy does it have?
   a) 15 Joules
   b) 25 Joules
   c) 50 Joules
   d) 55.5 Joules

48. The temperature at which all molecular motion stops is:
   a) −460 °C.
   b) −273 K.
   c) 0 K.
   d) 0C.

Science – ANSWER KEY

1. A	25. D
2. A	26. C
3. B	27. C
4. A	28. D
5. B	29. C
6. C	30. B
7. A	31. A
8. B	32. C
9. A	33. D
10. B	34. B
11. C	35. B
12. C	36. B
13. A	37. B
14. C	38. B
15. D	39. D
16. C	40. A
17. B	41. A
18. C	42. D
19. C	43. C
20. C	44. B
21. A	45. A
22. B	46. B
23. A	47. B
24. B	48. C

English & Language Arts

1. Which is correctly punctuated?
   a. They were scheduled to attend the lecture, but were unable to be there due to illness.
   b. They were scheduled to attend the lecture but were unable to be there due to illness.
   c. They were scheduled to attend the lecture but were unable to be there, due to illness.
   d. They were scheduled to attend, the lecture, but were unable to be there, due to illness.

2. Which is a simple sentence?
   a. Take the car to the car wash.
   b. He was going to wash the car, but didn't have time.
   c. You need to wash the car because we are leaving in the morning.
   d. The car is dirty, so it needs to be washed.

3. Which word best completes the sentence? Good _____ is essential to a safe and healthy hospital.
   a. Manners
   b. Etiquette
   c. Grammar
   d. Hygiene

4. Which changes the sentence from passive voice to active voice? The play was watched by John, Mary and Tim.
   a. The play watched John, Mary and Tim.
   b. The play is watching John, Mary and Tim.
   c. John, Mary and Tim watched the play.
   d. The play was viewed by John, Mary and Tim.

5. Which is correctly punctuated?
   a. Take a right at the gas station, then drive two miles to the parking lot.
   b. Take a right at the gas station then drive two miles to the parking lot?
   c. Take a right at the gas station then drive two miles to the parking lot.
   d. Take a right at the gas station; then drive two miles to the parking lot.

6. Which is correctly capitalized?
   a. The patient is ready for his MRI.
   b. The Patient, Mr. smith, is ready for his MRI.
   c. The patient, Mr. Smith, is ready for his mri.
   d. The patient is ready for his mri.

7. Which best defines chronic?
   a. New
   b. Ongoing
   c. Severe
   d. Mild

8. Which word in the sentence should be capitalized? I heard that jane was sick last week and had to go to the doctor.
    a. Sick
    b. Doctor
    c. Jane
    d. Week

9. Which has a correct subject-verb agreement?
    a. Mr. Smith has been experiencing a variety of symptoms.
    b. Mr. Smith were having a variety of symptoms.
    c. Mr. Smith have a variety of symptoms.
    d. Mr. Smith experience a variety of symptoms.

10. Which word best completes the sentence? Nursing school can be difficult and you will need to _____.
    a. Pernicious
    b. Persevere
    c. Perverse
    d. Perpetuated

11. Which is the correct pronoun and verb? _____ the Eiffel Tower when he visited Paris.
    a. They saw
    b. He seen
    c. They seen
    d. He saw

12. Which is correctly punctuated?
    a. Make a study plan to learn the parts of the respiratory system, the muscles, and the heart.
    b. Make a study plan to learn the : parts of the respiratory system, the muscles and the heart.
    c. Make a study plan to learn the parts of the respiratory system the muscles and the heart.
    d. Make a study plan to learn the parts: of the respiratory system, the muscles and the heart.

13. Which uses an apostrophe appropriately?
    a. Could'nt
    b. Shouldn't
    c. Shaln't
    d. Ain't

14. Which uses a third-person point of view?
    a. She carried the tools up the stairs.
    b. We carried the tools up the stairs.
    c. I carried the tools up the stairs.
    d. You carried the tools up the stairs.

15. Which is spelled correctly?
    a. Illustrious
    b. Illustrius
    c. Illustros
    d. Illustries

16. Which is spelled correctly?
    a. Examane
    b. Examine
    c. Eximine
    d. Examaine

17. Which best defines thorough?
    a. Lackadaisical
    b. Lazy
    c. Incomplcte
    d. Methodical

18. Which is grammatically correct?
    a. After a thorough examination, the patient were released.
    b. After a thorough examination, the patient was released.
    c. After a thorough examination the patient was released.
    d. After a thorough examination, the patient was release.

19. Which is correctly capitalized?
    a. I finished reading the introduction to the history of medicine.
    b. I finished reading the Introduction to the History Of Medicine.
    c. I finished reading the introduction to the History of Medicine.
    d. I finished reading the introduction to the History Of Medicine.

20. Which is the correct part of speech of the underlined word? If you miss a lab, you will lose ten points off of your <u>final</u> grade.
    a. Adverb
    b. Noun
    c. Verb
    d. Adjective

21. Which word best completes the sentence? The patient came to the emergency room complaining of _____ pain.
    a. Mild
    b. Acute
    c. Nonexistent
    d. Some

22. Which is a complex sentence?
    a. He turned his homework in to his teacher.
    b. He turned his homework in today, because he would not be in class the next day.
    c. He turn in his homework.
    d. He turned in his homework at the beginning of class.

23. Which has a correct subject-verb agreement?
    a. The homework assignment are due on Monday.
    b. The homework assignment dues on Monday.
    c. The homework assignment is due on Monday.
    d. The homework assignments is due on Monday.

24. Which ending would make the sentence a simple sentence?
    a. Take the laundry to the laundry room.
    b. Take the laundry to the laundry room, so you can finish cleaning your room.
    c. Take the laundry to the laundry room, and start the first load.
    d. Take the laundry to the laundry room, because I need to start a load.

25. Which is spelled correctly?
    a. Minimal
    b. Minimle
    c. Minimile
    d. Minimale

26. Which is spelled correctly?
    a. Unintelligable
    b. Uninteligible
    c. Unintelligible
    d. Uninttelligible

27. Which has a correct subject-verb agreement?
    a. The doctor's office is booked with appointments all day.
    b. The doctor's office are booked with appointments all day.
    c. The doctors' offices is booked with appointments all day.
    d. The doctor's office booked with appointments all day.

28. Which word best completes the sentence? _____ patients are less likely to seek out medical care.
    a. Insured
    b. Uninsured
    c. Unusual
    d. Ill

29. Which best defines Acute?
    a. Severe
    b. Agile
    c. Intelligent
    d. Ongoing

30. Which is grammatically correct?
    a. Patient care is a much important part of the job of a nurse.
    b. Patient care is the most important part of a nurse's job.
    c. Patient cares are the most important part of a nurse's job.
    d. Caring for patients are the most important part of a nurse's job.

31. Which word best completes the sentence? _____ programs are designed to provide end-of-life care.
    a. Hospital
    b. Hospice
    c. Hopeful
    d. Heritage

32. Which is correctly punctuated?
    a. The orthopedic hospital offers, a calm and well-organized environment.
    b. The orthopedic hospital offers a calm and wellorganized environment.
    c. The orthopedic hospital offers a calm and well-organized environment.
    d. The orthopedic hospital offers a calm and well-organized environment!

English & Language Arts – ANSWER KEY

1. a.
2. a. Complex and compound sentences have dependent or independent clauses.
3. d.
4. c.
5. a.
6. a.
7. b.
8. c.
9. a.
10. b.
11. d.
12. a.
13. b.
14. a. Third-person point of view uses he, she or they.
15. a.
16. b.
17. d.
18. b.
19. c.
20. d.
21. b.
22. b. A complex sentence has a dependent clause.
23. c.
24. a.
25. a.
26. c.
27. a.
28. b.
29. a.
30. b.
31. b.
32. c.

Reading

Regardless of the time of the year or the time of the day there are pies. The Pennsylvania Dutch eat pies for breakfast. They eat pies for lunch. They eat pies for dinner and they eat pies for midnight snacks. Pies are made with a great variety of ingredients from the apple pie we all know to the rivel pie which is made from flour, sugar, and butter. The Dutch housewife is as generous with her pies as she is with all her cooking, baking six or eight at a time not one and two.

The apple is an important Pennsylvania Dutch food. Dried apples form the basis for many typical dishes. Each fall barrels of apples are converted into cider. Apple butter is one of the Pennsylvania Dutch foods which has found national acceptance. The making of apple butter is an all-day affair and has the air of a holiday to it. Early in the morning the neighbors gather and begin to peel huge piles of apples that will be needed. Soon the great copper apple butter kettle is brought out and set up over a wood fire. Apple butter requires constant stirring to prevent burning. However, stirring can be light work for a boy and a girl when they're young and the day is bright and the world is full of promise. By dusk the apple butter is made, neighborhood news is brought up to date and hunger has been driven that much further away for the coming winter.

Food is abundant and appetites are hearty in the Pennsylvania Dutch country. The traditional dishes are relatively simple and unlike most regional cookery the ingredients are readily available. Best of all, no matter who makes them the results are "wonderful good."

1. Which is a logical conclusion?
   a. Pennsylvania Dutch housewives like to cook.
   b. Pie is the only food they eat.
   c. Food is an important part of Pennsylvania Dutch culture.
   d. Apple butter is used to make pies.

2. Which is a logical conclusion?
   a. Apples are a significant crop in Pennsylvania Dutch country.
   b. Pies require only butter, sugar and flour.
   c. Apple butter is made in the spring.
   d. Pennsylvania Dutch children all learn to cook.

3. Which is an opinion?
   a. Pennsylvania Dutch housewives frequently make pie.
   b. Pennsylvania Dutch children help make apple butter.
   c. Pennsylvania Dutch food is "wonderful good".
   d. Apple butter takes all day to make.

4. Which type of passage is this?
   a. Narrative
   b. Expository
   c. Technical
   d. Persuasive

5. What can be inferred?
    a. This is the introduction to a cookbook.
    b. This is the beginning of a history book.
    c. This is a book about Pennsylvania Dutch culture.
    d. This is a book about regional foods.

6. Which is a primary source?
    a. Interviews with Pennsylvania Dutch cooks
    b. Cookbooks
    c. People who have eaten Pennsylvania Dutch cooking
    d. History books

7. What is the first sentence in the passage?
    a. Main idea
    b. Topic
    c. Theme
    d. Supporting detail

I don't know whether you have ever seen a map of a person's mind. Doctors sometimes draw maps of other parts of you, and your own map can become intensely interesting, but catch them trying to draw a map of a child's mind, which is not only confused, but keeps going round all the time. There are zigzag lines on it, just like your temperature on a card, and these are probably roads in the island, for the Neverland is always more or less an island, with astonishing splashes of colour here and there, and coral reefs and rakish-looking craft in the offing, and savages and lonely lairs, and gnomes who are mostly tailors, and caves through which a river runs, and princes with six elder brothers, and a hut fast going to decay, and one very small old lady with a hooked nose. It would be an easy map if that were all, but there is also first day at school, religion, fathers, the round pond, needle-work, murders, hangings, verbs that take the dative, chocolate pudding day, getting into braces, say ninety-nine, three-pence for pulling out your tooth yourself, and so on, and either these are part of the island or they are another map showing through, and it is all rather confusing, especially as nothing will stand still.

8. What is the intent?
    a. Persuade
    b. Entertain
    c. Inform
    d. Express feeling

9. Which is a topic sentence?
    a. I don't know whether you have ever seen a map of a person's mind.
    b. Doctors sometimes draw maps of other parts of you, but catch them trying to draw a map of a child's mind, which is not only confused but keeps going round all the time.
    c. There are zigzag lines on it, just like your temperature on a card, and these are probably roads in the island.
    d. It would be an easy map if that were all, but there is also first day at school, religion, fathers, the round pond.

10. What can be inferred?
    a. The child's mind is being compared to Neverland.
    b. Neverland is an island.
    c. There are maps of Neverland.
    d. Neverland has chocolate pudding.

11. Which type of passage is this?
    a. Narrative
    b. Expository
    c. Persuasive
    d. Technical

Malvern Hill, a plateau a mile and a half long and half a mile wide, with its top bare of woods, commanded a view of the country over which the Confederates must approach. Around the summit of this hill McClellan had placed tier after tier of batteries, arranged like an amphitheater. On the top were placed several heavy siege guns, his left flank being protected by the gunboats in the river. The morning and early afternoon were occupied by several Confederate attacks, sometimes formidable in their nature, but Lee planned for no general move until he could bring up a force which he thought sufficient to attack the strong position of the Federals. The Confederates had orders to advance, when a signal shout was given by the men of Armistead's brigade. The attack was made late in the afternoon by General D. H. Hill, and was gallantly done, but no army could have withstood the fire from the batteries of McClellan as they were massed upon Malvern Hill. All during the evening brigade after brigade tried to force the Union lines. They were forced to breast one of the most devastating storms of lead and canister to which an assaulting army has ever been subjected. The round shot and grape cut through the branches of the trees. Column after column of Southern soldiers rushed upon the death dealing cannon, only to be mowed down. Their thin lines rallied again and again to the charge, but to no avail. McClellan's batteries still hurled their missiles of death. The field below was covered with the dead, as mute pleaders in the cause of peace. The heavy shells from the gunboats on the river shrieked through the timber and great limbs were torn from the trees as they hurtled by. Darkness was falling over the combatants. It was nine o'clock before the guns ceased firing, and only an occasional shot rang out over the gory field of Malvern Hill.

12. What is the intent?
    a. Persuade
    b. Entertain
    c. Inform
    d. Express feeling

13. Which is a likely motive for the author?
    a. To provide historical information
    b. To share opinions about the war
    c. To explain why the war ended slavery
    d. To persuade the reader that war was wrong

14. Which is a summary sentence?
    a. The Battle of Malvern Hill was a decisive Confederate victory.
    b. The Battle of Malvern Hill was a decisive Union victory.
    c. The Battle of Malvern Hill was a part of the Revolutionary war.
    d. The hill offered the Confederates a better position in the battle.

15. Which type of passage is this?
    a. Narrative
    b. Expository
    c. Technical
    d. Persuasive

16. Which accurately represents the historical context of the information in the passage?
    a. World War I
    b. The Civil War
    c. World War II
    d. The Revolutionary War

17. What can be inferred?
    a. This is part of a book about the Civil War
    b. This is a memoir of a Confederate soldier
    c. This is a memoir of a Union soldier
    d. This is a biography of a Confederate general

The following questions will test informational source comprehension.

18. After following the directions below, how many miles have you driven?
    1) Drive 2 miles to work
    2) Drive 3 miles to the gym
    3) Drive 5 miles to your home
    4) Drive 4 miles to the theater
    5) Drive 4 miles to your home

19. According to the table of contents below, is Differential Equations a heading or subheading?

Advanced Mathematics
Calculus
Pre-test 1
Practice Test 1
Differential Equations
Pre-test 2
Practice Test 2

20. According to the table of contents above, is Practice Test 1 a heading or subheading?

21. According to the map below, which direction is Ruby Stone Lake in relation to Camp Diamond?

22. According to the map below, which geographical feature is west of Camp Sapphire?

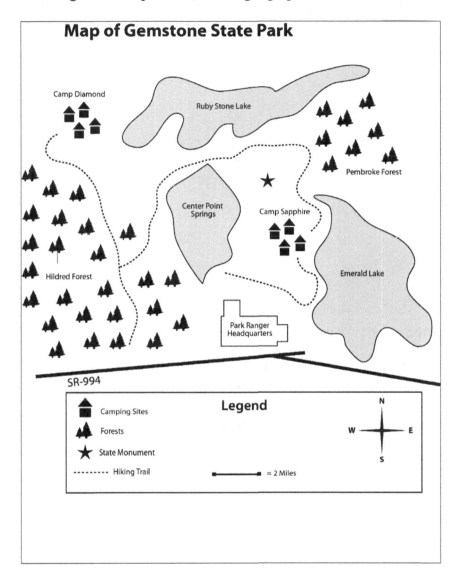

23. According to the map above, how many miles is it from Park Ranger Headquarters to the center of Emerald Lake?

24. According to the graph below, Food and Utilities account for how many dollars of expenses?

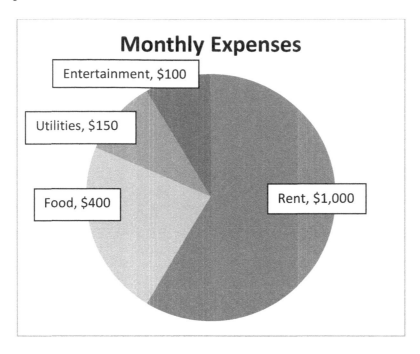

Monthly Expenses

Entertainment, $100

Utilities, $150

Food, $400

Rent, $1,000

25. According to the graph above, what is the largest expense?

26. According to the graph above, Rent and Entertainment account for how many dollars of expenses?

27. According to the index below, where can someone find how to lose weight?

> Health & Wellness, 52-103
>   cardio, 55-69
>   weight loss, 73-86
>   nutrition, 91-103

28. According to the index above, where can someone find how to improve endurance?

29. You start with 5 pennies in your pocket. After following the directions below, how many pennies do you have?
    1) You find 1 on the ground.
    2) You trade 5 for 1 nickel
    3) You find 3 under your bed.

30. A man needs to gain weight for health reasons. He needs to consume at least 5 grams of fat per meal. According to its nutrition label below, would this food satisfy that requirement?

Nutrition Facts

Serving Size 172 g

Amount Per Serving

Calories 200   Calories from Fat 8

	% Daily Value*
Total Fat 1g	1%
Saturated Fat 0g	1%
Trans Fat	
Cholesterol 0mg	0%
Sodium 7mg	0%
Total Carbohydrate 36g	12%
Dietary Fiber 11g	45%
Sugars 6g	
Protein 13g	

Vitamin A	1%	Vitamin C	1%
Calcium	4%	Iron	24%

*Percent Daily Values are based on a 2,000 calorie diet. Your daily values may be higher or lower depending on your calorie needs.

NutritionData.com

31. A woman is training for a marathon. She needs to consume at least 25 grams of carbohydrates per meal. According to the nutrition label above, would this food satisfy that requirement?

32. A man has too much iron in his blood and gives blood every month in order to remove iron from his body. According to the nutrition label above, would this food help or hinder his efforts?

33. According to the table below, which company offers the lowest base price?

Retailer	Base Price	Shipping & Handling	Taxes
Wholesale Footwear	59.99	10.95	7.68
Bargain Sales	65.99	5.95	5.38
Famous Shoes	79.99	0.00	4.89

34. According to the table above, which company has the lowest tax?

35. According to the table above, which company has the highest base price + shipping & handling combined price?

36. If the thermometer below indicated a temperature of 50° F, what would the temperature be in degrees Centigrade?

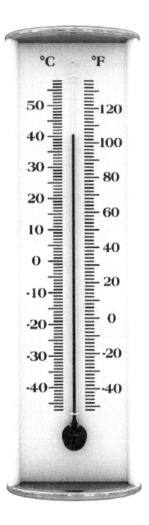

37. If the thermometer above dropped 30° C, what would the temperature be in degrees Fahrenheit?

38. Tina needs to purchase a dozen red or blue shirts, but has only $14. According to the table below, which company can accommodate her?

Company	Price	Color	Size
Maximum Tees	15.99/dozen	Red	M
Wholesale Tees	12.99/dozen	Blue	L
Total Tees	19.99/dozen	Green	XL

39. Robert wants to buy 4 dozen blue shirts. According to the table above how much will it cost?

40. According to the yellow page below, where is Spin Cycle Laundry located?

41. According to the yellow page above, how many companies are listed under Lawn & Garden Equipment?

42. According to the yellow page above, 227-1368 is the phone number for which company?